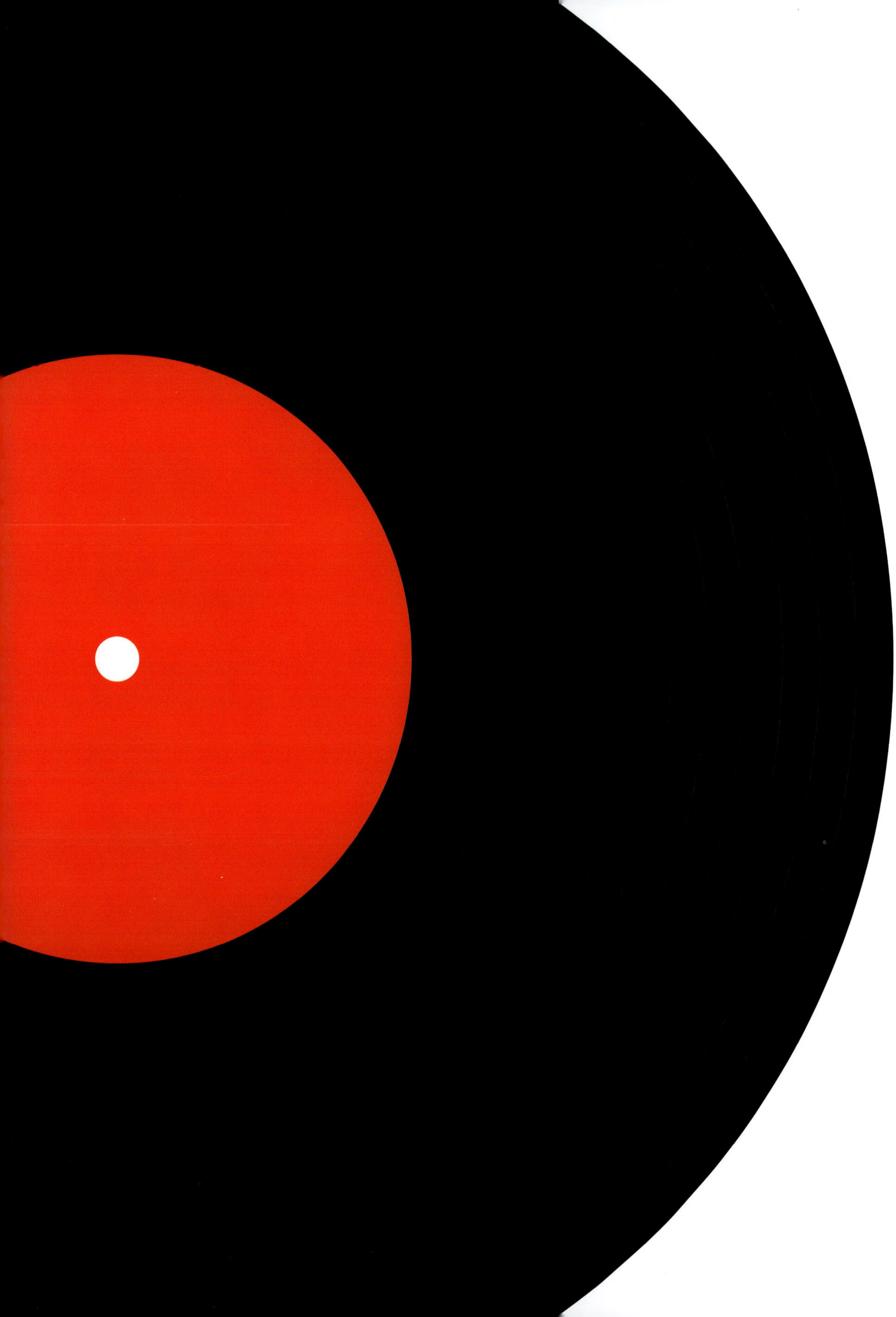

MUSIC OF RESISTANCE AND TRANSFORMATION

SONGS THAT CHANGED THE WORLD

ANDREW CLARKE

GELDING STREET PRESS

A Gelding Street Press book
An imprint of Rockpool Publishing
PO Box 252, Summer Hill
NSW 2130 Australia

geldingstreetpress.com
Follow us! @ geldingstreet_press

Published in 2026 by Gelding Street Press

Image credits: see page 230

ISBN: 9781922662361

Design and typesetting by Ethan Cohen Stoddart, Rockpool Publishing
Edited by Heather Millar

NATIONAL LIBRARY OF AUSTRALIA
A catalogue record for this book is available from the National Library of Australia

Printed and bound in China
10 9 8 7 6 5 4 3 2 1

TO MY PARENTS, MAGGIE AND GEOFF, FOR ENCOURAGING ME TO FORGE MY PATH IN THE WORLD. I MISS YOU BOTH, AND I'LL DO IT MY WAY.

AND TO ALL THE SONGWRITERS WITH SOMETHING TO SAY, THE WORLD IS RICHER FOR WHAT YOU CREATE.

CONTENTS

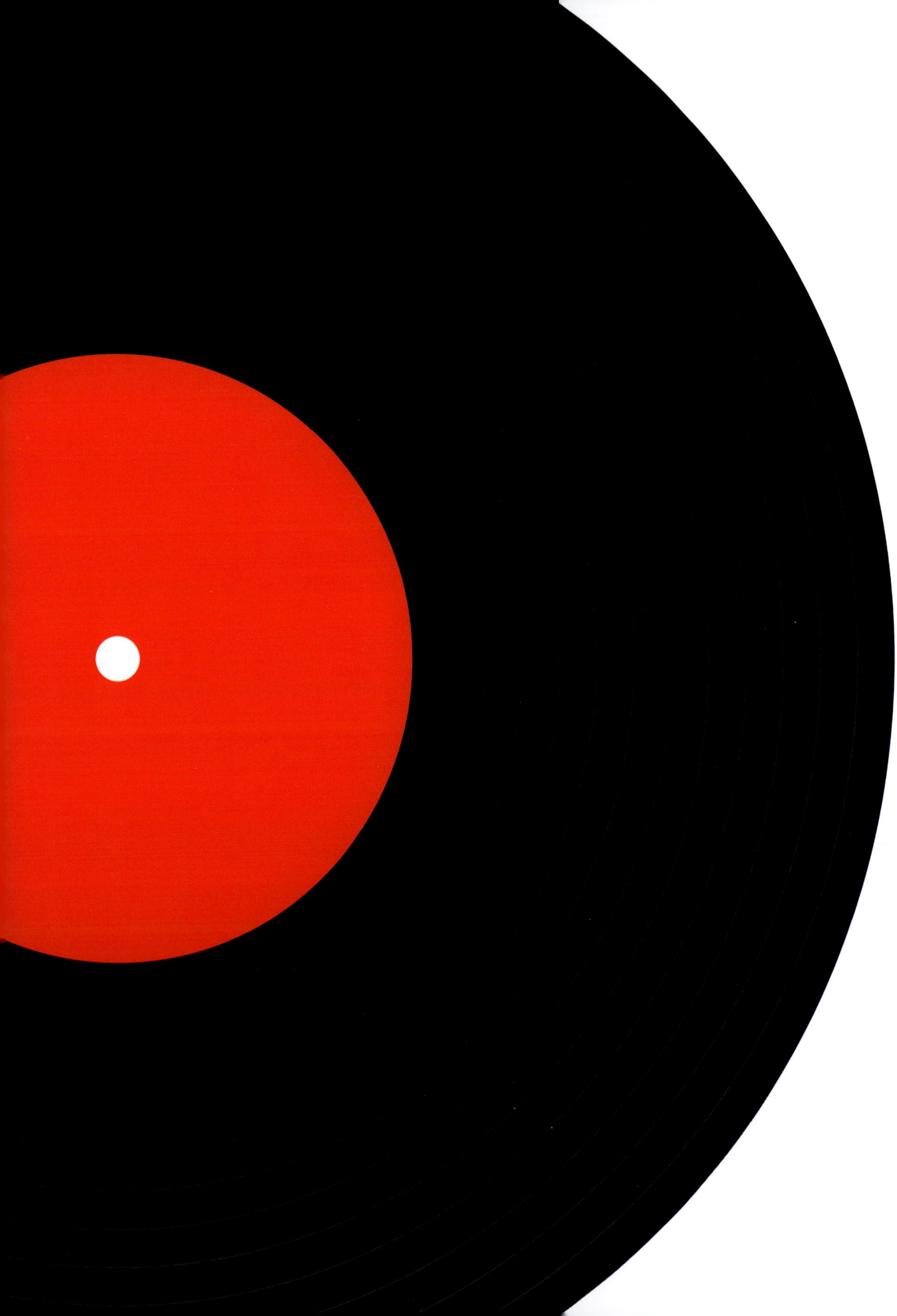

INTRODUCTION

This book has been growing in my mind for years. It started, stalled, and restarted more than once. I've always been fascinated with words, and meaning. When you combine words with meaning and music, as we have done for millennia, you get songs that change the world.

They can change the whole world, or just part of the world. And some of that micro impact is as important as the macro. "La Liberté" is as impactful a song as I can I find, even if to those outside Algeria it may not seem to be. However, what started local transcended so many barriers. I hope when you read its story it impacts you as it did me.

The true genesis of this book lies in Julien Temple's documentary *The Filth and the Fury* about the Sex Pistols. I knew I liked the band. I thought, as an 11-year-old in Australia when they arrived on our TV screens, that I even understood them. But I didn't. Not really.

Temple's film opened my eyes to the power of music, to the way lyrics could be more than stories. They could be statements. They could be catalysts for change. That anger is as much an energy as is love.

So I began making a list. The first version ballooned to a hundred songs before I worked it down to the 42 you'll find here. Why 42? Some of you will know why, and I'll have a sneaky smile with you.

And, as with any good list, I couldn't have done it without the editors and publishers at Gelding Street Press and Rockpool Publishing, who encouraged me to explore songs and sounds I'd never encountered, some of them requiring translation, but all demanding deep dives into history and meaning.

In cutting the list down, we considered both that macro and micro change. Some songs, such as "Big Yellow Taxi," speak to global concerns. Others, like "Beds Are Burning" by Midnight Oil, belong unmistakably to their country, yet resonate far beyond. Like Neil Murray wrote, it's about "my island home." Macro and micro. Global and personal.

This book isn't about the best songs. If it were, there'd be a lot more tracks by The Hold Steady. Craig Finn writes lyrics with layers of meaning, and songs like "The Birdwatchers" bristle with insight if you take the time to dissect. But they never changed the world, at least, not yet. This book is about impact. The moments when songs shifted thinking, sparked action, or gave people a voice they didn't know they had.

Some songs take on lives of their own, drifting far from the meaning their writers intended. That can be harmless enough, but sometimes the misreadings are staggering. "Fortunate Son" has been blared in triumph as though it were a patriotic anthem, when its sneer at privilege and power could not be plainer. "Born in the USA" was once claimed as a flag-waving celebration, despite being a lament for those left behind. And those are only the most famous examples: misinterpretations are scattered right across popular music.

Time, in many cases, has helped us to understand what may have been too subtle for some at the start. Some artists in this book could have easily appeared multiple times, while others were somehow overlooked. Bob Dylan wrote hit after hit that called for change. So did Nina Simone. Neil Young came close with songs like "Ohio," which remains a personal favorite of mine. But there had to be a cut line.

And then there's Pete Seeger, one of the earliest voices of protest featured here. His death in 2014 prompted tributes from around the world, which showcased the power of his voice and his songs.

Pete Seeger's music was regularly tied to the bigger story of America, capturing both its struggles and its hopes. His songs were used to back campaigns for workers and civil rights, to speak out against war, and to push ideas about caring for the environment. Just as importantly, he encouraged people to sing along, believing the act of joining voices together built strength.

Writers looking back, including Billy Bragg, have pointed out that Seeger never claimed songs could overturn the world on their own. What he argued instead was that music could shift how people felt and thought, and that shift might feed into larger movements. For him, a song was never the final answer, but it could open the door to change. Seeger left a lasting mark on both music and activism, and on many of the artists featured in this book, particularly those from the USA in the 1960s. What he was saying was that the music and song on its own isn't enough, but sometimes it can power the revolution.

Of course, social commentary in song didn't begin with Seeger. It's been there for as long as people have sung. Long before recording studios, radio airplay, or streaming, people used folk ballads, work songs, and protest chants to document injustice, oppression, and resistance.

In Egypt, more than 4,000 years ago, the *Ipuwer Papyrus* (The Admonitions of Ipuwer) laments social upheaval and criticizes the ruling class. Although there is no evidence that it was anything more than a poem, the transition to a song would have been relatively easy.

Then there's the *Book of Psalms,* where several songs are crying out against oppression and corrupt rulers. "Psalm 94" opens with the plea, "O Lord, God of vengeance, shine forth!" which is a direct call for justice. It is a voice of anguish and defiance, demanding that the powerful be held to account.

That same spirit of righteous fury would echo across the centuries. When Bob Dylan released "Masters of War" in 1963, its unflinching condemnation of those who profit from violence felt ancient in its cadence, biblical in its anger.

Dylan hurls a charge so severe it suggests the target's crimes lie even beyond Jesus's forgiveness, a blast of moral fury that sits comfortably alongside the psalmist's denunciation of those who crush widows, strangers, and the fatherless. There is a connection between songs, from one to the next, and from theme to theme. Do we get "To Be Young, Gifted and Black" without "Strange Fruit"? Do we get "I am Woman" without "Respect" and "Love Child"?

From Billie Holiday to Billie Joe Armstrong, music in the modern world has shaped moments and movements in ways few other art forms can. Since World War II, we've seen an extraordinary collection of songs leave their mark on the world. In many ways, Holiday started it. "Strange Fruit" shocked with its brutal imagery, forcing people to confront truths they would rather have ignored. It set a new standard: if this brilliant woman could sing about lynchings with a cry for justice, no subject from there was off limits.

With music, there is no place we can't go. No truths too hard to tell, no stories too difficult to sing.

Sometimes, though, we are just waiting for something to provide a spark. Perhaps sometimes, we don't know what we need until someone puts it in lyrics.

As I said earlier, this is just 42 songs and the list is subjective and it may not be complete. Surely there is more to come.

Please enjoy, and please think.

Andrew

1939, USA

STRANGE FRUIT

BILLIE HOLIDAY

ABEL MEEROPOL, COMMODORE MUSIC

RECORDED 1939 AT COMMODORE ONE, NEW YORK CITY

The introduction to the recording of "Strange Fruit" was slow and mournful, like a warning. Billie Holiday's voice then broke in and told the story of why this song was, in fact, mourning with imagery that was hard to ignore. The strange fruit at the heart of the stories was Black Americans being lynched by mobs in America's South, their blood staining the ground beneath after they were invariably beaten first. But the stains were not just on the ground; for Holiday and many others, it was a stain on the entirety of a nation that allowed this barbaric practice to continue.

"Strange Fruit" presented an unambiguous opposition to racial violence through its direct message, and Holiday gave the civil rights movement a voice. It stirred emotions in Americans of any color and represented a historical turning point that transformed music from entertainment to also serve as evidence, resistance, and social observation.

The music industry in the early 20th century avoided confrontations with harsh realities. Music was for dreaming, not for protesting. After "Strange Fruit," that was no longer the case, and artists started to emulate Holiday.

To understand "Strange Fruit" and its societal context, you need to step back into America in the 1930s. At that time, it maintained deep racial segregation across the nation. Some were enshrined in law, such as the South's Jim Crow laws, while the North had its segregation hidden below the surface.

Racism existed as an embedded institution throughout laws, housing policy, and education systems as well as everyday life. The US government actively worked to prevent Black Americans from progressing. The system of racial discrimination that controlled society remained strong during 1939 because it served the interests of white power holders.

Sadly, lynching continued to occur against African Americans in the 1930s with no signs of decreasing. On August 7, 1930, a white mob in Marion, Indiana, dragged J. Thomas Shipp and Abraham S. Smith from their jail cells, where they were being held on charges of murdering a white factory worker, Claude Deeter, and allegedly raping his companion,

Mary Ball. The evidence against them was tenuous at best. A third young man, James Cameron, was also accused but was spared by the mob and later fully exonerated.

A photograph showing Shipp and Smith's battered bodies hanging from a tree while white spectators grinned nearby became an image that haunted New York schoolteacher Abel Meeropol for years. The shocking brutality immortalized in that image inspired him to compose "Bitter Fruit" under his pen name Lewis Allan.

Meeropol adapted the poem into music under the new title "Strange Fruit" and performed it at New York leftist events. Billie Holiday (born Eleanora Fagan) discovered the song in 1939 when she was performing in the integrated Café Society nightclub of New York. She had established her place within the jazz world through her best-selling songs, too. She was a bona fide star.

"Strange Fruit" became her set closer; she wanted to leave her audience thinking. This song was treated differently from the rest

of her set: the audience experienced total darkness, the waiters stopped serving, and the spotlight revealed her face alone.

Eyes closed, she sang with that powerful visual imagery during the short, two-minute-long performance that the audience would find impossible to forget.

Columbia Records didn't want Billie Holiday to record the song because they feared potential backlash and dangerous consequences. However, they allowed her to partner with Commodore Records to create the record she had craved. She recorded "Strange Fruit" alongside Frankie Newton's Café Society band at Commodore Records on April 20, 1939. The song achieved Billboard chart success in the weeks following its release, en route to surpassing one million sales.

The musical world received "Strange Fruit," which brought its demand for attention to the forefront, in a positive light. *Time Magazine* in *TIME 100: Songs of the Century (*December 31, 1999) named it the Song of the Century.

The song's impact was no accident. Meeropol made deliberate choices when he wrote the poem. So did Holiday when she sang the song. The protest against lynching evolved into something greater than its original intention. The song provoked anger among many white Americans, yet strengthened Black communities with determination, and a staunch movement against lynchings gained its voice.

It was remarkable for a Black woman to present such defiant content within the confines of white cultural control during that time. It shattered expectations. The US government noticed. Harry Anslinger, who headed the Federal Bureau of Narcotics and exhibited racist views, considered Holiday a danger to society. He conducted a persistent war against her through continuous police arrests combined with extensive monitoring activities. She died in 1959 while being guarded in a hospital bed, and she was denied proper treatment during her final moments.

But the song endured. It changed attitudes towards lynching, it shifted the civil rights debate, and a cultural transformation began to emerge. The storm was coming: Brown v. Board, the Montgomery Bus Boycott, the rise of Malcolm X and Martin Luther King Jr. The song "Strange Fruit" was launched before these pivotal moments took shape. Through its existence, the song played a role in creating these historical events.

"Strange Fruit" revealed the harsh reality of a lack of racial harmony and equality through the era's false narratives, and the protest music of later generations built on this foundation.

It became more than music to Black Americans. The message declared that everyone understood what was happening and that they had each other's support. It validated the pain and suffering of others by giving their stories a dignified permanent expression.

The legacy runs deep. Paul Robeson sang it. Nina Simone made it part of her repertoire. Marvin Gaye, Gil Scott-Heron, Billie's goddaughter Lorraine Feather, and later Public Enemy, Erykah Badu, and Kendrick Lamar all drew from its well and had their own versions. The musical elements of "Mississippi Goddam" and "To Be Young,

Gifted and Black" and "What's Going On" by Marvin Gaye all resonated with the musical essence of "Strange Fruit." René Marie combined "Strange Fruit" with "Dixie" in her performance, even though "Dixie" served as a Confederate anthem for many listeners. The combination of these two opposing elements caused a shocking effect 60 years after the initial recording.

The backlash was inevitable too. Many radio stations banned it. Some venues asked her not to perform it. Yet the impact remained unchanged despite all attempts to eliminate it.

"Strange Fruit" became an integral part of academic resources, protest activities, and social movements throughout multiple decades. It served as a reference point in debates about federal anti-lynching laws until the Emmett Till Anti-Lynching Act became law in 2022 after an 83-year wait.

The music rules for what songs can accomplish underwent a fundamental transformation because of "Strange Fruit," which is why it leads this book. The metaphorical fruit does not grow on poplar trees but exists within police violence alongside mass incarceration and systemic inequality. The horror evolves, but the roots remain.

That's why "Strange Fruit" still matters.

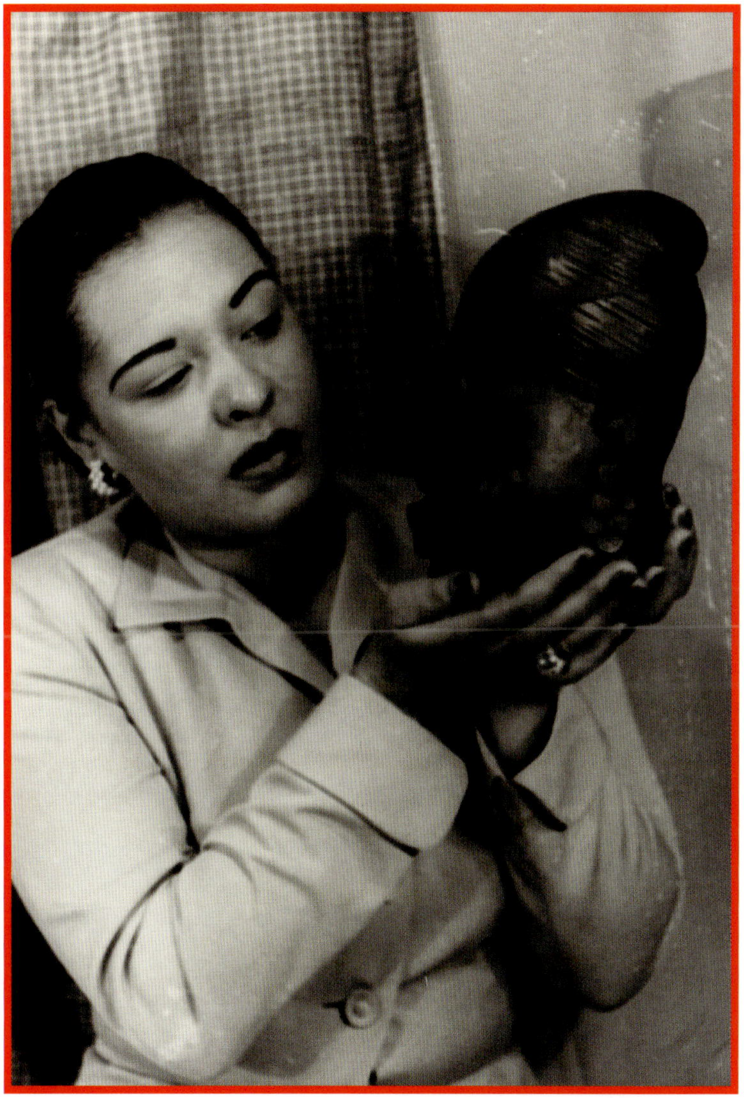

1953, ITALY

BELLA CIAO

EXACT ORIGINS AND SONGWRITERS ARE UNCLEAR

The story of "Bella Ciao" is one that is more myth than fact, but that doesn't diminish its power. Contrary to popular belief, it was not performed by *partigiani* (the Italian Resistance) in the hills during World War II. The wartime records of partigiani contain no mention of this song and wartime songbooks from the following years also lack any reference to it.

It cannot be found in Pasolini's *Canzoniere Italiano* of 1955 or the 1962 *Canti Politici* published by Editori Riuniti. According to historian Roberto Battaglia, the actual anthems of the movement were "Fischia il vento" and the Russian resistance song "Katyusha." "Bella Ciao" was conspicuous by its absence given the legend.

From its first notarized appearances in the early 1950s to the present day, it has gained widespread popularity with each passing year. Today, "Bella Ciao" is performed by several musicians, including exiled Argentine singer Mercedes Sosa, Spanish-French artist Manu Chao, Bosnian musician Goran Bregović, and Spanish tenor Manu Pilas, and guitarist Marc Ribot with Tom Waits in *Songs of Resistance* (2018).

"Bella Ciao" stands as a fundamental protest song of modern times, thanks to its simple folk melody and straightforward lyrics. It is performed at both public demonstrations and picket lines, as well as in school events and street protests. It exists in dozens of languages, which allows it to travel across different borders while transcending time periods. Although it was not the Italian Resistance's song, it has evolved into a worldwide protest anthem with its story rooted in the partigiani.

It begins with a simple verse about a morning invasion of the narrator's homeland. He says his final farewell to his beloved one by singing "Bella Ciao" (goodbye beautiful) before he departs to fight. If he dies in battle, he wishes to be buried on the mountain with a flower so passersby will understand he died for the sake of freedom.

It combines sorrowful expressions with a pledge and functions as the codicil to a last will.

For many years, people believed it originated spontaneously during World War II, as soldiers passed it among themselves during firelit gatherings and covert assaults. But that story doesn't hold. There are no documented stories of its existence prior to the early 1950s, and while many want to embrace the romance of the resistance, "Bella Ciao" made its first recorded public appearance in 1953 and was recorded in print for the first time in the Italian newspaper *l'Unità* in 1957. Although it may have appeared earlier, it is very unlikely that that is the case.

Italian singer Yves Montand (born Ivo Livi), while domiciled in France, recorded "Bella Ciao" in 1962. It was first released in Japan that year, and subsequently, it received broader distribution. But it wasn't until 1964 when Il Nuovo Canzoniere Italiano presented it at the Festival dei Due Mondi in Spoleto (the Spoleto Festival) that it gained momentum.

They presented it as a partisan anthem and as a musical expression of the "mondine women" (female workers) who labored in northern Italy's rice fields and sang this tune to protest their challenging working conditions. It obtained strength through its ability to serve dual purposes. It expressed resistance, but it also conveyed labor struggles and the determination to resist exploitation. At Spoleto, the reinvention was complete.

From that moment, "Bella Ciao" caught fire. After that, Montand became the embodiment of "Bella Ciao." As the son of Italian immigrants who escaped Mussolini's fascist rule, Montand brought an authenticity that extended beyond his musical performances. Through his singing, he infused it with meaningful strength, which spread throughout a war-torn European continent.

And "Bella Ciao" never looked back.

"Bella Ciao" has become a favorite among revolutionaries and reformers, students, strikers, climate activists, and unionists. But it is the Netflix series *La Casa de Papel* (a Spanish *Money Heist*) that brought it into the mainstream

recently via the recording by Manu Pilas. During the show's most intense moments, "Bella Ciao" became an anthem for rebellion and for lawbreakers who acted with integrity and for fighting against impossible challenges. That recording of "Bella Ciao" reached the No. 1 position in several international music charts, and remixes flooded streaming platforms. Teenagers danced to it on TikTok. It maintained its essence even though it became popular.

Today it continues to be a political symbol in Italy. It is sung with pride during leftist events as well as labor demonstrations and

anniversary celebrations on April 25th, which commemorates the end of fascist rule.

The feminist movement has also claimed "Bella Ciao" as part of its heritage. Through its origins in mondine music, it connects directly to the fight of working-class women. Today it serves to demonstrate how women face violence and economic inequality. It serves as an anthem for all defiant female voices who worked in the fields and spoke out against injustice, and continue to sing it today.

Although this history of the song is a myth, it continues to maintain its value beyond its factual inaccuracies. It has power not because of its supposed origins but because of what it says.

It passes from one language generation to another while retaining its direct yet powerful lyrics. The imagery is bold.

The concept of freedom exists as a choice that people must actively fight to obtain and protect. People must select freedom before they fight to defend it. Every time "Bella Ciao" is sung in the world, someone joins the endless, unbroken musical chorus. The mountains remain present even though the singers were not there in the mountains, nor hoping to be buried beneath a flower.

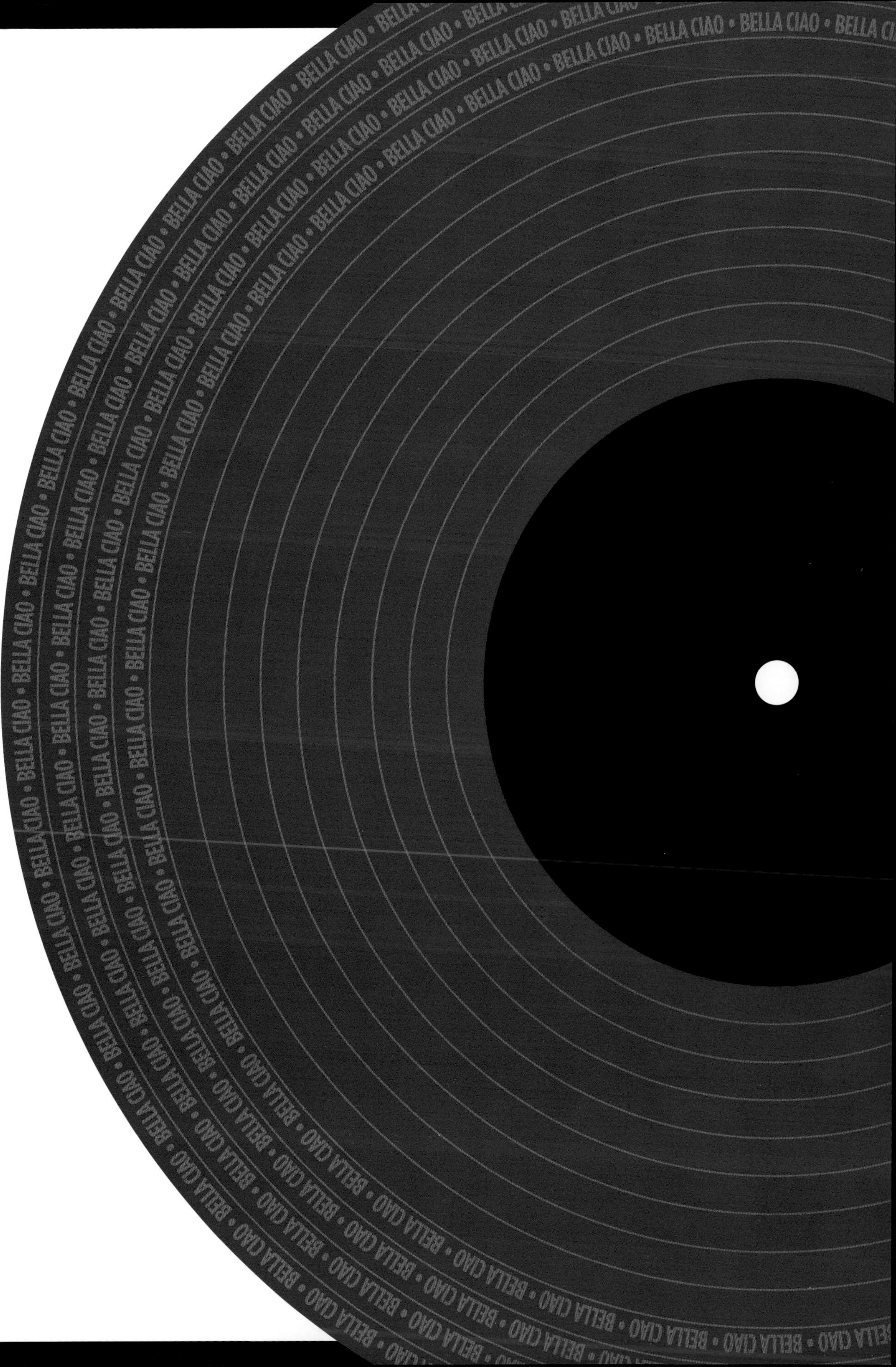
BELLA CIAO

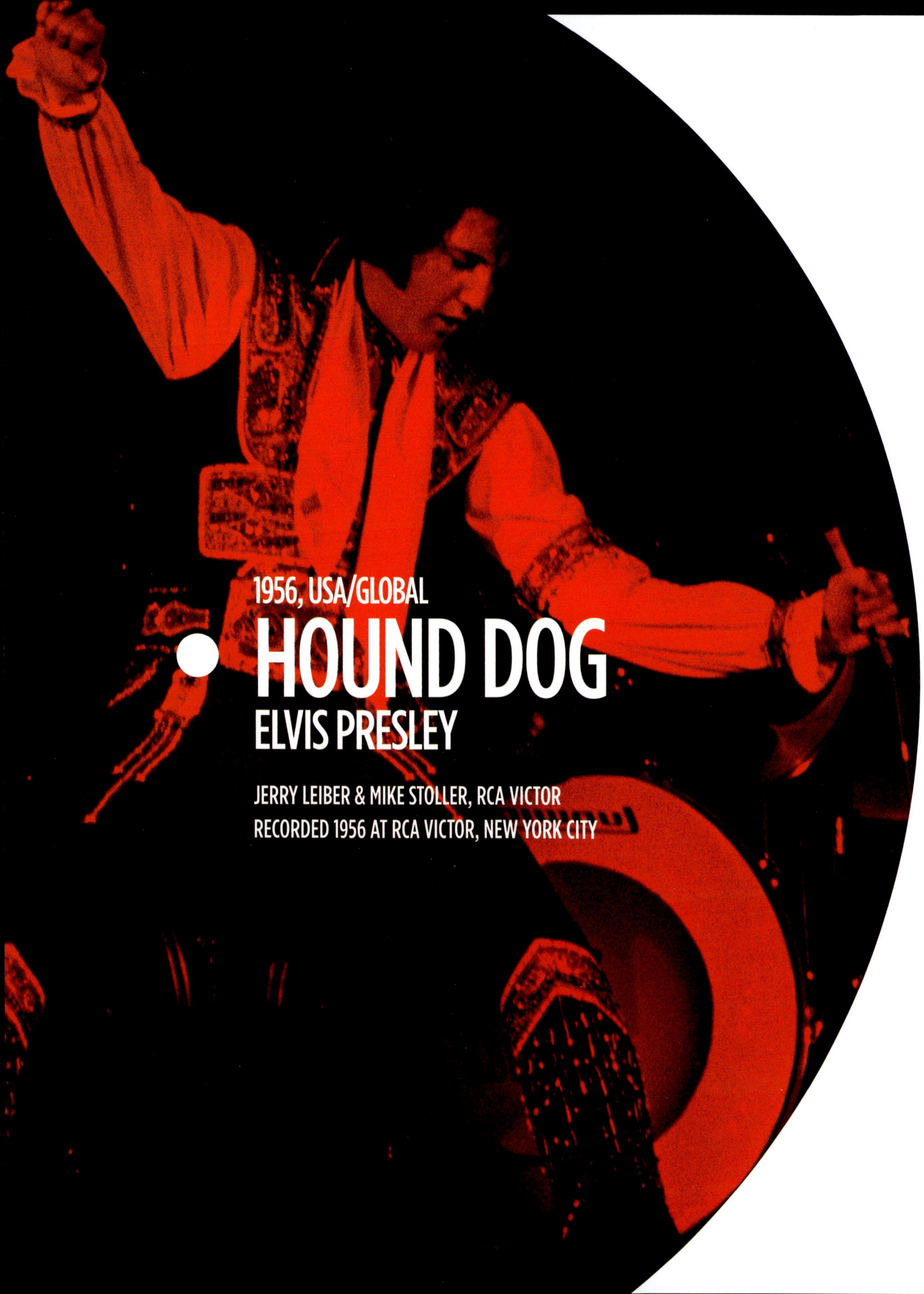

1956, USA/GLOBAL

HOUND DOG

ELVIS PRESLEY

JERRY LEIBER & MIKE STOLLER, RCA VICTOR
RECORDED 1956 AT RCA VICTOR, NEW YORK CITY

Sometimes, it is not the words or music in a song that change the world; it is the impact the song has on the world. Such is the case with "Hound Dog" by Elvis Presley. By the time he took to American television screens in 1956 with his now-infamous hip-thrusting rendition, Presley was already forging a new cultural path.

Throughout 1954 and '55, he had been building a following across the American South from his Memphis base, melding white country stylings with Black gospel and rhythm and blues, singing with urgency, and dancing with what one critic called "nervous energy."

But "Hound Dog" was something else entirely. It was not his first single, nor even his first No. 1 hit, but it was the lightning bolt that turned him from rising star into a cultural menace for some, and for others, a liberator for a restless teenage generation.

When Elvis appeared on *The Milton Berle Show* in June 1956 and performed "Hound Dog" without his guitar, America saw his hips in full, unrestrained motion. The performance split opinion straight away. Television reviewers and newspaper writers reacted with outrage, calling it crude, wild, and even unpatriotic. In *The New York Times*, Jack Gould dismissed Elvis as lacking any real vocal talent, arguing that what audiences saw was little more than a collection of gyrations and suggestive moves. The backlash was immediate and intense, yet it revealed just how profoundly he had shaken the cultural establishment.

It was during this time that the notorious tag "Elvis the Pelvis" took hold, a moniker he loathed. He rejected the idea that his movements were deliberately suggestive, insisting that his hips were not the focus of his act. For him, the energy and rhythm of the music simply carried him into motion, jumping, shaking, and moving with enthusiasm. He maintained that there was nothing lewd about it, only the natural expression of enjoying himself on stage.

But by then, it didn't matter. His body had become a battlefield. To the teenage girls screaming in studio audiences and gathering around television sets across America, his movement was pure electricity, liberation in human form. To their parents, preachers, and politicians, it was an existential threat. Suddenly, rock 'n' roll was not just loud music

with a backbeat; it had hips, and it moved.

PBS later captured the scale of the backlash in a 1956 retrospective, noting how religious figures denounced him from the pulpit, politicians floated the idea of banning him, and anxious parents demanded he be taken off television. Law enforcement filmed his concerts in places like Florida to find grounds for obscenity charges. Police warned him that further provocative movements could lead to arrest. In one concert, according to the PBS report, he was instructed to "stand still or else."

But the more they tried to stop him, the bigger he got.

Much of what was so provocative about Presley's dancing came from where it originated. His movements weren't invented in a Hollywood studio or on a Broadway stage, they were taken directly from Black American performance traditions. He had grown up poor in Tupelo, Mississippi, and later moved to Memphis, where he was immersed in gospel music and radio stations like WDIA that broadcast Black voices, and the pulsing rhythms of the blues. He watched and listened. He absorbed. And when he began

to perform, it came out not in imitation but transformation.

Presley's movements in those early years were largely unplanned. They erupted from the music. The leg shakes, the loose-limbed energy, the unfiltered bursts of motion came from nerves, instinct, and joy. But they also came from a place that White America had rarely seen on its own stages. By taking the ecstatic motion of Black gospel and blues performers and placing it in a white Southern body, on national television, Presley short-circuited a nation's sense of propriety and exposed its fault lines.

Later, as his career became more stage-managed and Hollywood beckoned, Presley's dancing evolved. Choreographers such as Alex Romero helped tame the wildness, most famously in "Jailhouse Rock." But even in its more polished form, the essence of Presley's style remained intact. It was never just about dance. It was about energy, rhythm, rebellion. It was vaudeville meets Pentecostal revival, Black church meets teenage angst, all channeled through a young man in makeup and hair product.

PBS pointed to the underlying tension, noting that while Black audiences were long familiar with such performances, White America found them startling. Elvis's style was not just about the sound, but also about the physical expressiveness he had absorbed from Black entertainers who had never been given the same platforms. This act of cultural borrowing, quintessentially American yet fraught with complexity, became both the foundation of his appeal and the spark for the outrage.

By 1957, the controversy had only grown. When *The Ed Sullivan Show* finally booked Presley, producers famously demanded that he

be filmed only from the waist up. The attempt to censor him only fed the legend. In a world before social media, when image and rumor carried enormous cultural weight, the decision turned his hips into myth.

What Presley proved, perhaps without meaning to, was that dance could be a political act. That how someone moved on stage could upset a nation. That the body itself could carry meaning more dangerous than lyrics. He made dancing matter. He made it a symbol of change. And he paved the way for every artist who used motion to shake the world, James Brown, Tina Turner, Michael Jackson, Prince, Madonna, Beyoncé, and Lady Gaga.

However, he also challenged views along racial lines with his blurring of style and the boundaries of teenage freedom and rights. It was the start of a revolution that continues to this day.

In 1956, the world was a decade removed from World War II, but other conflicts were emerging, leaving people uncertain of whether peace was truly secure. Into a world that was also retreating into moral conservatism came a hip-shaking, sexually provocative Elvis Presley and "Hound Dog." When he stepped onto a stage, wiggled his knee, and let loose a force that no one, least of all himself, could contain, his critics tried to lock him down while his fans screamed him onward. And in that collision, something shifted.

"Hound Dog" wasn't just a song. It was the start of a movement.

1961, JAPAN/1963, USA

UE O MUITE ARUKŌ

KYU SAKAMOTO

ROKUSUKE EI & HACHIDAI NAKAMURA, TOSHIBA/EMI

RECORDED 1961 AT TOSHIBA RECORDING STUDIO, TOKYO

In the summer of 1961, an unlikely sound floated across American airwaves, a gentle melody sung in a language few listeners understood, by an artist they'd never heard of. In America, the song was called "Sukiyaki," though that wasn't its real name. "Ue O Muite Arukō" (I Look Up As I Walk) was a soft, soaring ballad with a whistling interlude and a heartbreakingly sweet tone that masked its deeper, more political roots.

It was a protest song that provoked change not by its powerful words, but by its sound and ability to heal wounds. It sounded like it was from an American movie with Bing Crosby. Instead, it was performed by 21-year-old Japanese crooner Sakamoto Hisashi, more commonly known as Kyu Sakamoto, or just Kyu.

"Sukiyaki" became the first, and still only, Japanese-language song to reach No. 1 on the US Billboard charts. It has sold more than 13 million copies and has been covered numerous times, including one with a new set of lyrics. But beyond its chart-topping success, the song quietly achieved something more profound: it softened post-war American and Western perceptions of Japan, helping to warm a cultural and political relationship scarred by conflict.

"Ue o Muite Arukō" was written by lyricist Rokusuke Ei and composer Hachidai Nakamura in 1961, at a time when mass student protests gripped Japan.

The target of their anger was the Treaty of Mutual Cooperation and Security between Japan and the United States, which allowed the US to maintain a long-term military presence in Japan following World War II. The treaty's renewal in 1959 was a flashpoint, and demonstrators viewed it as a betrayal of Japan's sovereignty. Ei, having participated in those rallies, returned home disillusioned and began writing.

What emerged was a song cloaked in melancholy and quiet resilience. The lyrics describe a man walking alone, looking up at the sky so that his tears won't fall. He counts stars with tearful eyes, clings to memories of happier seasons, and tries to find hope beyond the clouds. On the surface, it reads like a heartbreak ballad. Beneath that, it's a lament for lost ideals, a coded protest in a country still

learning to balance tradition with the freedom of post-war democracy.

But when the song was released in America two years later, its complex origins were lost in translation, literally. The words didn't matter; what resonated in the song, renamed "Sukiyaki" (a word that doesn't appear in the song and refers to a Japanese hot pot dish) was that it was packaged as a charming curiosity from the East.

The name change, while seemingly absurd, likened by *Newsweek* at the time to calling "Moon River" "Beef Stew" if released in Japan, was in fact a calculated marketing move. Americans knew little of Japanese culture in the early 1960s, and the word "Sukiyaki" was recognizable, safe, and exotic all at once.

And yet, this repackaging did not diminish the song's power. Coming less than two decades after the end of World War II and just before Tokyo hosted the 1964 Olympics, "Ue o Muite Arukō" presented a radically different vision of Japan: not militaristic or menacing, but modern, tender, and human. Sakamoto, with his slicked hair and shy charisma, resembled American teen idols like Ricky Nelson or Bobby Darin. He was not the enemy. He was familiar, endearing.

The timing was perfect. Japan's economy was on the rise, its international image was shifting, and there was a cautious desire on both sides of the Pacific to move forward. For American audiences and others, "Ue o Muite Arukō" as "Sukiyaki" offered a bridge. It allowed them to connect with a Japanese voice not through politics or diplomacy, but through melody and emotion. In a sense, the song functioned as cultural diplomacy: it didn't lecture or apologize. It simply let Americans feel something deeply human from the other side of a long-finished war.

That emotional resonance gave the song incredible staying power. Artists like A Taste of Honey revived it for new generations layering their own lyrics atop the original melody. Yet the most powerful version remains Sakamoto's, the one sung in Japanese, with words many never understood but somehow still felt.

Ironically, the success of "Ue o Muite Arukō" also obscured the political grief that gave birth to it. Rokusuke Ei had penned the lyrics not just to express sadness, but to process national disappointment. The song's optimism, with lines like "Happiness lies beyond the clouds," was not blind. It was aspirational. It imagined a better future even while walking through political and emotional ruins. But it was that very ambiguity that allowed the song to travel so far. Americans heard melancholy; they didn't need the specifics. The universality of its mood created space for empathy.

Decades later, the story took a tragic turn. In 1985, Kyu Sakamoto boarded Japan Airlines Flight 123. The plane crashed shortly after take-off from Tokyo, killing 520 people, the worst single-aircraft disaster in history. Sakamoto was just 43. The nation mourned. And across the world, those who remembered that sweet, sad tune on the radio in 1961 felt a fresh pang of loss.

But his legacy endures. "Ue o Muite Arukō" remains a quiet monument to a complicated moment in history, a song born from protest, delivered with charm, and received as a healing balm. It helped humanize a former enemy. It offered Americans a glimpse of Japan not through the lens of Pearl Harbor or Hiroshima, but through a song about love, sorrow, and hope. It asked for no forgiveness, no explanation. It simply said: "I look up so the tears won't fall."

And somehow, that was enough, even though most people in the West had no idea what it was about.

1963, USA

WE SHALL OVERCOME

PETE SEEGER

ZILPHIA HORTON, GUY CARAWAN, FRANK HAMILTON & PETE SEEGER, LUDLOW MUSIC

RECORDED JUNE 1963 AT CARNEGIE HALL, NEW YORK CITY

Few songs have crossed so many boundaries, cultures, and generations as "We Shall Overcome." Its roots stretch deep into African-American spiritual tradition, but its journey, through labor strikes, civil rights marches, and global freedom struggles, has made it one of the most enduring and transformative protest anthems in modern history. More than a melody, it is a vow, a collective chant of hope, and a solemn declaration that justice will prevail.

The song supposedly began life as a gospel hymn, although there is little shared between the two versions. "I'll Overcome Some Day" was composed by the African-American preacher and composer Charles Albert Tindley in 1900. It drew from the sorrow songs of enslaved people and the redemptive tone of Christian worship, Tindley's version already carried the seeds of social and spiritual resilience.

The key switch was achieved by 1947 when "I" became "we," and it had shifted from an individual seeking guidance from God to a collective concept into "We Will Overcome" which was published in the *People's Songs Bulletin.* That version was first recorded as a refrain from the picket line at a tobacco workers' strike in Charleston, South Carolina, where Black women sang "We will overcome."

It was from these labor protests that the song passed into the hands of organizers and educators at the Highlander Folk School in Tennessee, an institution devoted to training grassroots activists in civil rights and labor leadership. There, Zilphia Horton, the school's music director, began teaching the song to her students.

It was Horton who shared the song with Pete Seeger in 1947. Seeger, a well-known political activist and popular folk singer recognized its power immediately. He made a subtle but meaningful change, altering the phrase "we will" to "we shall," a shift that gave the song a more solemn, inclusive cadence. That small change helped lift the song from a colloquial chant to a kind of sacred pledge. And from there, it began its journey across the country.

Throughout the 1950s, Seeger performed "We Shall Overcome" at union rallies, folk festivals, and church halls. His performances were never grandstanding; his soft voice and modest stage presence made the song feel communal. He didn't perform the song to

the audience; he invited them into it. This was essential to the song's spread: not through commercial charts or record sales, but hand to hand, person to person, voice to voice.

In fact, he didn't initially take it into the studio to record. The song's turning point came with Seeger's live recording at Carnegie Hall on June 8, 1963, just weeks before the March on Washington. That version, released on the album *We Shall Overcome*, gave the song global visibility and cemented its status as the unofficial anthem of the civil rights movement.

By then, the song had already taken hold among Black civil rights leaders and their communities. Dr. Martin Luther King Jr. heard it and understood its gravity. At marches from Selma to Montgomery, in jail cells and at sit-ins, the song became a kind of shield, a spiritual fortification against violence, humiliation, and despair. Its gentle but unyielding message, "we are not afraid," "we shall not be moved," "we shall overcome" was sung by protesters facing tear gas, police dogs, and batons.

In 1965, during a pivotal address to Congress advocating for the Voting Rights Act, President Lyndon B. Johnson invoked the song directly, concluding his speech with the words "And we shall overcome." Watching the speech, Dr. King reportedly wept.

While Seeger gave the song its cultural reach, Joan Baez gave it emotional purity. A young folk singer with a crystalline voice and unwavering conviction, Baez brought it to the steps of the Lincoln Memorial at the 1963 March on Washington for Jobs and Freedom, singing it after Dr. King's "I Have a Dream" speech.

Baez did not record the song as a studio single, but her live performances became some of the most stirring and visible renditions ever captured. As a white woman standing in solidarity with a Black-led movement, Baez represented the expanding moral coalition around civil rights. Her delivery was never theatrical; it was heartfelt, dignified, and achingly human. In her voice, the song's sorrow and its strength were laid bare. It wasn't just an anthem; it was a prayer.

"We Shall Overcome" did not stop with the US civil rights movement. Its message proved universal, and its melody was easy to learn, to translate, and to make one's own. It travelled far beyond American borders: in South Africa, it was sung by anti-apartheid activists; in Northern Ireland, it echoed through peace marches during The Troubles; in India, it was translated into regional languages during protest movements; in Eastern Europe, it inspired democratic dissidents under Soviet domination.

The song's capacity to cross language, religion, and culture is unmatched. It carries no overt ideology. It asks for no blood. It is powered not by anger but by determination, and that makes it endlessly adaptable.

Decades after its rise, "We Shall Overcome" remains a living song. It is sung in schools, at vigils, at protests, and in moments of national mourning. Its message still rings out wherever people gather to demand justice, whether that's on the steps of state capitols, in churches mourning victims of gun violence, or at climate marches led by a new generation.

It has never belonged to a single movement or era. That's what makes it revolutionary. It is a song that absorbs struggle and transforms it into courage. A few repeated words, we shall overcome, have outlasted empires, crossed oceans, and endured through every kind of resistance.

"We Shall Overcome" changed the world not through spectacle, but through simplicity. It offered a language of hope when language was under attack. It offered melody when the air was thick with fear. Pete Seeger made it a tool for unity. Joan Baez gave it a human voice. The Black church gave it soul. And millions of ordinary people gave it life.

As a song of hope, it is, and always will be, a song for those who believe that change is not only possible, but inevitable.

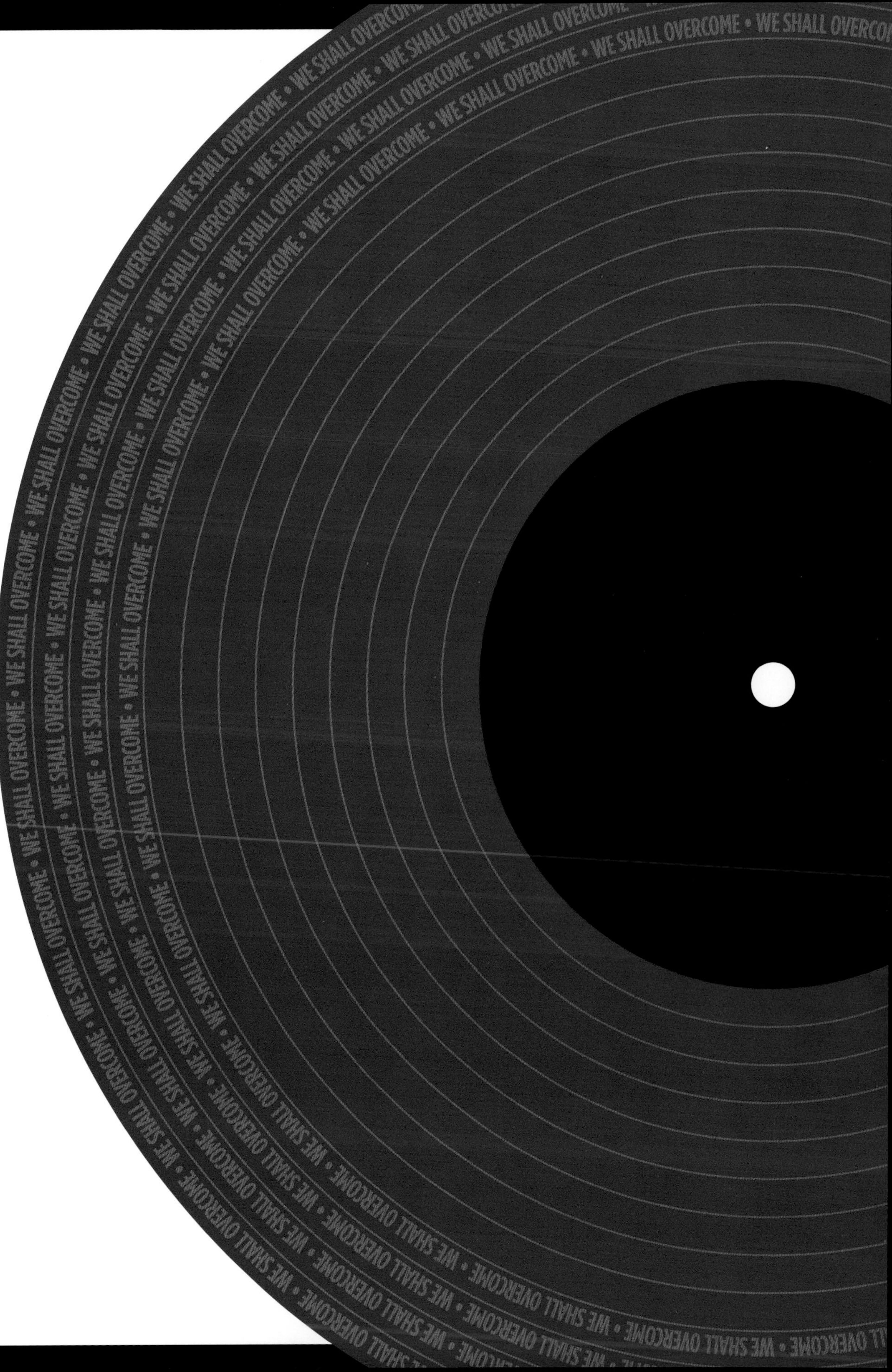
WE SHALL OVERCOME • WE SHALL OVERCOME • WE SHALL OVERCOME

1963, UK/USA

I WANT TO HOLD YOUR HAND

THE BEATLES

JOHN LENNON & PAUL MCCARTNEY, PARLOPHONE/CAPITOL

RECORDED OCTOBER 1963 AT EMI STUDIOS, ABBEY ROAD, LONDON

Beatlemania was the intense fan frenzy that surrounded The Beatles, starting in the early 1960s and lasting until the band's demise in 1970. It wasn't just a wave of popularity; it was a cultural eruption that reshaped music, celebrity, and youth identity on a global scale.

This was different from Elvis Presley, who had previously shaken the fabric with his hips alongside music, and from other chart-toppers. Beatlemania was a phenomenon, an irresistible surge of screaming teenagers and a global impact that lasts to this day. Four clean-cut lads from Liverpool dressed in suits – who would have guessed they'd spark a revolution?

And the spark for the global phenomenon was "I Want to Hold Your Hand," even though it wasn't the band's first success. In the United States, Australia, and several other countries, the band's second single, "Love Me Do," topped the charts. In the band's UK homeland, it was the fourth single, "From Me To You," that went No. 1.

In America, the path to the top was not so easily mapped. Capitol Records, an EMI subsidiary, was the label that should have released the band's recordings, but it resisted. So *Introducing . . . The Beatles* was sold through a licensing agreement with the label Vee-Jay, which was cancelled when it was alleged Vee-Jay didn't report royalties properly.

The first single taken up by Capitol was "I Want to Hold Your Hand," and the rest is history. The bigger label threw its weight behind the band and organized that first US tour.

The Beatles' arrival in the US on February 7, 1964 marked a seismic cultural moment, not just in music but in the broader fabric of American society. When their Pan Am flight touched down at New York's JFK Airport, they were greeted by more than 3,000 screaming fans, a wall of sound and hysteria that foreshadowed the media storm and fan frenzy to come.

Two nights later, their five-song performance on *The Ed Sullivan Show* drew an audience of over 73 million viewers, which was roughly 40% of the US population at the time, closing with "I Want to Hold Your Hand."

For many Americans, still mourning the assassination of President John F. Kennedy three months earlier, The Beatles offered a burst of joy, optimism, and youthful energy. Their charm, their wit, and their mop-top image captivated a generation overnight.

Over the next three weeks, The Beatles performed four short shows on the tour – one in Washington D.C., two at Carnegie Hall in New York City, and a final one in Miami – before a second appearance on *The Ed Sullivan Show*. Fan hysteria was sparked everywhere they went. Thousands camped outside their hotels. Police had to form barriers to contain screaming crowds. Radio stations played their songs nonstop.

In the days and weeks that followed, Beatles singles occupied the top of the Billboard charts, culminating in the unprecedented feat of holding the top five positions – "Can't Buy Me Love," "Twist and Shout," "She Loves You," "I Want to Hold Your Hand" and "Please Please Me" – on the *Billboard* Hot 100 on April 4, 1964, and 12 songs in total in the top 100. By the end of its sales cycle, "I Want to Hold Your Hand" had sold more than five million copies in the States alone.

Beatlemania wasn't just about music. It symbolized the rise of a new youth culture at a time of post-war optimism, economic prosperity, and social change. The Beatles' charm, wit, and style challenged norms, giving young people a fresh voice. Their haircuts and fashion sparked trends.

The Beatles' music broke down barriers and united people across generations and continents. Their songs initially explored timeless themes of love, peace, and self-reflection, with a sincerity that resonated with the human experience. In a world grappling with upheaval and change, their message of harmony struck a powerful chord, elevating them from pop stars to cultural icons and unlikely ambassadors of peace.

After the US, Beatlemania exploded globally. Canada and Australia were next. In Adelaide, the state capital of South Australia, it was estimated that more than 300,000 people welcomed The Beatles to the city. That was more than one-third of the city's population at the time, after a petition to get the band to Adelaide garnered more than 70,000 signatures.

The final wave was Europe, followed by Japan and South America, and it remained at its peak until 1966, when the band slowed its touring. It was the global reach that defined Beatlemania, regardless of language.

As the band's songwriting evolved, its fan base continued to embrace The Beatles' music until the band's demise in 1970. From "Nowhere Man" onwards, The Beatles took on a more socially aware edge too, with the first songs John Lennon and Paul McCartney had written that weren't love songs of sorts.

The Beatles sparked a significant discussion around topics such as loneliness ("Eleanor Rigby"), hypocrisy ("Baby You're a Rich Man"), religion ("Within You Without You"), and war ("Revolution").

In the end, Beatlemania was more than a cultural moment; it was a social revolution, and "I Want to Hold Your Hand" was the match that lit the fuse. That single song did not just introduce The Beatles to America; it introduced the world to a new kind of music, a new kind of fame, and a new kind of youth power.

From that first *Ed Sullivan* performance to the global stampede that followed, Beatlemania reshaped the pop landscape and laid the foundations for modern celebrity and fandom. The Beatles weren't just a band; they were a force that rewired culture, broke barriers, and offered a generation a soundtrack for awakening.

What started as four boys from Liverpool singing a catchy tune became a worldwide transformation, and it all began with one hand reaching out across the Atlantic, saying simply: "I want to hold your hand."

1964, USA

A CHANGE IS GONNA COME

SAM COOKE

SAM COOKE, ABKCO/DUCHESS MUSIC

RECORDED 1964 AT RCA STUDIOS, HOLLYWOOD

Soul legend Sam Cooke didn't live long enough to feel the full impact of his most profound words on a racially divided nation. At the age of 33, and just months after the release of the *Ain't That Good News* album, which included "A Change Is Gonna Come," Cooke was controversially shot dead in a Los Angeles motel.

Cooke was a chart-topping artist who had sold more than 10 million records at the time of his death, a number that has since tripled. In many ways, he was the voice of soul music, lifting it from the back blocks of gospel tradition to the top of the pop charts.

His voice was pure velvet, smooth, controlled, and effortlessly expressive. He could glide from a gentle croon to a soulful cry with stunning precision, blending the raw power of his gospel roots with pop elegance. There was a clarity in his tone, but it carried an emotional weight that conveyed heartbreak, joy, and yearning all within a single phrase.

He was the perfect voice to carry the arc from the romantic optimism of his 1957 breakout hit "You Send Me" to the haunting depth of "A Change Is Gonna Come," often referred to simply as "Change."

In those terms, "Change" was a humble posthumous release that has grown in stature over the decades. It reached a new zenith when America's first – and so far only – Black president, Barack Obama, had the song performed at the Lincoln Memorial during his inauguration festivities by Bettye LaVette and Jon Bon Jovi. On the night of his historic election victory, Obama also referred to it directly at Grant Park in Chicago: "It's been a long time coming, but tonight, change has come to America."

That moment arrived nearly five decades after Cooke had pleaded for change in song. But as powerful as that crescendo was, it also served as a reminder that there was more change to come, and more still needed.

In 1963, three events had a profound impact on Cooke. The first was Bob Dylan's "Blowin' in the Wind," a song that directly challenged racial injustice. Cooke, who later covered the Dylan song in his live shows, reportedly wished he'd dared to write something like it,

but feared alienating the white audience who bought his records.

But Dylan's boldness gave Cooke a sense of hope. If this young white folk singer could confront racism so openly, maybe change truly wasn't so far away.

The second was the March on Washington in August 1963, when Martin Luther King Jr. delivered his "I Have a Dream" speech, one of the most pivotal moments in civil rights in the USA. And finally, Cooke and his entourage were refused bookings at a motel in Shreveport, Louisiana, once the staff realized they were Black. After protesting loudly, Cooke was arrested for disturbing the peace under Jim Crow laws, a bitter reminder that things were not "separate but equal."

The convergence of Dylan's song, the March, and the motel arrest ignited something within Cooke. Just after Christmas that year, the lyrics to "Change" came to him in a dream, so deeply embedded was the longing and injustice he had experienced.

When he recorded it, it marked a dramatic shift from his usual pop fare. The track featured wlush, semi-orchestral arrangements, strings, horns, and melancholy harmonies underpinning Cooke's vocals. The lyrics were restrained yet full of longing and defiant hope.

At first, it was just an album track, opening side two of *Ain't That Good News* on March 1, 1964. There were concerns it might alienate the very audience that had made him a star. Cooke only performed it live once, on *The Tonight Show Starring Johnny Carson* on February 7, 1964, just weeks before the album's release. The arrangement, he felt, was too complex to reproduce in concert.

Cooke never lived to see its full impact. After his death, the song began to find its place, not as a chart hit, but as an anthem.

Its power lies in longevity. With one song Cooke had become, and today remains, one of the voices of a movement that continues to seek racial justice. "A Change Is Gonna Come" gave voice to pain, struggle, and, above all, hope, during the civil rights era as it still does today.

At a time when mainstream music rarely spoke to the Black experience, Cooke delivered a haunting and deeply personal anthem that became a collective testimony. It captured the exhaustion of a people burdened by segregation, violence, and second-class citizenship, but without bitterness or despair.

The lyrics became a sacred promise. It was sung at rallies, church services, and protest marches, offering strength to those who faced batons, jail cells, and water cannons. This was not a protest born out of anger; it was a protest shaped by grace, resilience, and hope, sharpened by suffering.

Notably, the song also helped shift the role of popular music itself. For a Black artist in 1964, especially one known for romantic ballads, to express such vulnerability and quiet defiance was a radical act. Cooke wasn't just singing about change. He was change.

Today, the song still echoes through the corridors of history. It is played at presidential inaugurations, civil rights anniversaries, and vigils for racial justice. It remains a timeless reminder that actual change, while often slow, is both necessary and unstoppable.

In 2007, "A Change Is Gonna Come" was inducted into the Library of Congress's National Recording Registry, recognized as "culturally, historically, or aesthetically significant." In 2021, *Rolling Stone* ranked it No. 3 on its list of the 500 Greatest Songs of All Time. And in 2025, it rose to the top of another *Rolling Stone* list, crowned No. 1 in The 100 Best Protest Songs of All Time.

It stands now above even Cooke's remarkable catalogue. Like "Strange Fruit" before it, "A Change Is Gonna Come" was a lightning bolt in the storm, an audacious, poetic act of witness from a Black artist willing to lay bare his hopes in a divided world.

1964, USA

THE TIMES THEY ARE A-CHANGIN'

BOB DYLAN

BOB DYLAN, COLUMBIA

RECORDED OCTOBER 1963 AT COLUMBIA 30TH STREET STUDIO, NEW YORK CITY

"The Times They Are A-Changin'" by Bob Dylan (Robert Zimmerman) is a powerful anthem of social and political transformation. Released in 1965, at the height of the American civil rights movement and just before the cultural upheaval of the late 1960s, it captures a moment of generational shift and growing resistance to the status quo.

It was Dylan's third single in some places, but it wasn't released as such in the USA. Instead, it was the title track of a watershed album by Dylan, a stark album that confronted racism, poverty, and social change. Dylan had lost his humor with this album, and with the title track, he wanted to write an anthem for change. And he did.

In the liner notes for *Biograph* (his 1985 compilation album), Dylan reflected that the song had been written with a clear purpose. He explained that its structure was shaped by the tradition of Irish and Scottish ballads such as "Come All Ye Bold Highway Men" and "Come All Ye Tender Hearted Maidens." His aim was to craft something expansive, built from brief, tightly written verses that built momentum through repetition. At the time, he noted, the civil rights struggle and the folk revival were closely connected, moving forward side by side.

At its core, "The Times They Are A-Changin'" is a warning and a call to action. Dylan urges listeners, especially those in positions of power, such as politicians, parents, and critics of change, to recognize that a wave of change is coming, whether they like it or not. The lyrics suggest that a rising tide of youthful dissent and democratic reform is sweeping away old systems, values, and hierarchies.

Dylan turns his attention to the political establishment, urging lawmakers to recognize the urgency of change. His warning is clear: those who resist or obstruct progress risk being swept aside by the unstoppable force of history.

The phrase "the times they are a-changin'" acts as both a prophecy and a challenge, signaling that social norms, racial inequality, war, generational authority, and outdated traditions are all under pressure. Dylan's use of biblical cadence and poetic simplicity gives

the song a timeless, almost prophetic weight, placing him in the tradition of folk singers as truth-tellers and moral witnesses.

Ultimately, it conveys the message that change is inevitable and resistance to it is futile. Whether in civil rights, anti-war protests, or youth counterculture, a new era is dawning. And those unwilling to listen, evolve, or engage with the demands of the latest generation will find themselves sinking "like a stone."

The early 1960s were a time of rapid social change in America, and this song served as a catalyst, a reflection, and a warning. Dylan's lyrics don't just reflect the social movements of the time; they press the issue, pushing listeners, particularly those in power, to confront the inevitability of change. With verses addressed to senators, mothers and fathers, and writers and critics, Dylan makes it clear that no one is exempt from the tide that's turning.

The power of "The Times They Are A-Changin'" lies in its ability to give voice to a generation that was no longer content to be polite or patient. Civil rights marches, student demonstrations, and the early stirrings of feminist and anti-war movements marked the 1960s. Dylan's words gave a poetic backbone to those protests. Activists and organizers adopted it not as background music, but as a rallying cry.

It was particularly resonant during the civil rights movement. Although Dylan was a white musician from Minnesota, his willingness to align himself with Black activists and causes made "The Times They Are A-Changin'" a bridge between folk music and direct social action. He performed at the 1963 March on Washington, prior to Dr. Martin Luther King Jr.'s "I Have a Dream" speech. "The Times They Are A-Changin'" wasn't played that day, but its spirit was unmistakably present.

As the Vietnam War escalated and political trust eroded, it gained new life. It became an anthem not just of hope, but of confrontation, used by young people to challenge the authority of parents, schools, churches, and governments that refused to listen. It was banned from some radio stations, criticized by conservative voices, and celebrated by protesters who believed Dylan was articulating what they were living.

The song's simplicity made it transcendent. There are no specific references to legislation or individual leaders. That's why it has remained relevant across generations, adaptable to struggles far beyond the 1960s. From the fight against apartheid in South Africa to modern climate protests led by young people, Dylan's message has remained relevant: the old ways are fading, and those unwilling to support change should step aside for the new generation pushing forward.

Socially, Dylan helped elevate songwriting as a serious form of political commentary. Before him, popular music largely steered clear of direct confrontation. It was a step beyond "Strange Fruit." After "The Times They Are A-Changin'," it was no longer radical to expect that a song could carry the weight of protest, dissent, or moral clarity. It inspired countless musicians, such as Bruce Springsteen, Joan Baez, Tracy Chapman, and Kendrick Lamar, to fuse music with activism.

"The Times They Are A-Changin'" crystallized the desire for change by Dylan, and it captured the mood of a restless generation and amplified the urgency of its demands. In doing so, it helped shift the cultural weather, giving voice to the voiceless and notice to the powerful. It's not just a song of its time. It's a song that changed how time itself could be challenged.

1966, CHILE

GRACIAS A LA VIDA

VIOLETA PARRA

VIOLETA PARRA, RCA VICTOR
RECORDED AUGUST–OCTOBER 1966; RELEASED NOVEMBER 1966
ON LAS ÚLTIMAS COMPOSICIONES

"Gracias a la Vida" (Thanks to Life) stands today as a suicide note for Violeta Parra. A potent song embracing all the things that matter while pointing a finger at those who wish to take away the basics of life, including freedom.

When it was released in 1966, it was a powerful commentary on her Chilean homeland as much as it was about herself. It expressed thanks for sight, sound, love, laughter, and even moments of sorrow, which she saw as life's simple gifts. Woven through the lyrics, though, is a quiet sense of emotional conflict, shaped by Parra's anguish over Chile's political unrest and the silenced voices that came with it, as well as her mental health struggle.

That all combined to explore the struggle between hope and despair gives the song its haunting power.

As with many songs in this book, it is both the song's use in protest and the music itself that lend it its gravitas. It gives them hope, and that is likely the point, as she slid into a fatal depression.

The song's verses praise life's gifts with unwavering appreciation. But with the benefit of hindsight, considering her struggles with depression and the political turbulence of 1960s Chile, it becomes clear that the song is not only a celebration but also a farewell. It also found its verse in defiance of the turmoil engulfing Chile at the time, with the left pressing for more equality, the right resisting change, and the democratic government in the middle getting squeezed from both sides.

Chile in 1967 was a country on the brink. Democratic but divided, hopeful yet unstable, it was a society where artists like Parra used music to express the sorrow, complexity, and latent power of a nation in transformation. "Gracias a la Vida" was born into this context, albeit written in La Paz, Bolivia, a work of gratitude composed amid political frustration and personal anguish. It remains, in part, a mirror of the Chile she saw: wounded and beautiful, with an underclass yearning to be heard.

Parra was born in San Fabián de Alico, a small town in Chile's Ñuble region, situated

at an elevation of approximately 600 m above sea level, partway up the Andes in central Chile, with a population of less than 2,000 residents. She was one of nine children and grew up singing traditional folk songs with her siblings and father, who was a music teacher.

At the age of two, the family moved to Santiago, then Lautaro and finally Chillán. The two rural towns suited the family more than the big city. As she grew, she recorded songs with her sister and experimented with Eurocentric music before returning to traditional Chilean folk music and writing her own material in that style. She was a big star in Chile, a national icon of folk revival and social song, who revived and preserved the Chilean rural music she grew up with.

"Gracias a la Vida" was written late in her career, and while not written to fuel a revolution, it did. Today, it is seen more as a suicide note, beginning with "Thanks to life, which has given me so much" and moving through a litany of gifts and experiences for which she expresses gratitude.

It is both gratitude and grief, expressed in a form that avoids bitterness while refusing to shy away from pain. That contradiction is what makes the song so powerful. It speaks to those who have suffered deeply and yet continue to find meaning in life . . . and hope.

Parra was a foundational artist in the *nueva canción chilena* (new Chilean song) movement, which merged traditional folk with political commentary and gave voice to the marginalized, particularly the working class and indigenous communities. She traveled Chile collecting rural and indigenous songs, preserving cultural heritage and asserting its importance in a modernizing, unequal society. Her music was radical not because it shouted, but because it insisted that stories of everyday people, especially women, mattered.

In many ways, "Gracias a la Vida" became a subtle act of resistance. It wasn't explicitly political; the messaging was more nuanced than explicit, and it was the time in which it was written, and by whom it was written, that gave it its political power. Latin American women in the 1960s were still expected to be silent, but Parra stood tall as an artist, a thinker, and a cultural protector for her country.

After her death, the song's reach only grew, becoming a resonant anthem across the Spanish-speaking world and far beyond. Argentine singer Mercedes Sosa recorded a cover version, which translated Chile's political issues into life under Argentina's military dictatorship. American folk icon Joan Baez performed it in both Spanish and English as a gesture of respect and solidarity.

Each time "Gracias a la Vida" was performed, it gathered new layers of meaning and transitioned to a new place. Whether heard at protests, funerals, peace rallies, or human rights vigils, it had the rare ability to mourn without surrendering to despair and to celebrate without turning a blind eye to suffering.

From Parra's time through the 1970s and '80s, Latin America endured dictatorships with protagonists exiled and grave human rights abuses. "Gracias a la Vida" became inseparable from the spirit of resistance. It gained strength from its quiet resolve and dignity rather than militancy. To give thanks for life, even in the darkest times, was itself a radical act of defiance.

Today, it endures through global expressions of reflection and resilience, extending well beyond its Chilean roots and into concerts, memorials, vigils, and activist spaces. It speaks to survivors of all kinds, those recovering from personal loss, political violence, or displacement. It offers a rare musical space where contradiction is welcomed, where sorrow and hope can exist side by side. It is a song of hope.

It was more than a folk song, even when it was written. It was a cultural testament through a personal expression that became collectively owned. Parra did more than just give her thanks for life. She redefined what it meant to live with both happiness and sorrow, and grace.

That unique position helped her create a song that has transcended time and is understood by many. We have a lot to be thankful for, but surely we deserve better than some of what governments present us with. Parra thought so.

1967, USA

RESPECT

ARETHA FRANKLIN

OTIS REDDING (COMPOSER), REARRANGED AND PERFORMED BY ARETHA FRANKLIN, AND RECORDED FEBRUARY 1967 AT THE ATLANTIC RECORDING STUDIOS, NEW YORK CITY

When Otis Redding wrote and first recorded "Respect" in 1965, one can only imagine he had no idea what Aretha Franklin, the Queen of Soul, would do with his humble little soul song two years later when she got her hands on it.

She flipped the song, redefined it, and transformed it into one of the most potent anthems of the 20th century.

Franklin turned "Respect" from a working man's cry into a declaration of self-worth with a few lyrical changes. An "I" to "you" shifted the balance. Redding wanted respect when he came home from work, while Franklin wanted respect when her partner came home from work. With that switch, a man's plea became a woman's demand. She took the sentiment of the original and gave it a shot of pure, unapologetic attitude. In doing so, she broadened it from one person to a group of people. It was about everyone who'd ever been undervalued or pushed aside, and for many, it was as much a feminist anthem as it was for civil rights.

Franklin recognized the song's broader meaning. Speaking in a 1999 NPR interview, she noted that although it later became an anthem for the civil rights movement, her own recording was framed more simply, as an exchange of respect within relationships, especially between men and women, with the expectation that it would be returned.

"Respect" was a banner for dignity, equality, and power, a song that echoed through streets, rallies, and living rooms alike.

The second wave of the feminist movement was gaining momentum. Betty Friedan's *The Feminine Mystique* had lit a fuse, and a new series of battlelines were being opened in what we would call the gender wars today. There was a backlash, but change can do that.

The civil rights movement had also stalled somewhat, despite still being far from achieving the progress necessary to even contemplate the concept of equality. The legal victories of the early 1960s hadn't translated into action, and frustrations often boiled over into violence. Those calling for peaceful

righteous fury. She wasn't asking for respect, she was demanding it.

And people listened.

"Respect" became a dual-purpose anthem, a rallying cry for both the civil rights and women's liberation movements. Aretha Franklin's voice, fierce, elegant, and commanding, cut through the noise of the era. It played from loudspeakers at marches. It appeared on protest signs. It entered the everyday lexicon. Saying "I want some respect" after 1967 meant something more. It meant: I know my worth. I won't be moved. And I'm not asking twice.

change, like Martin Luther King Jr., found themselves marginalized in an increasingly hostile political climate.

Black people in America did not feel respected.

Into this atmosphere dropped Franklin's "Respect," and the world was forced to pay attention. It became her first No. 1 on the Billboard charts, a feat she wouldn't match for another 20 years. It also earned her two of her 18 Grammy Awards. It kickstarted a career that would eventually see her ranked by *Rolling Stone* as the greatest singer of all time in both 2008 and 2023.

Her arrangement added even more fire. Backed by her sisters, Carolyn and Erma, on vocals, their urgent "sock it to me" chants turned the chorus into a call to arms. Unlike Redding's smooth, sensual take, Franklin delivered hers with gospel grit, sharp enunciation, and

Musically, "Respect" redefined what soul could be. It blended funk, gospel, and call-and-response with the spiritual urgency of a sermon. Recorded in New York City during February 1967, Franklin led the rhythm section through her vision of the arrangement and, with her sisters, developed vocal parts for the backing singers on the spot. The song continued to evolve in the studio until it was just right.

Reflecting on the song's place within the civil rights and feminist struggles, Franklin told the *Detroit Free Press* in 2017 that she never saw it as daring. To her, the call for respect was simply natural – something everyone deserves.

Socially, the song opened doors for Black women to take center stage in cultural and political conversations, not just as background singers, but as leaders with something urgent to say.

In the immediate aftermath, "Respect" became a rallying cry, not in the way slogans are pasted on placards, although it also was, but in how it became etched into the cultural psyche. Protesters sang it. Radio stations played it relentlessly. It echoed in marches, and its message was written on signs. It became a kind of shorthand for refusal: I will not be dismissed.

Globally, "Respect" landed like a lightning bolt. Although deeply rooted in the Black freedom struggle and the women's rights movement in the United States, its message resonated far and wide. The call for dignity, the demand for equality, and the voice of a woman asserting her worth unapologetically – these were not just American issues. They echoed from South Africa to Sweden, from Brazil to Britain.

Across Europe, especially in France, Germany, and the UK, "Respect" found a second life in student uprisings and feminist collectives. In Paris in 1968, amid massive protests against capitalism and patriarchy, "Respect" blared from dorm rooms and transistor radios. In London, second-wave feminists adopted the song in consciousness-raising sessions, finding in Franklin's voice a strength that mainstream pop rarely offered. It became a blueprint for a new kind of protest, less about marching feet and more about raised voices.

In apartheid South Africa, the song was banned from the radio. That made it even more powerful. Underground, Black South Africans heard a sound of defiance in Franklin that mirrored their own quiet resistance. She became a symbol of dignity and refusal.

In Latin America, during the rise of military dictatorships in the late 1960s and early '70s, Franklin's "Respect" sat alongside local protest songs, such as Violeta Parra's "Gracias a la Vida." It demonstrated how American soul music could also be a political force, how rhythm could carry revolution.

For many Black Americans, it stood alongside "We Shall Overcome" as a statement of identity and pride. For women, it carved out new territory, where soul, feminism, and Black excellence merged into something defiant, fresh, and undeniable.

What began as a personal reinterpretation evolved into a collective, global political statement. And decades later, its message still lands like a punch.

1968, USA

LOVE CHILD

DIANA ROSS & THE SUPREMES

R. DEAN TAYLOR, FRANK WILSON, PAM SAWYER & DEKE RICHARDS (THE CLAN), MOTOWN

RECORDED JULY–SEPTEMBER 1968 AT HITSVILLE U.S.A. (STUDIO A), DETROIT

"Love Child" by Diana Ross & the Supremes, released in 1968, marked a sharp turn in both subject matter and social impact for both the group and Motown. Departing from The Supremes' usual romantic fare, this song tackled the stigma of being born out of wedlock and poverty.

Its social impact was significant. "Love Child" gave voice to the experience of shame and exclusion felt by many in working-class and single-parent households. At a time when American pop music rarely addressed anything other than romanticism, Diana Ross's impassioned vocals humanized a topic that had long been hidden in silence.

After two singles by Diana Ross & the Supremes missed the top 20 on the charts, Motown boss Berry Gordy convened a team of writers and producers, including R. Dean Taylor, Frank Wilson, Pam Sawyer, Deke Richards, and Henry Cosby, but he didn't know what he was going to get. Known as The Clan, they set out to create a socially relevant hit. Instead of another love song, they crafted "Love Child," a track about a woman resisting sexual pressure, scarred by her own experience growing up poor and fatherless.

Diana Ross delivered the lead vocal brilliantly, with just enough pop to sell the record, and enough soul to sell the message. Motown's session group, The Andantes, handled the backing harmonies. Mary Wilson and Cindy Birdsong, who were now The Supremes, didn't appear on the record.

But most of the work was done in secret because Gordy didn't want anything that overtly political for his most successful act at the time. Gordy was worried about what making political statements could do to record sales, and he took some convincing. In fact, it was only when he was presented with the finished recording that he relented.

"Love Child" reached No. 1 on the *Billboard* Hot 100, proving that socially conscious messages could succeed in mainstream pop. Following its success, Motown developed a growing willingness to engage with real-world issues, subtly aligning with the broader civil rights and women's liberation movements.

It was a turning point song in so many ways, especially for Black female singers, taking the cry for "Respect" to another level.

The first female to record for Motown was Mable John. She signed with Berry Gordy in 1959 on the Tamla label, a Motown subsidiary. Her debut single "Who Wouldn't Love a Man Like That" was released in 1960, marking the beginning of Motown's journey with female performers.

From there, The Marvelettes, Mary Wells, Martha and the Vandellas, and, of course, The Supremes followed. But it was The Supremes who took it to the next level. "Where Did

Our Love Go" was a monster hit in 1964, and it was followed by "Baby Love," "Stop! In the Name of Love," "Back in My Arms Again," "You Can't Hurry Love," "You Keep Me Hangin' On," "Love is Here," "Now You're Gone," and "The Happening," which all went to No. 1 on the Billboard charts. The Supremes were one of the biggest recording acts in the world.

But they were all soft love songs, romantic pop if you like, until "The Happening," which was a bold, upbeat pop song about being disillusioned. It was an experiment with upbeat music that clouded the meaning of the words, and it marked a perfect turning point.

In 1968, the band was rebranded Diana Ross & the Supremes, with the poignant social commentary of "Love Child" as its first success in its new form. Released as the civil rights movement was at its height in the wake of the assassination of Martin Luther King Jr., "Love Child" was a multi-layered conversation as told by Ross as the narrator.

It touched on the stigma of illegitimacy and the pain of poverty. Sung from the perspective of

a woman born out of wedlock, or what was then known disparagingly as a "love child," the lyrics are a plea for dignity and self-determination in the face of shame and judgment.

The song's voice warns a partner that she cannot face the prospect of an unplanned child outside marriage, burdened by memories of her own upbringing marked by poverty, stigma, and the absence of a father.

Motown was happy to take a risk on this song and eventually encouraged the social comment. Lyrically rich, "Love Child" explored other taboos in addition to illegitimacy, such as sexual pressure and female agency in one pop song. Illegitimacy was at the forefront of the song and hard to miss. At the same time, the song connects sexual freedom with female autonomy, expressing enduring affection while demanding the right to personal boundaries and independence.

The narrator of the song is talking about desire, but also a woman's right to say "no," as well as "yes." She is in control.

Diana Ross herself was at the height of her fame then, performing a song that used veiled but unmistakable language of hurt and exclusion, with lines evoking shame, rejection, and social stigma.

So, while "Love Child" was a daring move for The Supremes and Motown, it was executed with such finesse that it not only avoided blowback but also topped the charts, becoming The Supremes' 11th No. 1 hit. That, in itself, was a revolutionary act: a socially conscious song about female sexual autonomy, sung by a Black woman, hitting No.1 in America!

While Motown was a money-making machine, it also became a vehicle of change. While she wasn't a songwriter, Diana Ross continued her journey with songs like "I'm Still Waiting" (1971), "Do You Know Where You're Going To" (1975), and "Love Hangover" (1976).

Stevie Wonder embraced the ability to comment rather than just make music, actively examining race, class, and inequality.

Marvin Gaye also took on the charge with his album *What's Going On*, which was a concept album filled with sorrow, protest, and soul-searching, ranging from war and police brutality to ecological ruin. It included a hit single of the same name that appears later in this book. Whether he could have recorded a song like this at Hitsville USA without "Love Child" will never be clear, but what is known is that "Love Child" opened the door for others to follow, crying out for acceptance and equality, lyrically catching people off guard while they danced and sang along.

Many others passed through that door. With "Respect" and "Love Child," the role of the female Black singer changed, and the messages were embraced.

1969, USA

FORTUNATE SON

CREEDENCE CLEARWATER REVIVAL

JOHN FOGERTY, FANTASY

RECORDED 1969 AT FANTASY STUDIOS, BERKELEY

From its pounding drumbeat and one of the most unmistakable guitar riffs in rock history, "Fortunate Son" by Creedence Clearwater Revival comes out swinging, a blistering indictment of privilege and the Vietnam War that left no room for misunderstanding. Then enters the voice, gritty, uncompromising, and sharp; delivering the opening words with force, slicing through the sound to expose a harsher truth.

Released in September 1969, at the height of the Vietnam War, and included a month later on the album *Willy and the Poor Boys*, "Fortunate Son" was more than just a hit record. It became a howl of protest, a two-minute and 21-second outburst of pure, electrified class warfare. Its target wasn't just the war in Southeast Asia, but the system that fed it, and more precisely, the people who never had to pay its cost.

John Fogerty, the driving force of CCR, had carried a skepticism of authority since childhood. In second grade, he was sent home to watch President Eisenhower's inauguration, but what struck him wasn't the ceremony or the words; it was the procession of sleek black limousines carrying the powerful. Even as a boy, he sensed something unsettling about those displays of privilege, later admitting he had always felt wary of people parading in such cars.

As Fogerty grew older, the unease sharpened whenever he watched the theatrics of political conventions. The repeated declarations from state delegates nominating their "favorite son" struck him as hollow and performative, a ritual celebrating privilege rather than people. From his working-class vantage point, such displays only reinforced his skepticism toward the wealthy and powerful who seemed far removed from everyday lives.

That suspicion became disgust when he was drafted during the Vietnam War. Though Fogerty himself found relative safety in a Reserve unit in 1966, the glaring injustice of the draft system stayed with him. Wealth and power, he saw, bought exemptions. The poor went to war. The privileged sons of senators and CEOs found deferments, desk jobs, or diplomatic outs.

CCR had been working on a song, and after weeks of fine-tuning, the music was

there. But Fogerty still needed to write the lyrics. He shut himself in a room and sat on the edge of his bed with a yellow pad to write "Favorite Son."

But something shifted, and he pivoted to "Fortunate Son" and the lines poured out in 20 minutes, the fastest he'd ever written a song's lyrics. The irony was that it came after weeks of rehearsal and musical preparation had been underway in the background.

What came out was a blistering, working-class anthem, defiant and uncompromising. Fogerty's delivery drove home a rejection of privilege, calling out the elites who cloaked themselves in patriotism while letting ordinary people bear the real cost of war. It wasn't a song against soldiers; it was a song for them. Against the corrupt system that sacrificed them.

The impact was immediate. "Fortunate Son" climbed to No. 3 on the *Billboard* Hot 100 and roared across American airwaves in an explosion of truth. It became the unofficial anthem of the anti-war movement and a battle cry for working-class Americans tired of being told to shut up and serve. It wasn't flower power, it was fury. Not kumbaya, but kickback.

Fogerty later admitted one person didn't inspire the song, but he'd had someone in mind. David Eisenhower, grandson of the former president and soon-to-be son-in-law of Richard Nixon, became a stand-in for privilege. Eisenhower did serve, but comfortably, on the

USS *Albany* in the Mediterranean. "Whether they liked it or not," Fogerty wrote in his memoir, "these people were symbolic . . . they weren't being touched by what their parents were doing."

For Fogerty, that symbolism was unavoidable. "You'd hear about the son of this senator or that congressman who was given a deferment from the military," he said. "They seemed privileged." The working class, meanwhile, got the draft notice and the body bags.

"Fortunate Son" didn't just explode the myth of equal sacrifice, it laid bare how the elite had weaponized patriotism to shame the poor into fighting their wars while college kids with connections stayed home. The unlucky ones got a free ticket to Saigon.

And while many '60s protest songs leaned on dreamy metaphors and love-ins, "Fortunate Son" came from a grittier place. CCR may have hailed from California, but their sound was Southern-fried and hard-edged. Fogerty's voice wasn't pleading, it was snarling. His protest wasn't abstract; it was razor-sharp and working-class to the bone.

Over the years, "Fortunate Son" has featured in nearly every major Vietnam War film and dozens of documentaries on the conflict, as well as *Forrest Gump*, *Born on the Fourth of*

July, and *Apocalypse Now*. It's been covered, sampled, debated, and dissected. And yet, despite all the accolades, including a place in the US National Recording Registry in 2013, its sharpness hasn't dulled.

In 2020, Fogerty was compelled to step in when Trump's campaign began using the song at rallies. He pushed back hard, arguing that the entire message had been twisted. What made it worse was that Trump seemed to revel in the reference to the presidential anthem, apparently missing the point that the song was mocking those in power who lived comfortably behind gates while sending others to the battlefield.

And yet, maybe that's the cruel brilliance of "Fortunate Son." It always hits hardest when the message is ignored by the fortunate. In a world where the powerful still dodge consequences and wrap themselves in flags to justify conflict, Fogerty's words remain a scorching reminder.

As long as war is waged by the poor on behalf of the rich, as long as patriotism is sold like a product, and if young people are asked to die for leaders who wouldn't dare send their own kids, "Fortunate Son" will never stop being relevant.

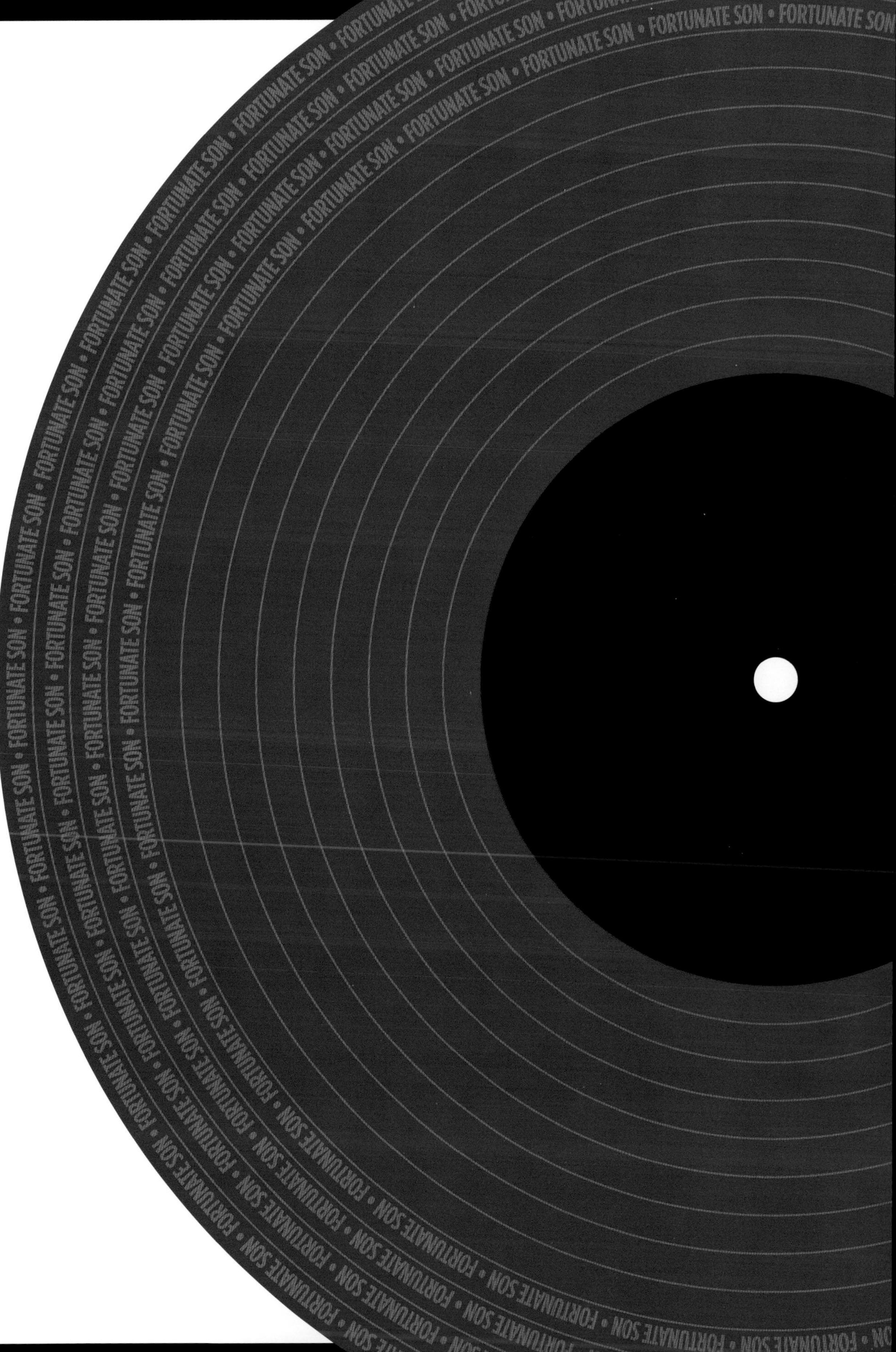
FORTUNATE SON • FORTUNATE SON • FORTUNATE SON

1969, USA

TO BE YOUNG, GIFTED AND BLACK

NINA SIMONE

NINA SIMONE & WELDON IRVINE, RCA VICTOR

RECORDED 1969 AT RCA STUDIO B, NEW YORK CITY

Nina Simone was one of the all-time great singing Black activists, and she wrote and sang many songs espousing the "rights of her people." She was involved at all levels of the fight for equality, even after leaving the States in the wake of the assassination of Martin Luther King Jr.

Born Eunice Waymon, she chose a stage name to provide distance between herself and her North Carolinian family after she began singing the devil's music in a nightclub in Atlanta. Flighty and fiery, she was a staunch defender of what she believed to be right.

Her music transitioned from classical and gospel to jazz, folk, and blues, and she was known for many years as the High Priestess of Soul. This forms the background to her transition from a nightclub singer to one of the most influential singers of her time, as she confronted social commentary head-on. Which brings us to 1969's "To Be Young, Gifted and Black," a moderate chart hit and her second biggest selling single in its time.

But before it was a song, it was a loss and a book.

Playwright Lorraine Hansberry was a friend of Simone's, and her death from cancer in 1965 left a hole in the world of Black writers, as well as in Simone's heart. Hansberry's play *A Raisin in the Sun* was the first Broadway play written by an African-American female, and the book and play *To Be Young, Gifted and Black: Lorraine Hansberry in Her Own Words* was released posthumously.

Simone took her grief and turned it into a roar. Four years later, with lyrics by her bandleader and frequent collaborator Weldon Irvine, she debuted "To Be Young, Gifted and Black" at the Harlem Cultural Festival in 1969. It was not just a tribute to Hansberry; it was a statement, an anthem, and a mission.

But it wasn't for everyone.

Simone made it clear that the song was not directed at white audiences, nor was it intended to disparage anyone. Instead, it deliberately centered on Black identity and pride, declaring itself as something created for her own community. It simply ignores them, the rest. She didn't care if mainstream America understood it, liked it, or played it on the radio.

This song wasn't interested in inclusion; it was an act of affirmation. An early statement that Black lives matter.

And affirmation was radical. In 1969, America was not in the mood for Black joy. MLK was gone. Malcolm X was gone. Medgar Evers, which was the assassination that fueled the civil rights movement, was already a fading news story. Black communities were still facing poverty, police brutality, and political betrayal on all sides. Civil rights had been signed on paper, but not lived in practice. What did it mean, then, to sing a song so bold?

Simone opened with a celebration of Black youth and talent, her voice lifted by rich choral harmonies that gave the song both warmth and power.

For young Black children listening, it was the opposite of what society was telling them. It told them they were brilliant. That they mattered, that their potential wasn't something to apologize for, it was something to protect, nurture, and fight for. It wasn't angry, like her earlier work "Mississippi Goddam." It wasn't cynical, it was quietly defiant. It sidestepped rage and instead offered something even more dangerous to the status quo: pride.

Hansberry believed in the need for cultural transformation alongside political change. That you couldn't simply legislate equality, you had to sing it into being, write it into stories, etch it into memory. Simone took that belief and gave it melody.

It spread like the gospel. Aretha Franklin recorded her own version in 1972, giving the song a rich, soulful glow that carried its message even further into American homes. Her album *Young, Gifted and Black*, which featured the cover, won the Grammy Award for Best Female R&B Vocal Performance.

The win was laced with irony: the year before, Franklin with "Don't Play That Song" had beaten Simone in the same category for the album *Black Gold* that featured Simone's original. Franklin dominated those awards, winning seven straight, and was the darling of the music world. Simone, by contrast, was far more confrontational, openly aligning herself with Malcolm X's belief that violent revolution might be necessary.

Franklin reflected the song's gospel and jazz roots, but Donny Hathaway, not long after Simone's original, proved its versatility and power with a smooth and soulful version. The song appeared at school graduations, rallies, theater shows, and Sunday services. Teachers used it. Preachers used it. Organizers used it. It slipped into the culture and stayed there.

But it was never just a song; it was a worldview. Simone was not singing for entertainment. She was testifying. Her activism wasn't a side hustle; it was the backbone of her art. She played Carnegie Hall and called out American hypocrisy. She

appeared on television and spoke with the moral clarity of someone who had no patience for half-truths. She was complicated, unyielding, and often bruising. However, in "To Be Young, Gifted and Black," she found a space to be vulnerable and powerful simultaneously.

The song's influence was carried beyond America's South and Harlem and into any country still wrestling with colonial hangovers, where being Black was equated with inferiority. It reminded listeners that their value wasn't conditional on the color of their skin. That their beauty wasn't niche, and their intelligence wasn't an exception.

Decades later, the song hasn't aged. It was played and shared widely during the 2020 Black Lives Matter protests, often remixed, sampled, or quoted in speeches and performances. But it never needed updating. It has never been out of time. It was never trendy. It was always *true*.

During a television interview on WKCR-TV in 1968, hosted by Harold Channer, Simone said, "An artist's duty is to reflect the times in which we live." This quote has since been widely used in documentaries, books, and cultural commentary, especially in the documentary *What Happened, Miss Simone?* as it perfectly encapsulates Simone's belief that music and art cannot be separated from social and political struggle.

However, with "To Be Young, Gifted and Black," she did more than reflect the times; she gave us something to carry forward. She turned Hansberry's legacy into a living message. She gave young Black children a song that didn't ask them to be anything but themselves. It was an affirmation that her people should not be ashamed of being brilliant.

1970, CANADA/USA

BIG YELLOW TAXI

JONI MITCHELL

JONI MITCHELL, REPRISE

RECORDED 1970 AT A&M STUDIOS, LOS ANGELES

Much like "Love Child" smuggled a hard truth inside an irresistible pop melody, Joni Mitchell did the same with "Big Yellow Taxi." This bright, bouncing tune masked a deeply pointed protest about the destruction of the environment. At its heart is a stark image of natural beauty destroyed for the sake of concrete convenience – simple, brutal, and impossible to forget.

Playful on the surface but piercing in its intent, the song is both a political statement and a personal lament. It landed in 1970, at the dawn of the modern environmental movement, and helped soundtrack a cultural shift. Mitchell even closes the track with a feigned laugh after the final run of "ooh, bop-bops," a knowing chuckle that underscores the bitter irony of what she's singing.

This was satire, sharpened to a point.

Though Mitchell was born in Canada, she was living in California when she wrote the song. She wasn't a chart-dominating superstar, "Big Yellow Taxi" was just her third single, and she never chased singles success, preferring the depth of the album format. But she already had a reputation that made people listen.

And the real power of "Big Yellow Taxi" isn't just what it meant in 1970, although it quickly became an unofficial anthem of the emerging green movement; it's how it has grown in meaning over time. Its message hasn't faded; if anything, it has become more urgent and as relevant as ever.

In a 2004 interview with the *Los Angeles Times*, Mitchell explained that "Big Yellow Taxi" was born during her first visit to Hawaii. After arriving by taxi, she awoke the next morning to a striking contrast: lush green mountains in the distance, and directly below, an endless stretch of asphalt. The jarring sight inspired the song's central image of paradise lost to development.

From there, the images tumble out, shiny hotels, slick little boutiques, all the signs of "progress," but not the good kind. Then comes the tree museum, most people figure it's pointing to the Foster Botanical Garden in Honolulu. And the twist at the end: you're better off chewing on a crooked, ugly apple than choking down the poison that comes with chemical farming.

Released the same year as the first Earth Day, 1970, "Big Yellow Taxi" arrived just as environmentalism was becoming a political force in North America. It echoed Rachel Carson's *Silent Spring,* which warned of ecological disaster, and public unease over pesticides, pollution, and unthinking development was growing.

Yet while most protest music of the era targeted war or racial injustice, Mitchell trained her gaze on the planet itself. It was one of the first times that mainstream pop music addressed environmental issues, making environmental concerns feel like part of daily life, not just academic policy, in a way that was both listenable and culturally digestible.

But "Big Yellow Taxi" wasn't just a song about trees and poisoned apples. The final verse throws a curveball that's still argued about today: the sudden sound of a door slamming and a man being carted off in a yellow cab. Some point out that in the 1950s and '60s, police cars in parts of Canada, including Saskatoon, where much of her childhood was spent, were painted yellow. Was she hinting at an arrest? Or was it just another image of loss, slipped in at the end?

She hints at the latter. In interview after interview, she insists it was just that: a literal taxi. A symbol of personal loss, not legal trouble. Her old man simply left.

And that's the brilliance of it. The way it folds the personal into the political, love entwined with landscape, is a cry of regret that resonates on every level. Forests cut down, orchards poisoned, relationships lost, it all lands the same. You don't realize the value until it's already slipped away.

Success in music is often measured by numbers such as chart positions, record sales, and radio play. And they are important, but if you want to send a message, legacy counts, and perhaps the most accurate test of a song's power is how deeply it embeds itself in the cultural fabric. By that standard, "Big Yellow Taxi" may be the most enduring achievement of Joni Mitchell's extraordinary career.

It peaked at No. 67 on the *Billboard* Hot 100, and the week it debuted at No. 100, "(They Long to Be) Close to You" by the Carpenters started a four-week run at the top. Not to diminish the Carpenters, but I'd suggest "Big Yellow Taxi" is the better-known song today.

It became a cultural landmark, transcending time to become a reference point across generations. It has been quoted in newspapers when talking about environmental issues, echoed in protests, and endlessly referenced in think pieces and public discourse. It has been frequently used in films, television commercials, and environmental campaigns, often ironically, by the very forces Mitchell was criticizing. Yet that only deepens its legacy: it has become part of the polluted air we breathe, its warning cry embedded in the soundscape of modern life.

Over the years, "Big Yellow Taxi" has been covered by a wide range of artists, from Amy Grant's 1990s rendition to Counting Crows' 2002 version featuring Vanessa Carlton, which brought the song to a whole new generation, even if the music press slammed it at the time for completely missing the original's subversive intent. What had once been a satirical, bittersweet protest song was reimagined as a chirpy pop duet, stripped of its irony and edge. Critics were scathing. *Rolling Stone* called it "toothless," and it was later included in several 'worst songs of the 2000s' lists, with many accusing it of turning one of Joni Mitchell's sharpest statements into background music for shopping malls.

Yet even that backlash proved its significance. You can't ruin something that doesn't matter, and this song mattered. But each interpretation

speaks to the song's adaptability and its ability to resonate with different eras and different audiences while retaining its core message.

Perhaps most strikingly, it has become a kind of shorthand for ecological regret. Today if someone speaks of paving paradise to put up a parking lot, almost everyone knows exactly what you mean. It's a line that has outlived the song that birthed it, serving as a condensed critique of unchecked development and environmental destruction. That's not just songwriting, that's cultural imprinting.

Everyone knows the sting of that line about not realizing what you've got until it's gone. The difference here is simple: this song isn't going anywhere. It's dug in, timeless, and it'll outlast all of us.

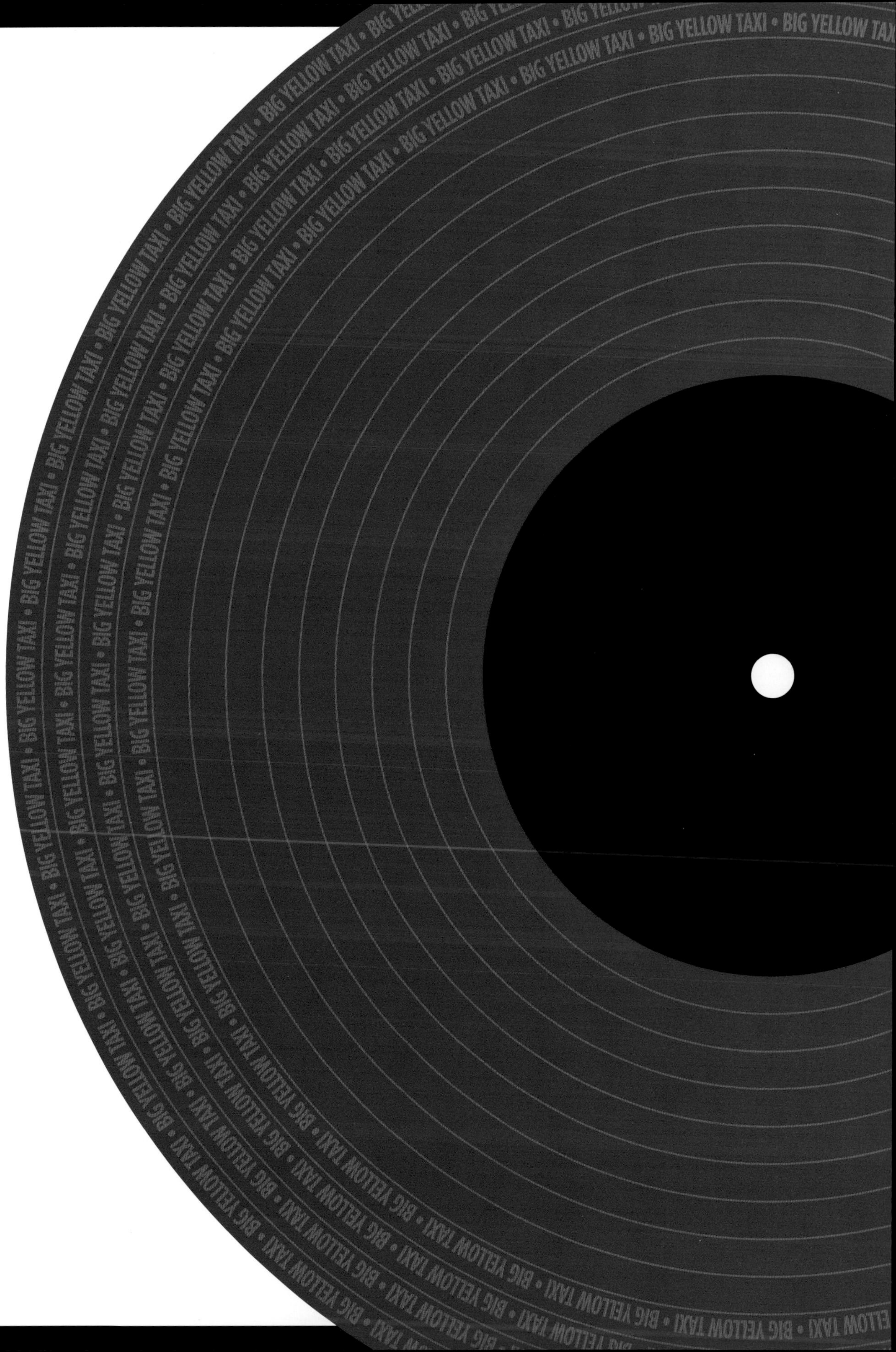
BIG YELLOW TAXI • BIG YELLOW TAXI • BIG YELLOW TAXI

1971, BRASIL

CONSTRUÇÃO

CHICO BUARQUE

CHICO BUARQUE, PHILIPS/UNIVERSAL
RECORDED 1971 AT PHONOGRAM STUDIOS, RIO DE JANEIRO

Construção was the title of Chico Buarque's eighth studio album. It was written, in part, during his exile in Italy and also in his native Brazil. It emerged in the heart of a repressive era, when Brazil was firmly under the grip of a military dictatorship that had been in place since 1964.

The regime imposed strict censorship, dissolved Congress at key moments, and used the Institutional Acts, especially AI-5 in 1968, to legalize repression, torture, and surveillance. The regime imposed strict censorship on the press, literature, theater, and music, and opposition figures, students, intellectuals, and journalists were imprisoned or disappeared.

It was from this environment that Buarque was exiled in Italy.

While freedom was lost, Brazil was experiencing what the regime proudly called the Milagre Econômico, the Brazilian Miracle, a period of rapid GDP growth and grand infrastructural expansion. New highways, buildings, and cities grew, and the people who built them, laborers and bricklayers, were being left behind, both economically and in the national narrative. The title track, "Construção," stepped directly into this contradiction and exposed it with elegance, venom, and artistry.

On the surface, it tells a simple story in which a construction worker kisses his wife goodbye, goes to his job, and falls to his death, as if inspired by "Bella Ciao" whereby the process is about heading off to war. But its form and language reveal a much more profound critique.

Buarque uses anaphora to haunting effect with repeated sentence openings like "And he kissed his wife," "And he walked into the building," "And he floated in the air," each time altering only the end, mirroring the mechanical and monotonous rhythm of working-class life in a hypnotic rhythm.

The worker doesn't even get a name. Just gone. No story, no dignity. Dead in the wrong lane, holding up traffic. Not remembered as a person, just an inconvenience, something in the way. That line keeps coming back, over and over, and each time it hits harder, because it's never just one man. It's a whole class, ground down, spat out, written off so the world can call it progress.

Brazil's censorship laws prohibited overt political protest. But Buarque, like many great artists of his time, found a way to resist without being obvious. "Construção" was, at its core, just a song about a man and his job. But to listeners who lived in the shadows of dictatorship, it was a cry of pain and protest.

Somehow it slipped past the censors, but not the people. In households, on radios, and in quiet conversations, the meaning was understood. It was a song that said more with suggestion than others dared say with slogans.

At the time of its release, the regime was celebrating Brazil's development as a triumph. International economists praised the country's growth, and the government beamed with pride at the image of a modern, industrious nation.

Brazil's regime was celebrating the iconic imagery of skyscrapers in São Paulo and Rio, but Buarque wasn't impressed by GDP when it came with such a human cost. The man in "Construção" is the very worker who built this "miracle" with his hands, only to be discarded, unnamed, unmourned, erased. The title itself is a bitter pun: "Construção," construction, is both the man's job and the machine that destroys him. He is not only building the nation; he is being built into it, brick by brick, until he vanishes.

What makes "Construção" extraordinary is that it does not rage, it mourns. Its repetition, its subtle linguistic shifts, and its slow musical build all contribute to a feeling of entrapment. The song loops upon itself like the workday. It mimics the grind of a system that cannot be

escaped. By the end, the listener is exhausted, not by volume, but by inevitability. The emotional weight is cumulative. The political message is devastating due to its weight.

Musically, Buarque broke new ground by combining traditional Música Popular Brasileira (MPB, or Brazilian pop music) with lush orchestral arrangements, creating a sound that was rich and theatrical. The instrumentation swells as the song progresses, building like a city under construction, until it suddenly drops, flat and final, like the man falling from a scaffold. The artistic control is absolute.

Its legacy is vast. "Construção" is now taught in schools, analyzed in universities, and held up as a masterclass in how music can carry meaning under oppression. It proved that lyrics could be literature, that melody could be defiance, and that a voice, carefully used, could still cut through the noise of authoritarian control. It inspired other musicians, writers, and filmmakers to find ways to say what could not be said aloud. In the years that followed, even as censorship persisted, Brazilian art became increasingly layered, poetic, and coded. Buarque showed the way.

Above all, the song gave dignity to the forgotten. The worker in "Construção" is no longer unseen. In song, he becomes a symbol of every man crushed by the weight of a system that values production over people, buildings over bodies, and growth over justice. His fall is not just a death; it is a national tragedy. And in that fall, repeated endlessly in Buarque's brilliant refrain, Brazil was forced to hear what it had been trained to ignore.

"Construção" remains one of the most potent expressions of resistance in Latin American music. Its genius lies not in its volume, but in its restraint. It whispered truth in a time of lies. And more than 50 years later, it echoes anywhere the ordinary person is lost to a system.

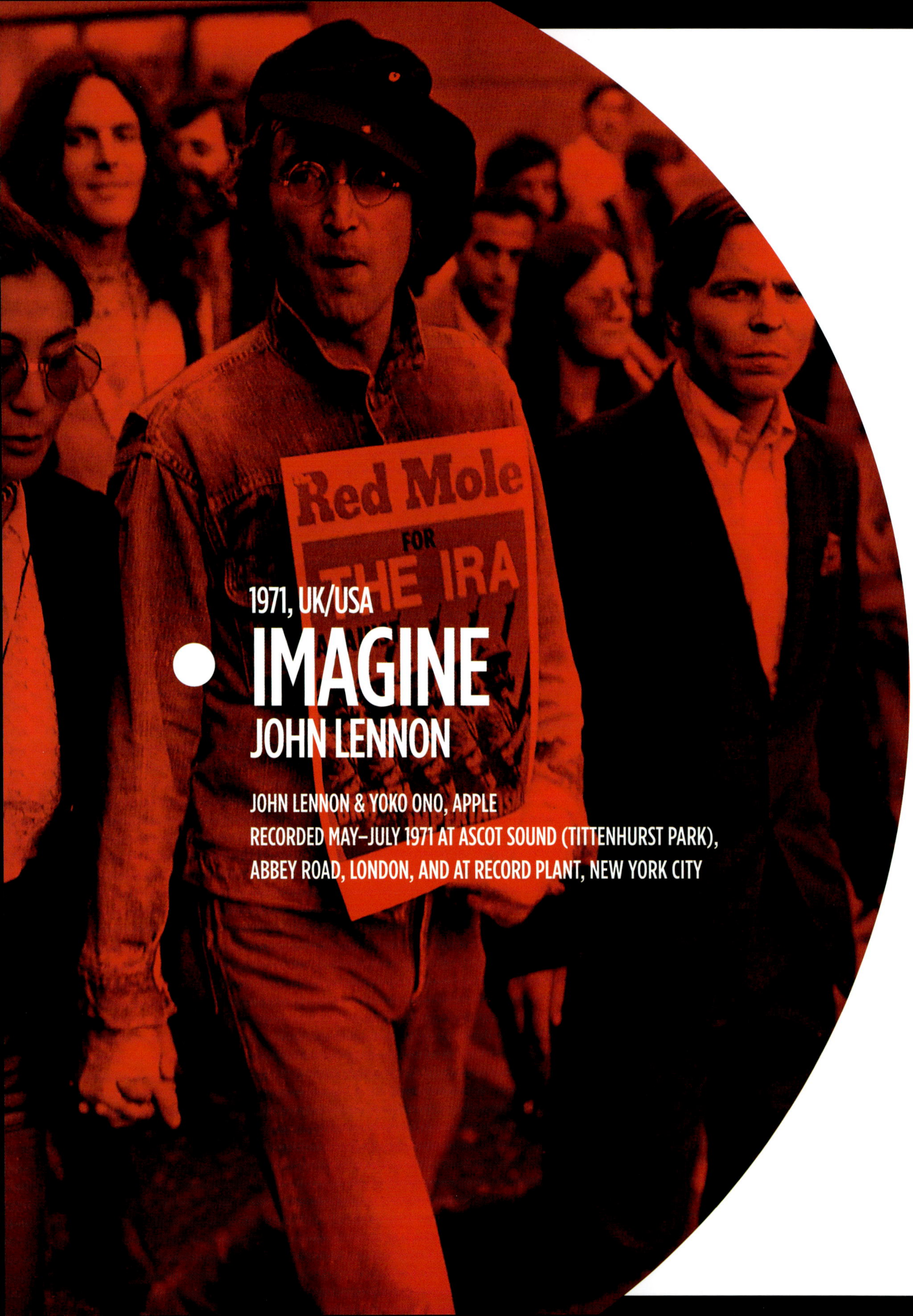

1971, UK/USA

IMAGINE

JOHN LENNON

JOHN LENNON & YOKO ONO, APPLE
RECORDED MAY–JULY 1971 AT ASCOT SOUND (TITTENHURST PARK), ABBEY ROAD, LONDON, AND AT RECORD PLANT, NEW YORK CITY

By the early 1970s, the dream of the 1960s counterculture was beginning to fray. The peace movement hit rigid walls, civil rights gains were under siege, the Vietnam War raged on with no clear end, and the optimism of Woodstock gave way to the brutality of Altamont. In the Western world, young people remained politically engaged, but they were increasingly disillusioned with the lack of, or the slow pace of, change.

Richard Nixon sat in the White House and was escalating an increasingly unpopular war in Vietnam, and protests against it filled the streets. Trust in government was eroding fast, with revelations of secret bombings in Cambodia and the release of the Pentagon Papers fueling public outrage, and this was before Watergate.

Globally, Cold War tensions lingered, while the US inflation, inequality, and racial unrest exposed the limits of post-war prosperity. The establishment, once seen as unshakeable, now looked increasingly fragile. Idealists from the '60s weren't just protesting; they were searching for something entirely new. Nirvana, perhaps.

That's the world John Lennon saw in 1971 when he sat at his white Steinway piano and wrote "Imagine." It wasn't a passive song. It was a provocation, quiet and melodic, almost lullaby-like, yet ideologically sharp. Lennon was not describing the world as it was but deliberately imagining the opposite and the world he wanted. Where nationalism, religion, capitalism, and borders divided people, Lennon offered a vision of a borderless, secular, classless utopia.

In a 1980 interview with *Playboy*, Lennon reflected that "Imagine" carried ideas as radical as any political manifesto, even if he wasn't aligned with communism or any formal movement. What made it work, he admitted, was its sweetness and the way a message of upheaval was delivered gently enough for people to embrace it.

In other words, Lennon understood that to communicate radical ideas, you often need to disarm people first. Where earlier protest songs shouted slogans and drew clear political lines, "Imagine" asked its audience to pause, reflect, and dream. The melody was gentle and meditative, unlike "Fortunate Son" which expressed anger. "Imagine" proposed the dismantling of nearly every institution that held up the modern world.

It was a bold move, but not an isolated one. Lennon's journey toward "Imagine" began in 1969, with "Give Peace a Chance," his first solo hit after leaving The Beatles. That track was recorded not in a studio, but in a Montreal hotel room during his and Yoko Ono's famous "Bed-In for Peace." Surrounded by reporters, friends, and fellow activists, Lennon led a makeshift choir through what would become the most enduring anti-war chant of the era.

With only handclaps, a cardboard-box drum, and raw room acoustics, the song captured the messy, spontaneous spirit of late-1960s activism. Its simplicity was its strength and the title of the song repeated. Just one line, over and over, offering a hopeful refusal rather than a complex political doctrine. It quickly became the unofficial anthem of the anti-Vietnam War movement. Folk legend Pete Seeger famously led over half a million demonstrators in singing it during the November 15, 1969, Moratorium to End the War in Vietnam protest in Washington, DC, a moment that crystallized the song's power.

"Give Peace a Chance" worked because it gave people a tool for collective action, and its simplicity allowed anyone, anywhere, to join in. It was a chant, a slogan, something to hold onto in a time of despair and rage. But it didn't offer a roadmap. That's where "Imagine" stepped in.

Where "Give Peace a Chance" was reactive, opposing war and calling for a break in hostilities, "Imagine" was visionary. It wondered what a truly peaceful world would look like. Lennon's answer was radical and challenging. No religion, nations, or personal property were postulated. They weren't gentle suggestions; they were direct challenges to the foundations of modern Western society. Yet millions embraced the song not as a manifesto, but as a soothing anthem for hope.

It initially received a modest reception, as it challenged many social norms, so that was perhaps expected. It was released in October 1971 and reached No. 3 in the US, receiving mixed reviews. Some listeners and critics embraced the song's ethereal, utopian quality, while others, especially within conservative religious groups, reacted strongly against its dismissal of organized faith. The suggestion of a world without religion struck them as deeply provocative and even threatening. Several American radio stations refused to play the track, especially in the Bible Belt. Yet over time, the song's message grew in relevance and reach.

By the 1980s, "Imagine" had been adopted around the world as a universal call for peace. It was played at the fall of the Berlin Wall. It echoed through Olympic ceremonies and United Nations events. It became a staple at candlelight vigils and peace rallies. And after Lennon's assassination on December 8, 1980, it became something even more powerful: a eulogy for the man himself.

Still, "Imagine" has never lost its edge. Its lyrics remain challenging, especially in a world still gripped by war, religious extremism, and economic inequality. After 9/11, US radio stations stuck "Imagine" on a no-play list. Not because it was angry, it wasn't. It was calm. Too calm, maybe. The problem was the words. In a country suddenly praying on every corner, a song that questioned heaven was a bit too raw. Too close to the bone.

That tension, that a song can be both comforting and radical, is why "Imagine" endures. It doesn't just ask us to hope for peace; it asks us to let go of everything that stands in its way. It's not a call to arms, it's a call to unarm, to dismantle, to dream harder.

And crucially, it wouldn't have happened without "Give Peace a Chance" first. That earlier track gave Lennon his voice as a solo artist and proved that music could still

mobilize people even after The Beatles. It was direct, unsophisticated, almost childlike, and that was the point. It built the bridge between the visceral protests of the 1960s and the more introspective, philosophical vision of the early 1970s.

One song asked for a moment of pause. The other offered an entirely new future.

Together, "Give Peace a Chance" and "Imagine" trace a path from collective protest to individual awakening. They represent two sides of Lennon's public evolution, from agitator with a guitar to philosopher at the piano. And in a world still struggling to choose peace over power, they remain as relevant now as they were then.

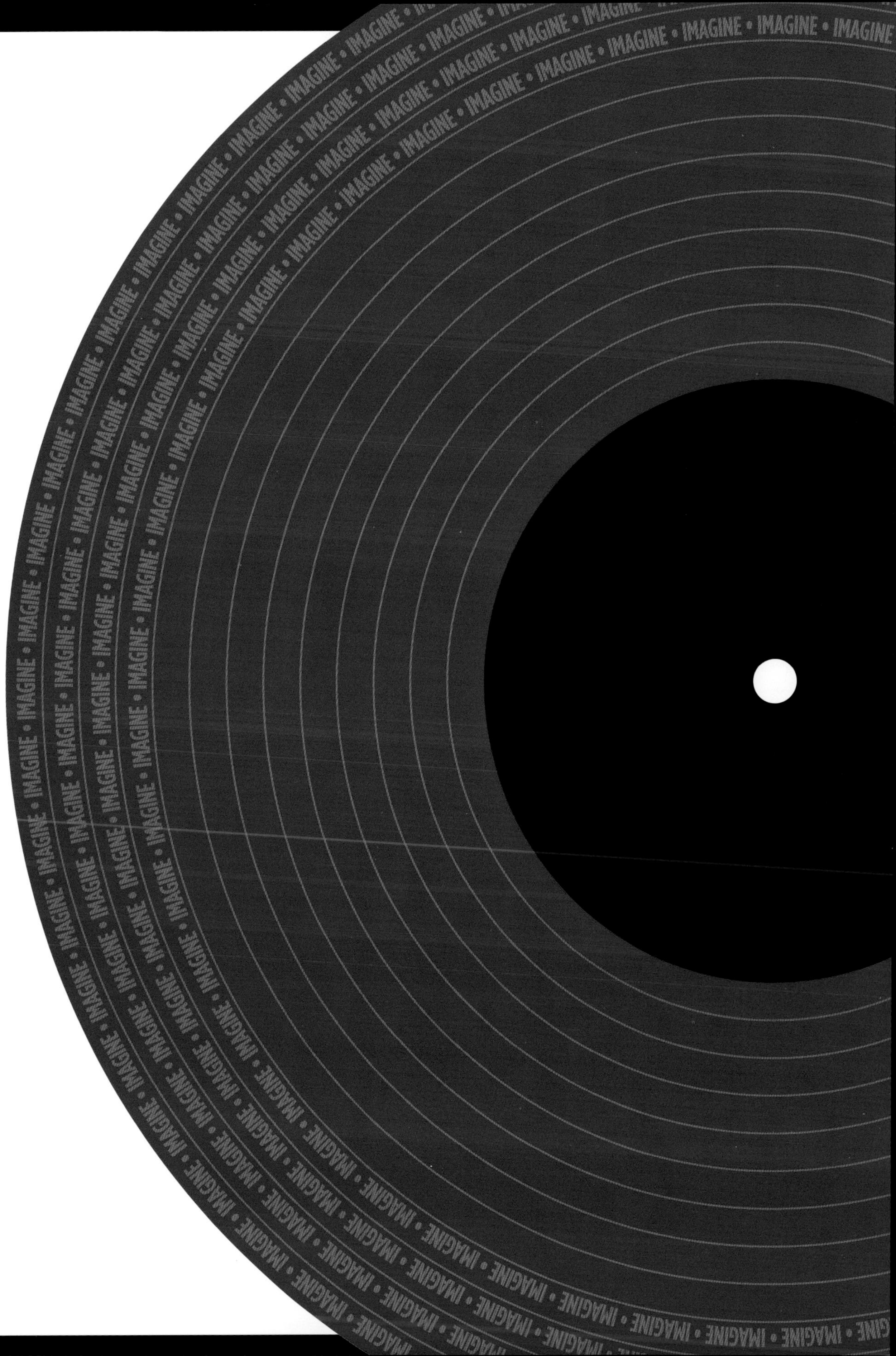
IMAGINE • IMAGINE • IMAGINE

1971, USA

MAN IN BLACK

JOHNNY CASH

JOHNNY CASH, COLUMBIA

RECORDED FEBRUARY 1971 AT COLUMBIA RECORDING STUDIOS, NASHVILLE

"Man in Black" is one of the most revealing and enduring songs Johnny Cash ever wrote. It was also pivotal for country music, and for the first time stretched the genre and opened the door for songs like "The Pill" by Loretta Lynn and "Jesus was a Capricorn" by Kris Kristofferson. Cash had dabbled before with social statements in songs like "The Ballad of Ira Hayes," but "Man in Black" was a next-step manifesto for one of the biggest stars in the American music scene at the time.

Released in 1971, it was a public explanation, in his own words, of why he always wore black, and what that color had come to symbolize in his life and music. He said he'd love to wear a rainbow, but instead he needed to carry darkness on his back.

Cash had long been known for his somber wardrobe, but with this song, he gave the decision a political and moral clarity that cut deeper than any fashion choice.

And the message didn't stand alone. The *Man in Black* album, Cash's 38th, an extraordinary output by any measure, was one of his most politically charged bodies of work. This wasn't a one-song statement. It was an entire record built around conscience. Tracks like "Singin' in Viet Nam Talkin' Blues" dealt bluntly with the war and the soldiers coming home in pieces, mentally and physically. "Ned Kelly" mythologized the Australian outlaw as a symbol of rebellion against authority. Even the cover image, stark and austere, reinforced the idea that Cash was no longer singing for entertainment; he was singing as witness.

That made "Man in Black" all the more startling within the landscape of country music at the time. Nashville wasn't exactly known for protest songs. In the late 1960s and early '70s, mainstream country tended to avoid social commentary and, in fact, pushed back against it. Where rock, folk, and soul were alive with civil rights anthems and anti-war protests, country radio was playing "Okie from Muskogee" and "The Fightin' Side of Me" which waved the US flag, of which Merle Haggard, a brilliant chronicler of the working class, was so proud. He aimed at the counterculture, and President Nixon was so impressed he invited Haggard to the White House.

Not Cash, though; instead, Cash broke the Nashville mold as he carved his own path. And he wasn't doing it from the margins. He was a Grand Ole Opry star, a chart-topping veteran, a household name with his own television show. Yet here he was, declaring allegiance not to power, but to those society had left behind. "Man in Black" was no fashion statement. It was a rejection of silence.

But the seeds of that song had been planted years earlier. In 1964, Cash released *Bitter Tears: Ballads of the American Indian*, a concept album unlike anything else in country music. It was a pointed and painful reckoning, seven songs that told stories of betrayal, removal, and resilience, written to give voice to Native Americans whom American history had tried to silence. The album included "As Long as the Grass Shall Grow," about the forced displacement of the Seneca people, and "Apache Tears," which mourned the death march west. Most famously, it featured "The Ballad of Ira Hayes," the story of a Pima US Marine who helped raise the flag at Iwo Jima, only to return to Arizona and be ignored, alienated, and destroyed by the very country he served.

Radio stations refused to play it. The country music industry turned away. Cash responded the only way he knew how, head-on. He took out a full-page ad in *Billboard* magazine condemning the cowardice of DJs and programmers who celebrated myths of cowboys and conquest but couldn't stomach the truth of what those stories had cost. He didn't just wear black, he *stood* in it.

Cash had long believed he had Cherokee ancestry, a piece of family folklore passed down without evidence. Later research would prove it untrue, but the belief had shaped his sense of identity for decades. More importantly, it forged a lasting empathy. Whether the bloodline was real or imagined, the kinship was genuine. He saw in the stories of dispossession and resistance a reflection of his values, loyalty, pride, and survival in the face of power. *Bitter Tears* wasn't a commercial move. It was a moral reckoning. And it laid the groundwork for the song and the album that would come to define his public persona.

He dressed in black for a reason. In 1971, he laid it out: the poor, the beaten down, the ones living on the hungry side of town. He wore it for prisoners, for the war dead, for the kids shipped off to Vietnam while the rich sat safe at home. And then he cut deeper. The verse that struck hardest tied straight back to *Bitter Tears,* honoring those who died believing God was on their side, and the countless more who were slaughtered believing the nation was. A line that went right to Native America, to faith betrayed and lives destroyed.

"Man in Black" was not a protest song in the usual style of the era. It didn't borrow from the folk poetics of Dylan or the gospel fire of Nina Simone. Cash didn't do abstraction. He wrote like he spoke, plainly, directly, and without apology. He first performed the song publicly at Vanderbilt University, just months after returning from Vietnam and playing to inmates at Folsom and San Quentin. He described it as a song centered on the urgent issues in society, a reflection on what demanded transformation. He explained that his choice of color was a stand-in for sorrow, solidarity, and stubborn resistance. It was not anti-American. It was pro-truth.

Cash had never been a joiner. He wasn't a politician. He didn't campaign or preach. But he was always watching. And when something wasn't right, he couldn't let it slide. That was the force behind "Man in Black." It was a song of witness. He wasn't moralizing, he was standing beside the wounded, the outcast, and the forgotten. In black. Always in black.

What made "Man in Black" so compelling was that Cash wasn't playing a character. He *was* the character. His prison concerts weren't PR stunts; they were personal. His battles with addiction and depression were central to his identity and were visible to all. So you believed him when he said he'd keep wearing black "until things are brighter" because he'd already shown you what he stood for.

In the decades since, "Man in Black" has become more than a song. It's a cultural emblem and a phrase that means honesty, sorrow, and resistance. It's been quoted by artists and politicians, punks and pastors. And it stands today as a blueprint for what it looks like when fame is fused with purpose.

1971, USA

THE REVOLUTION WILL NOT BE TELEVISED

GIL SCOTT-HERON

GIL SCOTT-HERON, FLYING DUTCHMAN
RECORDED OCTOBER 1970; RERECORDED APRIL 1971
AT RCA STUDIOS, NEW YORK CITY

Gil Scott-Heron's "The Revolution Will Not Be Televised" hit like a cultural thunderclap in 1971.

Though built on a sparse jazz-funk groove, it wasn't a song in the conventional sense; it was a spoken-word broadside aimed at the complacency of a television-addicted America. Near hypnotic in its rhythm, its delivery is seen as a modern precursor to rap and hip-hop.

Music historian Brian Priestley observed in *Jazz on Record* (1988) that Scott-Heron's early output was essentially rhythmic poetry, laying the groundwork for what would later be recognized as rap.

Spoken word has always sat at the heart of Black culture, and Scott-Heron tapped straight into that, mixing it with the backbeat and the urgency of civil rights and Black Power. He wasn't talking in riddles or dressing it up as metaphor. His "revolution" was plain enough, change only comes if people get involved, if they struggle for it. In his work, he turned the language of advertising and popular culture back on itself, using it to expose the emptiness of consumerism at a time when Black Americans were confronting police violence, entrenched racism, and deep social and economic divides.

"The Revolution Will Not Be Televised" was the first song on his debut album *Pieces of a Man*, marking his transition from life as a poet to that of a recording artist. The recording was unlike anything else that had been released at the time, an intriguing mix of R&B, soul, jazz-funk, and proto-rap.

Scott-Heron's point was blisteringly clear on "The Revolution Will Not Be Televised": the real revolution, whether against racism, class oppression, or systemic injustice, wasn't going to unfold neatly on TV screens, sandwiched between ads and news bulletins. The revolution would happen in the streets, among the people, and by the people.

At the time, the United States was awash with images of the civil rights movement, Vietnam protests, and Black Power demonstrations. Yet, these were often filtered, softened, or spun by mainstream media. The news was increasingly being delivered by television, and while its reach was massive, it also felt filtered to Scott-Heron and untrustworthy.

So he flipped the lens back on itself, warning against passivity and mass media's capacity to sanitize or distract.

His cultural references, from *The Adventures of Rocky and Bullwinkle and Friends* TV series, which attacked the Cold War through satire, to Richard Nixon, who fueled the Cold War, punctuated the idea that revolution could never be a spectator sport. And the phrase itself, "The revolution will not be televised," has since transcended the song to become part of the political language of protest.

His verse about Nixon predates Watergate, proving the American president was already divisive and worthy of progressive scorn. Cynically, Scott-Heron cast Nixon and his leadership group into a ridiculous scene of political theatre. This verse painted the so-called leaders of the system as part of the problem. Nixon wasn't about to lead any revolution for justice; the idea of him doing so was absurd.

He took aim at Nixon for a reason. To Scott-Heron, Nixon was the last bloke you'd ever trust to lead a revolution. He kept a war going that nobody wanted and stomped on civil liberties the second people pushed back. The picture he painted, Nixon and his cronies chewing through soul food ripped out of Harlem, was pure sarcasm, a jab at leaders happy to exploit Black culture while giving nothing back.

It didn't matter, though. If Nixon appeared "presidential" on TV, dropped a sound bite or two between ad breaks, the machine kept rolling. America was sold as if it were just another product, sandwiched between petrol slogans and Coke jingles.

"The Revolution Will Not Be Televised" did not chart on the *Billboard* Hot 100, nor did it sell in the millions like the Motown hits of its era. Yet its impact, cultural, political, and artistic, was profoundly outsized compared to its commercial footprint.

It gave voice to a rising frustration within Black America in the early 1970s. Scott-Heron channeled the energy of the post-civil rights movement generation, angry, disillusioned, and suspicious of mainstream media and governments doing nothing. He captured the shift from peaceful protest to radical critique. His message wasn't designed for pop radio but for street corners, college campuses, and activist circles.

Second, its format changed music. Scott-Heron fused spoken word, poetry, and a jazz-funk backbeat into a delivery style that would become a blueprint for hip-hop and rap. Chuck D of Public Enemy called him "the first rapper," and hip-hop's pioneers, from KRS-One to Mos Def, have traced their lineage directly back to this song.

Third, its title became a slogan. "The Revolution Will Not Be Televised" entered the

social and political lexicon, quoted by activists, educators, journalists, and artists. It came to symbolize grassroots resistance and the idea that real change doesn't happen on TV or in curated media but in the streets and in people's lives.

One of the most remarkable aspects of its legacy is its flexibility. Activists, artists, and educators continue to reinterpret its meaning. For some, it is a call to direct action; for others, it is a critique of how capitalism commodifies even radical movements. During the 2020 George Floyd protests, the phrase was revived on social media, now juxtaposed against the reality that revolutionary moments can indeed be "televised," but not necessarily with the depth or justice Scott-Heron envisioned.

Ultimately, the song's influence permeated global protest culture. Even in Australia, Britain, and South Africa, its title was invoked in anti-apartheid rallies, Indigenous rights movements, and the underground press. It wasn't a chart hit, but it was a cultural wake-up call.

In the decades since its release, "The Revolution Will Not Be Televised" has been

archived by the Library of Congress as a work of cultural and historical significance. Universities teach it as a text that bridges the Black Arts Movement, the civil rights struggle, and modern media criticism. Its opening lines alone are instantly recognizable: an index of how deeply the piece has penetrated collective consciousness.

Ultimately, the song's enduring power comes from its uncompromising truth: change is not a spectacle; it is lived and fought for. It refuses to be softened by nostalgia or commodification. Even half a century later, Gil Scott-Heron's voice still cuts through with clarity, a reminder that we cannot wait for someone else to deliver justice to us in a neat, packaged broadcast. He didn't just write a song; he etched a warning into the culture:

Real change doesn't come packaged. It comes when people stop watching and start moving.

He ended on a note of optimism, insisting that real change would unfold in lived experience, not in advertisements or on television screens.

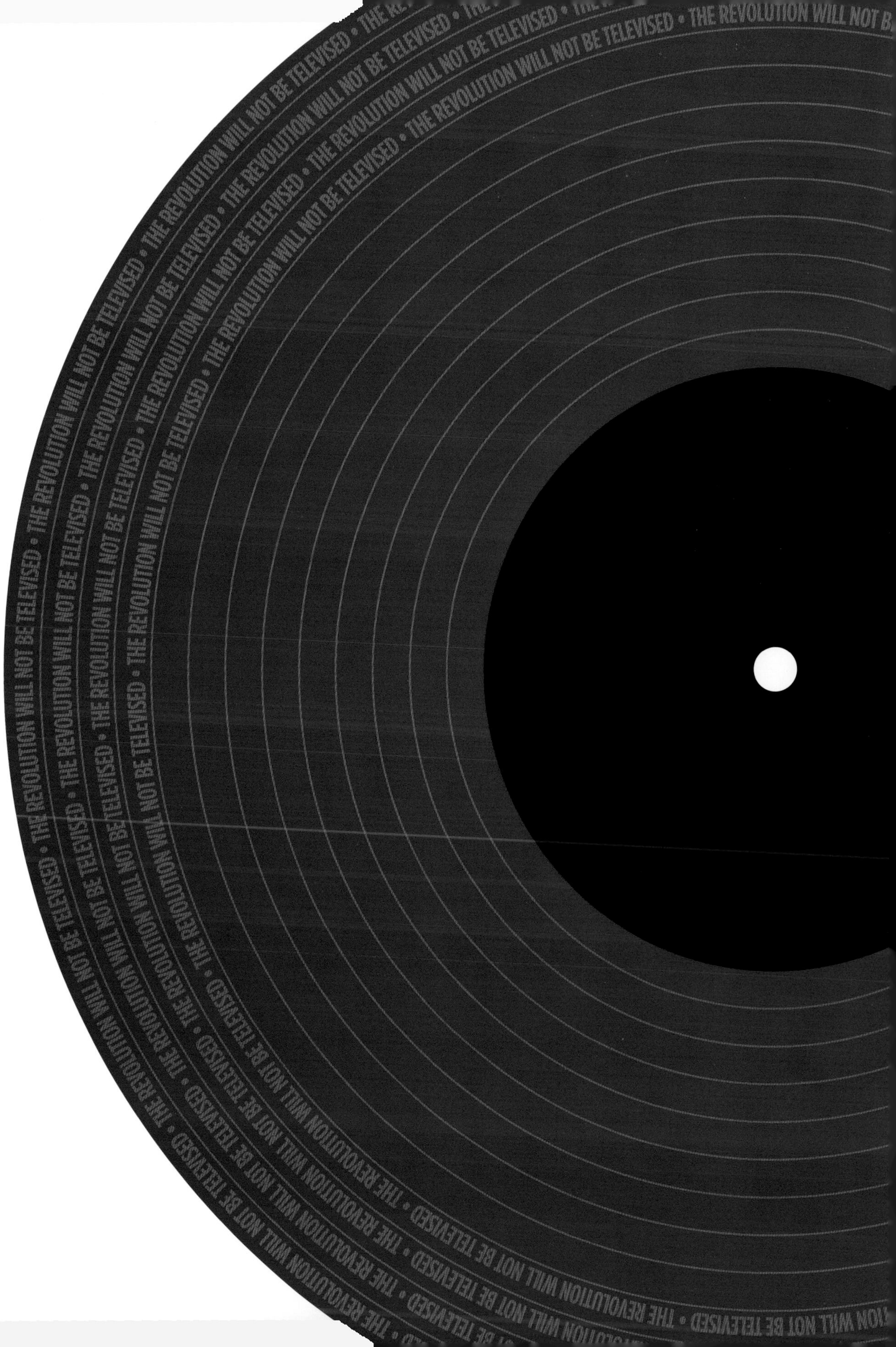
THE REVOLUTION WILL NOT BE TELEVISED

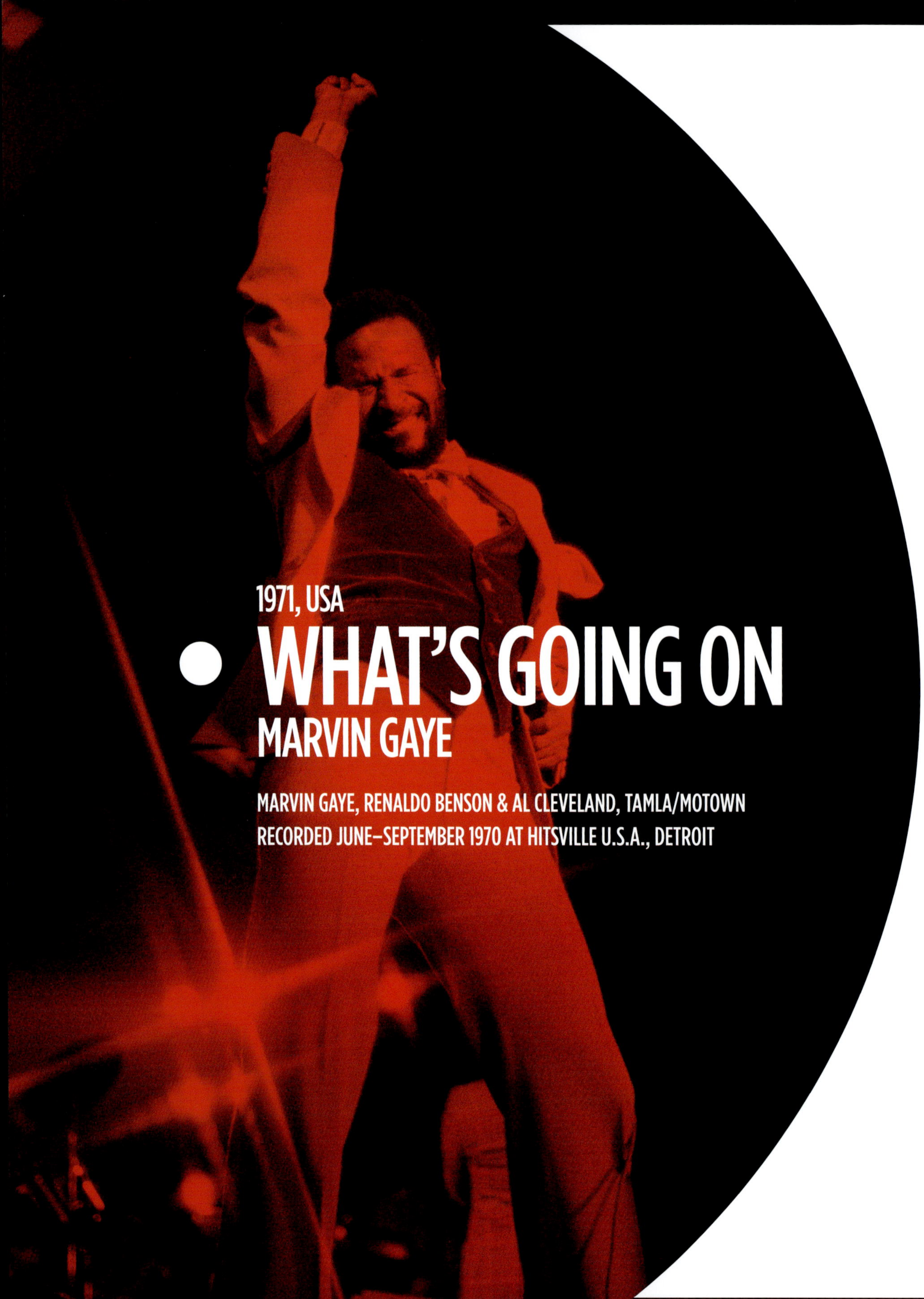

1971, USA

WHAT'S GOING ON

MARVIN GAYE

MARVIN GAYE, RENALDO BENSON & AL CLEVELAND, TAMLA/MOTOWN
RECORDED JUNE–SEPTEMBER 1970 AT HITSVILLE U.S.A., DETROIT

When "What's Going On" was released as a single in January 1971, it sent a shockwave through American popular music. This was Marvin Gaye, Motown's prince of smooth soul, the velvet-voiced hitmaker with domestic and foreign No. 1 singles, stepping away from love songs to confront the burning questions of his time: racism, war, poverty, and environmental destruction.

Motown founder Berry Gordy tried to block its release as he did with "Love Child" a few years earlier, fearing a political song would ruin Gaye's marketability. But Gaye refused to back down. The song was inspired in part by his brother Frankie's stories of Vietnam, the police brutality Gaye had seen on the streets of Detroit, and the growing violence toward anti-war protesters.

When Four Tops member Renaldo "Obie" Benson brought Gaye a fragment of a song he'd been working on with writer Al Cleveland, Gaye reshaped it into a mournful yet melodic plea. Benson witnessed police brutality at what is now known as Bloody Thursday, when the police used deadly force to quell the anti-war protest in People's Park at the University of California. He started writing this song in the `aftermath.

Benson rejected the idea that it was a protest song; in his eyes, it was a love song.

Gaye grasped the song and its intent, framing it in warmth. He altered the melody, added some extra lyrics, and gave it a title. He wasn't planning on recording the song, but Benson convinced him to make it his own. Over five recording sessions between June and September 1970, at Hitsville and mixed at Motown's Center, the song that *Rolling Stone* magazine named the greatest song of all time in 2020 was recorded.

The track opened with party chatter from people like Detroit Lions players Mel Farr and Lem Barney, as well as musician Elgie Stover, who would gain more fame as a caterer for Bill Clinton than he did as a musician. It gave it a semi-live feel with a deceptively gentle saxophone intro (recorded, for the most part, in one take by Eli Fontaine as a bit of "goofing around") and a loose, soulful rhythm that masked the anguish at its heart.

Gaye's vocals were also the result of a mistake by Kenneth Sands, who was engineering the song, when he accidentally put comparative

vocals over the top of each other and provided a lush sound that Gaye loved and later adopted for many of his recordings.

He starts the song by calling out to his mother, carrying the weight of grief that so many felt. It was a sharp turn from the love songs he was known for, suddenly facing a world where brothers were being killed and fathers were urging their sons to hold back – to stay safe, stay quiet, keep their heads down. The point wasn't hidden, war solves nothing. What mattered was compassion, some sense of unity. The single's release stunned Motown, but the public responded immediately. It climbed to No. 2 on the *Billboard* Hot 100 and No. 1 on the R&B charts. Here was proof again that a Motown song of conscience could succeed in the mainstream. It sold out the original 100,000 pressing in days, and then the second 100,000 within the first week, eventually selling more than two million copies and becoming the fastest-selling Motown single of all time.

After a journey of self-awareness that began in the mid-1960s, Gaye's transformation from a soulful singer of love songs into an agenda-setting agent of change for the 1970s was complete.

"What's Going On" was more than a hit; it was a line in the sand. For Motown, it ended once and for all the unwritten rule that Black artists should steer clear of politics, a door first opened by Diana Ross & the Supremes with "Love Child." It then allowed for Gaye's full concept album of the same name, released in May 1971. That record, flowing seamlessly through songs about war, injustice, drug abuse, and environmental ruin, redefined what soul music could be.

What's Going On became a landmark work, often hailed as the greatest protest album ever recorded. Critics and historians have repeatedly placed it at the pinnacle of socially conscious music, not only for its lyrical content but for how it reshaped the boundaries of soul and popular music.

In 1985, David Ritz published *Divided Soul: The Life of Marvin Gaye,* attempting to capture what made "What's Going On" so distinctive. For him, it was Marvin pouring his own pain into something bigger, a record that was as much about faith and doubt as it was about politics. It wasn't soul music in the old sense. It was Marvin turning himself inside out, and in the process inventing something new.

The legend has only grown since. *Rolling Stone* would go on to crown it the greatest album ever made, calling out the way it stretched soul into something both beautiful and bruised, art and conscience in one. And on the 40th anniversary, Alexis Petridis wrote in *The Guardian* that it flipped the idea of protest music, proving it didn't have to shout. It could evoke grief, offer consolation, or sound like empathy.

Its influence can be measured beyond critical acclaim by the number of artists, from Stevie Wonder and Curtis Mayfield to Lauryn Hill and Kendrick Lamar, who have cited it as a touchstone for socially aware music.

What set "What's Going On" apart was its delivery. Gaye wasn't shouting slogans; he was singing prayers, questions, and reflections. The seamless symphonic production created a haunting backdrop that gave his message universal reach. If you were lulled into the song by his voice, you would eventually consume the lyrics.

In this way, he transformed the idea of a protest album from an overtly political manifesto into something profoundly human and spiritually charged.

As a song, the power of "What's Going On" was driven by its compassion and request for a new non-violent way. In an era where protests were met with violence and the nation seemed to splinter, Gaye's voice invited empathy.

That empathy has kept the song alive for more than 50 years. Its central question still demands an answer in a world scarred by war, police violence, and environmental crises. Songs like this that don't shout for a revolution prove there is a different path to express disappointment and sorrow. You could ask, reflect, and still shake the world.

"What's Going On" didn't just change Motown. It changed the role of the soul singer. And it stands today as a timeless plea for understanding in a world still struggling to listen.

1972, USA/AUSTRALIA

I AM WOMAN

HELEN REDDY

HELEN REDDY & RAY BURTON, CAPITOL

RECORDED 1971; RERECORDED 1972 AT SUN WEST STUDIO, HOLLYWOOD

"I Am Woman" gave the women's liberation movement something it hadn't yet had: an anthem. Helen Reddy, the Australian-born singer building her career in the United States, co-wrote the song with Ray Burton after voicing frustration at the lack of songs that spoke directly to women's experiences and the feminist cause. A brief version appeared on her 1971 debut album, but it was the fuller, rerecorded single in 1972 that captured the public imagination.

Helen Reddy's anthem voiced a clear and unapologetic assertion of female strength and resilience, perfectly capturing the spirit of second-wave feminism as it surged through the 1970s. It wasn't poetic ambiguity or soft-focus radio fare; it was a direct, defiant statement of identity, strength, and solidarity.

Released in mid-1972, "I Am Woman" didn't charge up the charts. It climbed slowly, knocking resistance out of the way with every step. Radio programmers, especially in conservative markets, were wary of its feminist theme. Some flatly refused to play it, calling it too political, too provocative, or just not commercial enough for mainstream airplay, which was a cop out.

The pushback didn't kill the song; it only made it hit harder. That's how it goes with music tied to change. Reddy later said she wrote it because nothing else out there spoke the way she needed it to. No song gave voice to the kind of strength and self-belief she felt as a woman. So she wrote one herself. And it didn't rise on slick promotion or label hype. It spread because women kept calling radio stations, demanding to hear it, until eventually the stations caved and played it.

The song's progress through the second half of 1972 was steady, buoyed by demand the industry hadn't anticipated. By December, "I Am Woman" had climbed to No. 1 on the *Billboard* Hot 100, making Reddy the first Australian-born artist to top the US charts. And No. 1 is a rare spot for songs in this book; most of the songs that changed the world have done so through longevity, rebellion, or by just hitting a nerve.

But far from a fleeting pop hit, "I Am Woman" became a cultural anthem that transcended music charts and entered the lexicon of the women's liberation movement. "It's not just about me," Reddy said in Rachel Brodsky's *I Am Woman: The Story Behind The Song*. "It's every woman who ever felt she couldn't do something, and then found out she could."

Roaring women entered everyday language, a phrase that symbolized strength, resilience, and solidarity. When Reddy accepted the Grammy Award for Best Female Pop Vocal Performance in 1973, she famously thanked "God, because She makes everything possible," a moment that delighted feminists and scandalized traditionalists. In a seemingly casual comment, Reddy became a spokesperson for women's rights, and, however unexpected that role was, she embraced it.

Its impact stretched beyond its chart success. As a touchstone for the global women's rights movement, which was growing louder and more assertive, much to the chagrin of the patriarchy, it was sung at rallies, marches, and International Women's Day events . . . and still is. The *Los Angeles Times* later called it "the anthem of the women's rights movement" of the 1970s. Its influence was so enduring that when the 2019 biopic of Helen Reddy was released, it bore the same title, *I Am Woman*.

In hindsight, "I Am Woman" might sound unremarkable to contemporary ears, but in 1972, it was revolutionary, a feminist statement inside a No. 1 pop hit. It legitimized the idea that pop music could carry a powerful social message and empower millions in the process. With "I Am Woman" the women's movement found its voice, and the song's legacy echoes in every feminist anthem that followed.

Second-wave feminism emerged in the 1960s and 1970s to challenge deep-seated gender inequities. While the first wave of feminism had fought for suffrage and fundamental legal rights in the late 19th and early 20th centuries, the second wave struck at the cultural norms and systemic discrimination that kept women subordinate. Following the release of *The Feminine Mystique* by Betty Friedan, the second wave pushed for equal pay, reproductive rights, no-fault divorce, protection from domestic violence, and the right to define women's roles beyond the confines of the home.

Each battle was there, and in some ways, those battles still remain, which is why "I Am Woman" retains its resonance.

But on release, it gave further voice to "Respect" by Aretha Franklin and inspired and influenced many songs about female empowerment. That legacy echoed through tracks like Chaka Khan's "I'm Every Woman" (1978), Aretha Franklin and the Eurythmics' "Sisters Are Doin' It for Themselves" (1985), and No Doubt's "Just a Girl" (1995). Each took the baton in its own style, from disco to rock to pop, but all carried the DNA of Reddy's declaration.

Across the decades, the language of empowerment has shifted with the times while holding to the same core demand for liberation and equality. Beyoncé's "Run the World (Girls)"

in 2011 framed female strength as a global force, while Emmy Meli's viral "I Am Woman" in 2021 re-energized the theme for the digital age. Though expressed differently, both carried forward the same insistence first ignited in 1972, that women would no longer be confined, but claim their place as powerful and free.

The second wave of feminism wasn't just about changing laws; it was about changing minds. Helen Reddy's "I Am Woman" became its soundtrack: a declaration of autonomy, strength, and collective power that gave voice to a global movement.

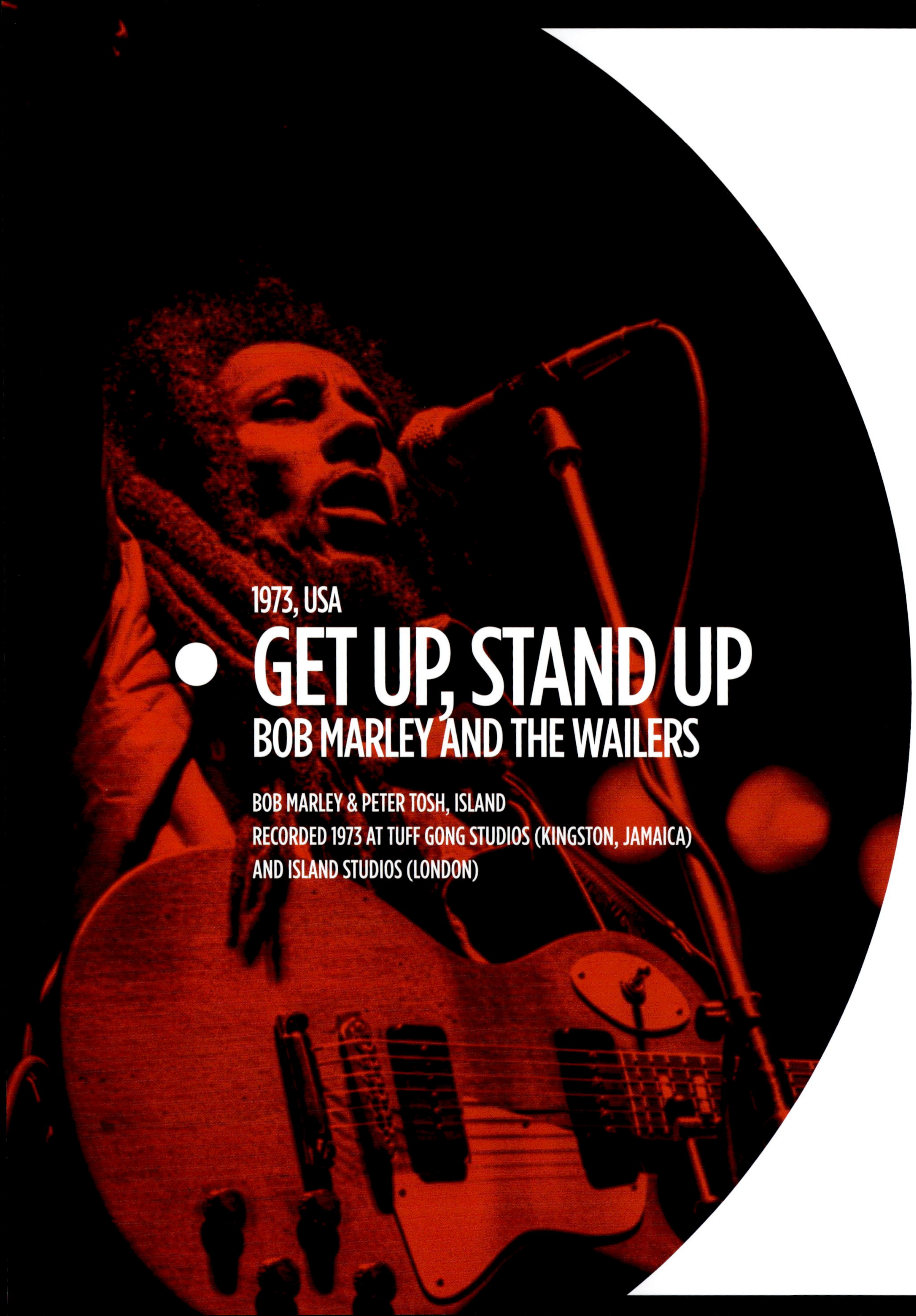

1973, USA

GET UP, STAND UP

BOB MARLEY AND THE WAILERS

BOB MARLEY & PETER TOSH, ISLAND
RECORDED 1973 AT TUFF GONG STUDIOS (KINGSTON, JAMAICA)
AND ISLAND STUDIOS (LONDON)

When Bob Marley co-wrote "Get Up, Stand Up" with Peter Tosh in 1973, it wasn't penned for radio or wrapped in commercial gloss. It was born of outrage, sparked by what Marley saw in Haiti, a country ground down by poverty and political oppression. In terms of its impact on the charts, this is probably the least successful entry in the book; yet that lack of numbers does not lessen its significance.

The song became a defiant cry for action, first released on The Wailers' 1973 album *Burnin'*. It wasn't subtle, and it wasn't meant to be. From the opening lines the message was clear. Marley was demanding rights for everyone, even the oppressed of Haiti who were suffocating under the brutal dictatorship of Jean-Claude "Baby Doc" Duvalier, who had inherited power from his father, François "Papa Doc" Duvalier.

The regime ruled through fear, enforced by the notorious Tonton Macoute militia. Arbitrary arrests, torture, and political repression were everyday realities. The economy was dire, and Haiti was the poorest country in the Western Hemisphere, with a massive gap between the corrupt elite and the destitute majority. Most Haitians lived in grinding poverty, denied fundamental rights and services.

When Bob Marley visited that year, he saw this harsh reality firsthand. The visit shook him, sharpening his sense of injustice and feeding directly into "Get Up, Stand Up," a song born from witnessing a nation where standing up for one's rights was both a necessity and a risk.

Unlike many protest songs that relied on metaphor or poetic phrasing, "Get Up, Stand Up" hits with blunt force.

The chorus was relentless, a demand to rise and keep pushing, no matter the cost. That line evolved into a chant, rolling through rallies in Kingston, Cape Town, and beyond, becoming an integral part of anti-apartheid marches and human rights protests around the world.

But Marley and Tosh weren't just throwing slogans around. The verses cut harder, calling out the way religion was used to pacify the oppressed, selling the lie that pain now would be rewarded in some distant afterlife. They tore into that complacency. And they went

after the politicians, too, the ones who lived fat off the suffering, the ones who thought they could keep people fooled forever. The song flipped it back; justice had to be demanded here and now.

He wasn't rejecting belief, as such; he was rejecting the idea that belief should pacify the oppressed, and that meant taking a broad swipe at both. He carried his Rastafarian beliefs from Jamaica into his lyrics, and he insisted that spirituality demanded action. In his eyes, standing up for your rights was a sacred duty, not a political choice.

Rastafarian ideology is explored in his music, with biblical imagery and references to Babylon (representing oppression) and calls for Zion (a spiritual homeland) to frame messages of justice, unity, and African identity. Through reggae, Marley and fellow artists like Peter Tosh transformed Rastafarian beliefs into powerful global protest anthems. In contrast, much of the world fixated on Marley's use of marijuana

– a shallow reading of a man whose music carried far deeper spiritual and political truths.

And this is where "Get Up, Stand Up" fed directly into the cultural phenomenon that Marley became. This was the song he chose to close his shows with, a time when black and white, rich and poor, could stand together and chant messages of peace and love.

He brought reggae and Rastafarian ideology to the world not just as a collection of songs, but as a way of life. His dreadlocks, faith, and unapologetic use of cannabis became part of a larger cultural force. This was never about escape; it was about waking people up. "Get Up, Stand Up" is not passive.

His influence didn't stop at reggae. "Get Up, Stand Up" laid down a blueprint for how music could move a movement. Its rebellious energy flowed directly into early hip-hop, with DJ Kool Herc, another Jamaican expat, carrying Marley's spirit into the Bronx block parties that gave birth to rap. The song's defiant spirit pulses in everything from Public Enemy's "Fight the Power" to Kendrick Lamar's "Alright." Marley proved that standing up for your rights could, and should, sound good doing it.

Through all the fire and fury of life around him, Marley never abandoned the idea of love. His message wasn't just about tearing down oppression; it was about building something better. Otherwise, what is the point? "One Love," "Could You Be Loved," and "Is This Love" weren't naive fantasies; they were radical ideas in a world guided by division. He believed that love, unity, and joy were acts of resistance. He saw "Get Up, Stand Up" as a defense of love and a fight for a world where love didn't have to hide behind fear.

When Marley asked why we chose conflict over love, it was a challenge that demanded justice, peace, and love could coexist.

Fittingly, "Get Up, Stand Up" as his most significant song was also the last he played live, closing out a set at the Stanley Theater in Pittsburgh on September 23, 1980, two days after being told that his acral lentiginous melanoma (a form of skin cancer) had spread to his brain, lungs, and liver. He died less than eight months later and never played live again, despite having planned a world tour.

"Get Up, Stand Up" remains timeless because Marley's vision of freedom is still unfinished, with wars and oppression across the globe fueling the injustices he raged against. Its chorus still hits like a rallying cry, as vital now as it was in 1973. Marley knew music wasn't just for moving feet but for moving hearts, and this song was his ultimate call to rise.

1975, USA

THE PILL

LORETTA LYNN

LORETTA LYNN, MCA

RECORDED JULY 1972 AT BRADLEY'S BARN, MOUNT JULIET

In April 1975, the release of "The Pill" did more than ruffle feathers: it tore straight through the heart of conservative America, particularly in the South, where churches in country towns seemed more plentiful than pubs in Australia. Loretta Lynn, the coal miner's daughter turned queen of country music, wasn't a protest singer by label. But with this song, she became one by deed.

Wrapped in a bouncy honky-tonk beat, "The Pill" delivered a message most country women had never heard put so bluntly: your body, your choice.

The song opens with a wry dismissal of old clothes and old roles, set to a jaunty country shuffle that undercut the seriousness of its subject. It was a cheeky broadside at conservative America, where the church often dictated the rhythm of small-town life. In a world built on faith, family, and appearances, "The Pill" broke the silence, handing women a sharp, witty anthem about control over their own bodies and futures.

No metaphor. No sugar-coating. Just a coal miner's daughter from Butcher Hollow, Kentucky, declaring she was done with endless pregnancies and was ready to reclaim her life. Loretta Lynn didn't wrap her message in allegory or veil it behind genteel phrases; she sang it with the grit and honesty that had defined her career. And in America's Bible Belt, a region where a woman's virtue was measured by her obedience, faith, and ability to bear children without complaint, her message struck like a tornado.

The Pill, as a method of birth control, wasn't just frowned upon in the regions where evangelical Protestants and country music thrived; it was practically a dirty word. The pulpit wielded as much power as the courthouse, and radio airplay often ran through an invisible filter of moral acceptability. It was in this world that Loretta Lynn strode with guitar in hand, daring to say out loud what millions of women only whispered in private: enough was enough.

The backlash came fast and loud. Radio stations banned it, not just a handful, but over 60 across key country markets. Entire networks blocked it. Preachers worked it into sermons, condemning it as an affront to family values and an incitement to sin. Nashville's establishment, wary of offending the powerful conservative radio networks, looked on with barely concealed discomfort.

And yet, "The Pill" stormed the charts anyway. It defied the boycott, reaching No. 5 on the *Billboard* Hot Country Singles chart. It became Loretta Lynn's highest-charting crossover hit, peaking at No. 70 on the *Billboard* Hot 100, a rare achievement for a traditional country song at a time when pop radio rarely touched Nashville acts.

The bans, far from killing the song, made it a sensation. Word of mouth spread in beauty parlors, church socials, and kitchen-table conversations, and women bought the single in record numbers. More than 500,000 copies were sold, a staggering number for a song that radio wouldn't touch. It wasn't just a hit record; it was a form of quiet rebellion.

"The Pill" drew a line in the sand. If "I Am Woman" helped women to roar, "The Pill" in the post Roe v. Wade era asked for their right to choose. They could tell their truth and be heard. In a world where the weight of tradition often fell heaviest on women's shoulders, Loretta Lynn had opened a door that wouldn't easily be closed again.

She'd already hit the top of the country charts with songs like "Coal Miner's Daughter," "Fist City," and "One's on the Way," but "The Pill" was something else again. It was sly, sharp social commentary wrapped in a cheeky country shuffle, and it proved just how strong a songwriter she was.

This one went straight into the culture war that most country stars wouldn't touch. Lynn played it with humor, poking fun at the grind of endless pregnancies, and then dropped the hammer with the raw truth: years stuck at home while the men had all the fun.

It wasn't a polite hint at social change. It was a direct challenge to the unspoken rule that a woman's body belonged to her husband, to the church, and to the community. In small towns across the South, where family honor and religious authority walked hand in hand, that kind of truth wasn't just uncomfortable. It was revolutionary.

The backlash was fierce. But quietly, women responded by buying the record and singing it in kitchens. For many, "The Pill" wasn't just a song; it was permission. A crack in the wall of silence. Proof that someone, somewhere, understood their fight.

Johnny Cash, the Man in Black, didn't publicly champion "The Pill," but his long-standing support of artists who rattled cages gave Lynn a degree of cover. If Cash could sing about prisoners and political injustice, maybe there was room for a woman to sing about birth control.

"The Pill" joined a wave of songs that, in different ways, fought for a woman's right to be heard. Aretha Franklin's "Respect" (1967) flipped a man's plea into a woman's demand. Helen Reddy's "I Am Woman" (1972) gave feminism its anthem. The Supremes' "Love Child" (1968) cracked open taboos about illegitimacy and poverty.

But in many ways, "The Pill" hit harder because it came from inside the heartland, from a woman who lived by its rules, calling them out in the language and music of the people who upheld them.

Loretta Lynn wasn't a feminist firebrand. She was a wife, a mother of six, and a country singer steeped in the traditions of her world. That made "The Pill" all the more dangerous. It came wrapped in a voice America trusted, a voice now telling the truth America didn't want to hear.

It didn't topple laws or spark marches. But it pried open a conversation the South couldn't ignore. And in doing so, "The Pill" earned its place among the songs that truly changed the world.

1977, UK

GOD SAVE THE QUEEN

SEX PISTOLS

JOHN LYDON, STEVE JONES, PAUL COOK & GLEN MATLOCK, VIRGIN RECORDS
RECORDED MAY 27, 1977, AT WESSEX SOUND STUDIOS, LONDON

England was a fading empire in the mid-1970s, clinging to the past and the belief that it could be "great" again. Unemployment was at its highest level since the war, and the youth from outside the upper class faced an uncertain future; they were angry but didn't know how to express it.

Enter the Sex Pistols.

In late 1976, the Sex Pistols released "Anarchy in the UK," and with it, vocalist Johnny Rotten, born John Lydon, to those not safety-pinned, declared in an engineered rhyme, "I am an Antichrist, I am an anarchist." For most of polite British society, it was the musical equivalent of a Molotov cocktail lobbed into Buckingham Palace.

But "Anarchy" was a warning shot fired across the bow of staid old England, and it rattled the windows before "God Save the Queen" blew the doors off their hinges.

Released during Queen Elizabeth II's Silver Jubilee in May 1977, "God Save the Queen" was everything the establishment feared punk might be: angry, articulate, wildly popular, and aimed directly at the heart of the British hierarchy. Where "Anarchy in the UK" had been a raucous shout from the underground, "God Save the Queen" was a coronation riot in three minutes flat.

The Britain in which the Sex Pistols were born was struggling to keep itself together. The 1970s were a dismal decade of despair for a generation of young people who were told there was no place for them. Politicians were out of touch, bin bags were left to rot on the curbs, and a national identity had been forged in an empire that was falling apart at the seams.

Lydon wasn't born angry. He earned it. A childhood bout of spinal meningitis left him hospitalized for nearly a year, temporarily blind and prone to vivid hallucinations. When he returned home, the slums of North London felt more alien than ever. That sense of disconnection, combined with a sharp wit and a sharper tongue, shaped the performer he would become: defiant, cerebral, and not remotely interested in making anyone feel comfortable.

Even before joining the Pistols, Lydon was styling his hair into random spikes, ripping clothes for effect, and pushing back against the moral codes of school and society.

And yet it sold furiously. Officially, it peaked at No. 2 on the UK Singles Chart. Unofficially, it was No. 1, but the listing was left blank. Even the charts were too scared to admit what the country was listening to.

Lydon would later explain that "God Save the Queen" was never about hating England. It came from a place of anger and frustration at seeing ordinary people mistreated, a protest born out of a rough kind of love for his country rather than contempt.

It's hard to remember now just how shocking it really was. Back then, the monarchy was off limits. You could dissent, sure, but only if you whispered it. The Pistols didn't whisper. They spat, they snarled, they screamed it. Rotten dragged Britain's fantasy of past glory through the gutter. And he didn't stop at the Queen; he smashed the whole post-imperial myth to bits.

He stood out. Lydon couldn't sing by traditional standards, but he could sneer like a master and deliver lyrics with scalpel-sharp clarity.

This brings us to "God Save the Queen." Its arrival, just seven months after "Anarchy in the UK," came at the height of Britain's royalist self-celebration. The Jubilee was meant to be a soothing balm to national discontent. The Sex Pistols instead treated it like an open wound.

When Johnny Rotten snarled out his attack on the monarchy, it was meant to shock, and it did. The fury in his voice offended many, but it also struck a chord with those ready to hear it. The BBC banned the track. Retailers refused to stock it. Radio stations wouldn't play it.

The cultural impact was nuclear. "God Save the Queen" became punk's defining anthem and catapulted the Pistols from cult notoriety to national menace. Politicians raged, newspapers screamed, and protesters sang hymns outside venues. Meanwhile, youth across Britain and beyond dyed their hair, tore their clothes, and picked up guitars.

It also marked the beginning of the end for the Sex Pistols. The chaos they inspired turned inward. Their infamous appearance on Bill

Grundy's *Today* program in December 1976 had already drawn blood; Grundy was sacked, and the press had a field day. Their first major UK tour, the Anarchy Tour, was more notable for the venues that canceled than the ones that went ahead. EMI signed them, then panicked and dumped them. A&M did the same. Virgin Records held its nerve, and got *Never Mind the Bollocks, Here's the Sex Pistols* into shops later that year.

By that point, the Pistols were already starting to unravel. Original bassist Glen Matlock was replaced by Sid Vicious, who looked the part but could barely play. Vicious's heroin addiction spiraled. The band limped through an American tour that ended in collapse at Winterland in San Francisco in January 1978. Rotten, fed up with manager Malcolm McLaren's manipulations and Vicious's decline, dropped the mic at the end of a one-song encore with a final sneer: "Ever get the feeling you've been cheated?"

Less than two years after they'd started, the Sex Pistols were done after igniting the punk movement in a way no one else could. The Clash, Siouxsie and the Banshees, Chrissie

Hynde, and countless others drew inspiration from the Pistols' audacity. Fashion changed. Attitudes changed. Youth culture would never again be as willing to do what it was told.

It wasn't just about the music. The Pistols embodied the punk ethos of DIY rebellion. Their look, characterized by ripped shirts, safety pins, and offensive slogans, became a global style. Their sound, raw, stripped back, and unapologetically loud, became a template for others to follow. And their message, that anyone could pick up a guitar and scream about the world, still resonates.

It became a global symbol of defiance, giving disenchanted youth a voice. The song ignited class and generational conflict, turbocharged punk rock in Britain and beyond, and exposed the absurdity of a country so trapped in its past that the official music charts left a blank space where the best-selling single in the nation should have been.

"God Save the Queen" didn't just shake the foundations. It cracked the crown and gave voice to millions who'd never been heard.

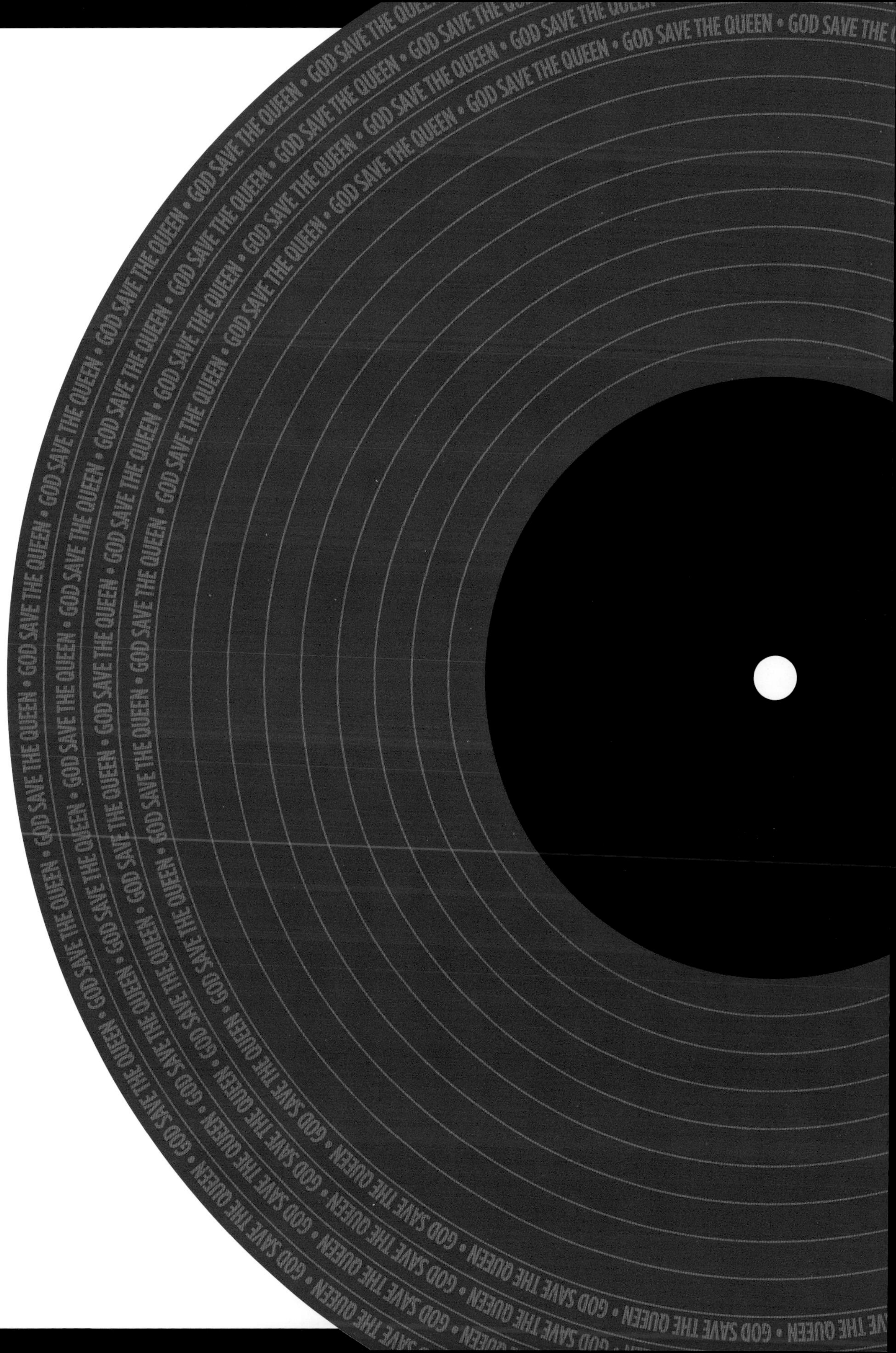
GOD SAVE THE QUEEN • GOD SAVE THE QUEEN • GOD SAVE THE QUEEN

1978, USA

Y.M.C.A.

VILLAGE PEOPLE

JACQUES MORALI & HENRI BELOLO, CASABLANCA

RECORDED 1977–78 AT SIGMA SOUND STUDIOS, NEW YORK CITY

When Frenchman Jacques Morali first conceived the Village People, he wasn't chasing subtlety; he was chasing spectacle. Inspired by the costumes, codes, and camp of New York's gay nightlife, Morali, alongside business partner Henri Belolo, set out to create a group that blended pop accessibility with the unspoken language of queer subculture. In 1977, they struck gold with "San Francisco (You've Got Me)," but it was just the beginning.

The Village People's concept was as bold as it was simple: assemble a cast of hyper-masculine archetypes, the leatherman, the cowboy, the construction worker, the policeman, the Native American, and the GI, and give them irresistibly catchy disco anthems. They were a pop act, a camp parody, and a living billboard for gay-coded culture, all rolled into one.

Victor Willis was out front in police gear, but the band wasn't just a novelty act, and it became a cultural and musical phenomenon that topped charts and changed attitudes.

The band was originally a set of dancers, but Morali, Belolo and Willis knew early in the band's history it needed more, so they advertised for singers with a simple ad that hinted at the aesthetic, "Macho Types Wanted: Must Dance And Have A Moustache."

The costumes weren't random. The leatherman character, famously clad in black leather with a horseshoe mustache, drew directly from the dress code of The Mineshaft, the notorious New York BDSM leather club, as later noted by author Jack Fritscher. Glenn Hughes, who portrayed the leatherman, was known to frequent the venue himself. The Village People took subculture and spun it into pop gold, walking a razor's edge between caricature, just as Kiss had done in rock music, and celebration.

And the world couldn't get enough.

When "Y.M.C.A." hit the charts in November 1978, it wasn't just a song; it was the crowning moment of a phenomenon. Morali had brought the idea to Willis with a straightforward brief: write a song about the Y.M.C.A., a place well known in New York's gay community as a social hub and, discreetly, a cruising spot.

Willis later insisted in interviews that the song was about "youthful fun." He denied it was intended as a gay anthem. Whether this was a creative spin or a public relations defense remains contested. The lyrics, the delivery, and the band's onstage image left little doubt about its meaning for those who recognized the world it portrayed.

The formula was classic Village People: catchy hooks, a sing-along chorus, and a driving beat built for dance floors. But "Y.M.C.A." worked on a deeper level. Where "Macho Man" played with masculine tropes and "In the Navy" sailed with cheeky innuendo, "Y.M.C.A." danced through the mainstream as disco's Trojan horse. This song celebrated freedom and camaraderie while the world sang along, initially unaware.

A worldwide sensation, complete with an iconic arm-spelling dance that solidified its place in pop culture, and a subtext that shouted gay pride before that was a thing, it reached No. 2 on the *Billboard* Hot 100 and topped charts everywhere.

The reaction wasn't limited to Western culture. In 1985, just two months before Mikhail Gorbachev rose to power, the Soviet Communist Party's youth wing issued a secret blacklist of artists deemed ideologically harmful.

The Village People was on that list with music that was reportedly condemned as "violent" when nothing could be further from the truth. The blacklist was reported by Western media as part of a sweeping cultural crackdown, highlighting the group's unexpected reach into global political tensions.

At home, the contradictions kept coming. While "Y.M.C.A." became a permanent fixture at weddings, sports games, and Pride parades, Willis repeatedly distanced the song from its queer associations. In December 2024, Willis publicly declared his intent to sue any news organization that called "Y.M.C.A." a "gay anthem." According to his statement, widely reported by the music press, the song was never intended as such, a claim that seemed almost quaint in light of decades of cultural evidence.

The critics had their say. Robert Christgau of *The Village Voice* dismissed the band as a "humorous annoyance" before later admitting, after hearing their 1978 album *Cruisin'*, that their over-the-top camp was impossible to resist. *AllMusic's* Ron Wynn summarized them as "part clever concept, part exaggerated camp act," a band that became global sensations during disco's heyday and revived time and again like a pop phoenix.

"Y.M.C.A." didn't need to wave a protest banner. It won hearts and shifted cultural ground by osmosis . . . by dancing straight past resistance. It gave coded gay culture a global stage and became, whether Victor Willis liked it or not, a banner for LGBTQ+ pride.

The song's impact echoed far beyond the charts. *VH1* ranked it among the 100 Greatest Dance Songs. *Paste Magazine* crowned it the No. 1 Dancefloor Classic in 2017. *Rolling Stone* and *Billboard* both enshrined it in their lists of all-time dance and sporting anthems. The Library of Congress inducted it into the National Recording Registry in 2020, praising its resonance with LGBTQ+ experiences and its "evocation of gay male culture."

And the Village People themselves became woven into the fabric of pop culture, parodied, imitated, and celebrated in everything from *Wayne's World 2* to *Married . . . with Children*, from U2's "Discothèque" video to *Despicable Me 2*. The leatherman alone became an enduring pop icon.

"Y.M.C.A." stands alongside "Respect," "I Am Woman," "Love Child," and "The Pill," songs that turned private battles into public conversations. Where Aretha Franklin demanded dignity, Helen Reddy gave voice to feminism, The Supremes tackled shame and poverty, and Loretta Lynn challenged patriarchal control, the Village People smuggled coded gay culture into the mainstream, all with a smile, a dance beat, and a song the world couldn't stop singing.

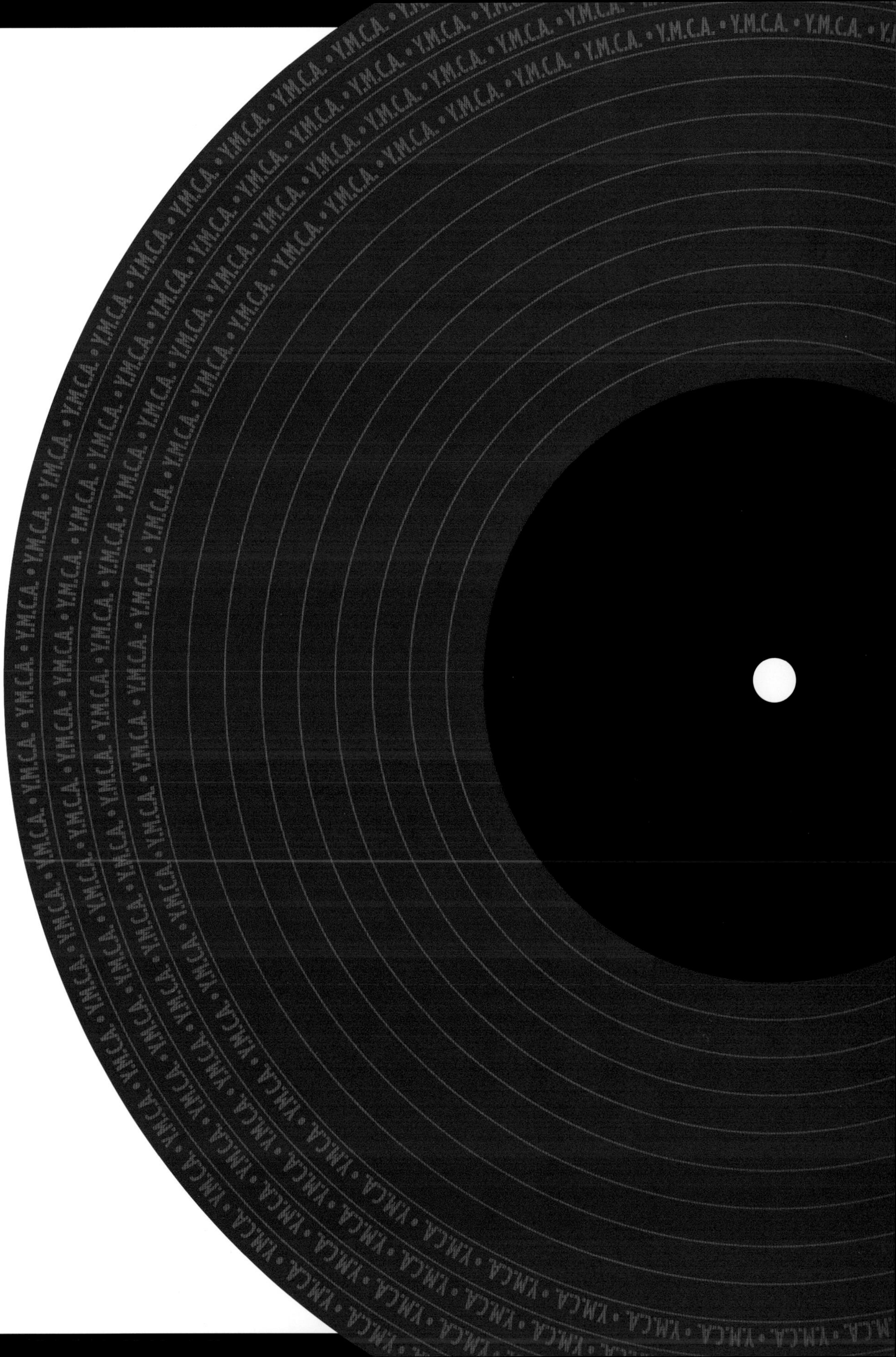
Y.M.C.A. • Y.M.C.A. • Y.M.C.A.

1980, GERMANY

99 LUFTBALLONS

NENA

CARLO KARGES, CBS

RECORDED 1983–84 AT SPLIFF STUDIO, WEST BERLIN

Floating into the German charts in 1983, "99 Luftballons" wasn't carried by protest or politics. At least, not at first. Written by guitarist Carlo Karges and performed by Nena, the song began as a sharp-edged pop anthem with a deceptively playful hook: a story about 99 red balloons drifting into the sky, triggering a catastrophic military overreaction that spirals out of control into a global war.

But beneath its punchy new wave sound and sing-along chorus, "99 Luftballons" struck a raw nerve in Cold War Europe, particularly in divided Germany, where the fear of sudden, senseless conflict was never theoretical. The song's narrative wasn't an allegory. It was a mirror held up to the precarious balance of power between NATO and the Warsaw Pact, with West Germany caught right in the crosshairs.

The impact was immediate in Germany, and "99 Luftballons" went to No. 1 in its first week on the West German singles chart and held the top spot for two months. It repeated the feat in Austria, Switzerland, and the Netherlands, becoming an anthem of anti-war sentiment among a generation who had grown up in the shadow of barbed wire and border checkpoints. It captured the helplessness of the nuclear standoff and the idea that the world could end not with a deliberate attack, but with a stupid and meaningless mistake.

In West Berlin, where the wall divided families and friends, it became a particular rallying point for youth disillusioned with both Soviet oppression and Western military escalation. The song didn't just tap into anti-war feeling; it gave it a voice that felt urgent, relatable, and human.

Its breakthrough into the English-speaking world came with "99 Red Balloons," a direct translation penned by Kevin McAlea and released in 1984. But while it carried the same melody and basic storyline, the English version subtly reshaped the message, softening the sharpest edges of the original's political bite.

In "99 Luftballons," the lyrics tell a blunt, cynical tale of militarism gone mad. Ninety-nine balloons float over the Berlin Wall, and when mistaken for UFOs, they inadvertently trigger a catastrophic military response.

By the second verse it's already spiraling. Balloons in the sky and suddenly the military's on edge. Fighters scrambled, orders barked, and a general sent out like the world's about to end, all because of a few bits of rubber floating on the horizon.

The tone is sardonic, bitter, and an apparent jab at the hair-trigger paranoia of Cold War politics. The German lyrics conclude in a wasteland of destruction and irony.

By contrast, the English version of "99 Luftballons" (with 'red' added simply for rhythm) feels more abstract, almost poetic. It speaks of alarms ringing and war machines set in motion, but avoids naming political leaders or generals directly. Even the closing verse softens, ending with the image of a single balloon released into the sky as a gesture of remembrance and loss.

Where the German narrator finds the last balloon in the ruins of a world destroyed by idiocy, the English version leaves the ending open, more wistful than damning, more reflective than outraged.

The sharp German political commentary, with its thinly veiled references to NATO, the Bundeswehr (the unified armed forces of West Germany), and the Soviet threat, is blurred in English into a general anti-war sentiment, safe for radio and accessible to a global pop audience. The shift didn't weaken the song's power entirely, but it did make it palatable enough to break into the Anglophone charts without provoking the same level of political discomfort.

The dual-language release became a perfect study in how protest songs travel, raw and pointed at home, adapted and softened abroad.

In Germany, "99 Luftballons" sounded like a direct challenge. In the English-speaking world, "99 Red Balloons" felt like a cautionary tale. And perhaps that was why it worked in both places, each version hitting its audience in precisely the way they were prepared to, or needed to, hear it.

In the United Kingdom, "99 Luftballons" went to No. 1 on the UK Singles Chart, holding the spot for three weeks in March 1984. In Australia, it climbed to No. 1 on the Kent Music Report. In Canada, it reached No. 1 on the RPM Singles Chart. Even in the United States, notoriously resistant to foreign-language and European acts, "99 Luftballons" cracked the *Billboard* Hot 100, peaking at No. 2, a staggering result for a German band at the height of Cold War paranoia.

Together, the two versions did what few songs had managed before: they localized a global anxiety. In Germany, it was personal. In Britain and America, it was a catchy, sobering reminder of how close the world sat to disaster. The song succeeded where political speeches and protest marches often failed: it made Cold War fear feel immediate, universal, and absurdly dangerous.

It didn't chant slogans, and it didn't call for revolution; "99 Luftballons" simply told a story. In doing so, it reached a generation alert to the threat of nuclear war but numbed by political rhetoric. It became a war cry for anti-nuclear demonstrations across Europe, with crowds singing it at rallies, and the message echoed in pubs and clubs.

Unlike "Wind of Change" by Scorpions, which later serenaded the fall of the Berlin Wall, or "Sunday Bloody Sunday" by U2, which raged against specific violence, "99 Luftballons" captured a floating, pervasive anxiety, the fear of an unstoppable machine spiraling out of human control.

Decades later, it endures as both a Cold War time capsule and a warning that still feels alarmingly current. The balloons may have been metaphorical, but the threat never was.

1983, IRELAND/UK

SUNDAY BLOODY SUNDAY

U2

PAUL HEWSON, DAVE EVANS, ADAM CLAYTON & LARRY MULLEN JR., ISLAND

RECORDED SEPTEMBER–NOVEMBER 1982 AT WINDMILL LANE, DUBLIN

"Sunday Bloody Sunday" launched as the lead track of *War* in March 1983 and propelled U2 from three promising Irish rockers to the forefront of political music in the 1980s. *War* went to the top, removing Michael Jackson's *Thriller* from No. 1 on the British charts, went top 10 in Australia, New Zealand, Canada, the Netherlands, Sweden, among others, and peaked at No. 12 on the US Billboard charts. As a single release, "Sunday Bloody Sunday" reached top 10 positions across all major markets.

U2 had arrived.

The song rose from the shadows of Northern Ireland's sectarian violence to confront directly the Bloody Sunday massacre that occurred 10 years earlier when British paratroopers killed 14 unarmed civil rights marchers in Derry. Bono (Paul Hewson) steered clear of using partisan language and nationalist rhetoric throughout the song. "Sunday Bloody Sunday" used its lyrics to highlight the tragic effects of violence. It was not a rebel anthem; Bono said it himself on stage. No sides, no neat blame game. The hit came from the question underneath. How many bodies? How many funerals before anyone says enough? That was the punch. Not right or wrong. Just violence that never stopped, grinding on. No end. No winners.

The Edge's (Dave Evans) guitar riff together with Larry Mullen Jr.'s military drum pattern created a powerful sound that perfectly represented the song's emotional depth. Their stage was often adorned with white flags when they played it live; this was a song of peace, not one of defeat.

The band achieved worldwide exposure when their live video of thc song from *Live at Red Rocks: Under a Blood Red Sky*, which is still one of my favorite live recordings, became a permanent fixture on MTV. Images of Bono waving a white flag while pleading for peace through the mist of rain, which could easily have been the smoke of war, are as iconic as it gets.

The power of "Sunday Bloody Sunday" stemmed from its universal appeal to all people rather than its particular message. The song demanded action from every group of people, not just the Irish, instead of making accusations by inviting all people to witness the futile nature of war.

However, its influence proved more intense and complicated within Ireland, both in Northern and the Republic territories.

"Sunday Bloody Sunday" resonated deeply with Irish citizens in the Republic because it expressed the widespread disappointment of people who supported the Northern nationalist cause yet felt exhausted by the ongoing violence. During the early 1980s, Ireland maintained a divided condition from partition. Yet, people generally avoided discussing "The Troubles" because of a mix of fear, political exhaustion, and intense anger.

The song served as an outlet for individuals seeking peace without entanglement in politics. Through its musical language, the song conveyed human sadness and emotional pain that surpassed political divisions. Young Irish listeners identified U2 as their musical mirror during this period, and "Sunday Bloody Sunday" emerged as their collective sorrowful anthem and scarce declaration of neutrality during a time of strict allegiance.

"Sunday Bloody Sunday" received widespread acceptance for its message of peace, although not everyone shared this belief.

Irish Republican communities received the song with doubt, while parts of that community displayed active hostility toward it. Some people in the community viewed the song as a form of betrayal because it refused to identify an oppressor, but that was its point. There were accusations of Republican allegiance from conservative and loyalist British audiences, even though U2 maintained a neutral stance.

The communities of Northern Ireland received the song with deep-seated pain when it arrived in their region, with Bloody Sunday massacre memories revived among civil rights supporters and nationalists who vowed to keep these painful events alive. The song created discomfort for loyalists together with British soldiers and their backers, who wanted to view the event as a tragedy rather than an example of oppression.

Every word and symbol used in the song ignited existing tensions throughout Belfast, Derry, and other regions of Northern Ireland. "Sunday Bloody Sunday" became an exceptional cultural dialogue contributor because it chose not to endorse violence or take sides in the Irish and UK dialogue. It sparked discussions that most people had

tried to avoid. The song gained mass audience recognition for its desire for peace, as it targeted both conflict resolution and freedom from ideological obligations, thereby breaking the repeated cycles of retaliation.

The Cranberries ventured into the political and cultural minefield a decade later using an entirely different musical approach.

"Zombie" emerged as a scathing protest song in 1994 after the 1993 Warrington bombings led to the IRA killing two English children. Dolores O'Riordan channeled her anger into a raw, almost screamed vocal, choosing confrontation over sorrow. The song's refrain tied the moment back to a cycle of conflict stretching as far as the Easter Rising of 1916, insisting that the old battles were still being fought inside people's heads.

"Zombie" attacked the mindless hatred that sustained ongoing violence, while "Sunday Bloody Sunday" mourned victims and sought unity between communities. "Zombie" directly attacked the militants who brought innocent civilians into their conflict by stating they maintained a dead cause. The song emerged as a straightforward anti-IRA track during a dangerous time in early 1990s Ireland.

Both songs received intense opposition when they were performed at home. They reached mainstream success, which compelled Ireland and the world to face the bloodshed happening in their streets. The Cranberries responded to U2's song by declaring that the conflict should have ceased many years ago. The two songs created an opposing cultural dialogue that urged Irish people to face the violence inflicted by their countrymen.

"Sunday Bloody Sunday" transcended Derry's streets to become a universal anthem after its creation. The theme introduced in this song would appear throughout U2's subsequent musical creations. The musical works "Pride (In the Name of Love)" honoring Martin Luther King Jr., and "Mothers of the Disappeared" mourning victims of Latin American dictatorships, and the equally brilliant "Miss Sarajevo" with Brian Eno and Luciano Pavarotti (released under the pseudonym "Passengers," and later U2 with Luciano Pavarotti) focusing on the Bosnian conflict, all maintained a humanitarian focus. The song "Sunday Bloody Sunday" established U2 as leaders in their advocacy for human rights, while their music made them famous.

Perhaps more than any other song of its era, "Sunday Bloody Sunday" established that rock music could function as a tool for conscience instead of rebellion during that musical period. Through U2's hands, the weapon functioned as an unyielding tool for promoting empathy, human dignity, and peace.

1984, USA

BORN IN THE USA

BRUCE SPRINGSTEEN

BRUCE SPRINGSTEEN, COLUMBIA

RECORDED MAY–JUNE 1982 AT THE POWER STATION & THE HIT FACTORY, NEW YORK CITY

One of the greatest songwriters and storytellers in American history, Bruce Springsteen has never wavered from his quest to hold America accountable, not only with the clenched fist of a rock concert, but with a guitar and a voice that refuse to flinch. Across six decades, through sold-out stadiums, stripped-back solo tours, and award-winning memoirs, Springsteen has pursued a singular mission: to sing for the people America forgets.

It is Heartland Rock. A voice for the workers discarded by a shifting economy, the veterans sent to fight and then left behind, and the communities hollowed out by broken promises. His overt political stance, sharpened by activism, charity work, and a lifetime of social commentary, has never been about partisanship. It has always been about fairness, about asking the country he loves to live up to its own ideals. And nowhere has that mission rung louder, or been more misunderstood, than with "Born in the USA."

Springsteen's early songs hinted at politics only in the margins, telling romantic street tales of restless dreamers and working-class strugglers. By *The River* (1980), he had become America's chronicler of blue-collar disillusionment. *Nebraska* (1982) pushed him into darker, starker territory, with tales of desperation, dead ends, and systemic failure that underscored how fragile the American Dream had become for millions.

"Born in the USA" in 1984 was the culmination of that evolution. Springsteen wasn't just documenting hard times; he was confronting the forces that created them. The song carried the weight of everything that had come before, exploding with stadium-sized force, anthemic, universal, impossible to ignore. From the echoing snare drum to the fist-pumping of a blue-collar singer in a sleeveless denim jacket, this song was designed for stadiums and the mass selling of the message.

But when it dropped into the American consciousness, it sounded like a patriotic roar. The official video began with a fluttering US flag, and Reagan's America latched onto it, holding it up as a symbol of national greatness.

But this song was no celebration. It was a bitter, unflinching portrait of working-class despair and the betrayal of Vietnam veterans. The song wasted no time setting its tone. From the first lines it painted a picture of hardship and struggle, a life that seemed to begin already beaten down.

Even the chorus, "Born in the USA," was a bitter refrain. The more it rang out, the more it sounded like a taunt. Springsteen, who avoided the draft through a failed induction physical, later spoke openly of his guilt and his empathy for those who served. His protest came not from battlefield scars but from solidarity with the men discarded by a nation that called them heroes, then turned its back.

Where "Sunday Bloody Sunday" mourned the sectarian dead of Ireland, "Born in the USA" turned its gaze inward, a challenge to an America that waved the flag while gutting its factories and abandoning its veterans. Springsteen wasn't attacking his country. He was demanding that it live up to its promises.

The imagery was just as powerful. Annie Leibovitz's album cover, Springsteen's faded jeans, white T-shirt, and a red cap stuffed in his back pocket, standing before the American flag, looked like a salute. But it was a study in contradiction: the battered American worker before a symbol of a country that promised everything and delivered little.

The ambiguity of the catchcry often left it misunderstood, but that became part of its legacy. Reagan's 1984 campaign tried to claim Springsteen as a symbol of conservative pride, a move that only sharpened his resolve; Reaganism was not his idea of America. His pointed interviews and fierce live performances made sure the truth behind the roar wasn't lost. The song became a Trojan horse, a protest anthem hiding in plain sight.

At first, it fooled people. Big noise. Big drums. Looked like flag waving. Sit with it, though, and the mask slips. Not pride. Betrayal. Kids were shoved off to fight a war they never asked for. Families living under smoke and wire, prisons on one side, refineries on the other. Rust is creeping over everything. The dream sour, gone. That's the sting. The music lifts, but the words pull you straight down.

The song's irony resonated. What began as a catchy anthem morphed into a Trojan horse of dissent, subtle, subversive, and deeply felt. Over the decades, the more people played it, the more they realized its power and pain. The song seeped into the background of American culture, its message becoming harder to ignore the longer it echoed.

Its social impact was lasting. "Born in the USA" gave voice to forgotten Vietnam veterans and forced working-class America into the cultural conversation. It highlighted the growing disillusionment with economic inequality, political spin, and a country too often blind to its own contradictions. It didn't change the nation overnight, but it cracked the surface of American complacency.

Springsteen's activism has never stopped. From labour rights to racial justice, he has carried the message of "Born in the USA" forward, in song, on stage, and in action. The song became part of the soundscape of American protest, heard in union halls, veterans' marches, and movements for social change.

The impact is measurable. "Born in the USA" has been streamed over 550 million times on Spotify, and its message resonates across generations. He wants you to think that every time you stand and recognize the US veterans, as I have when attending car

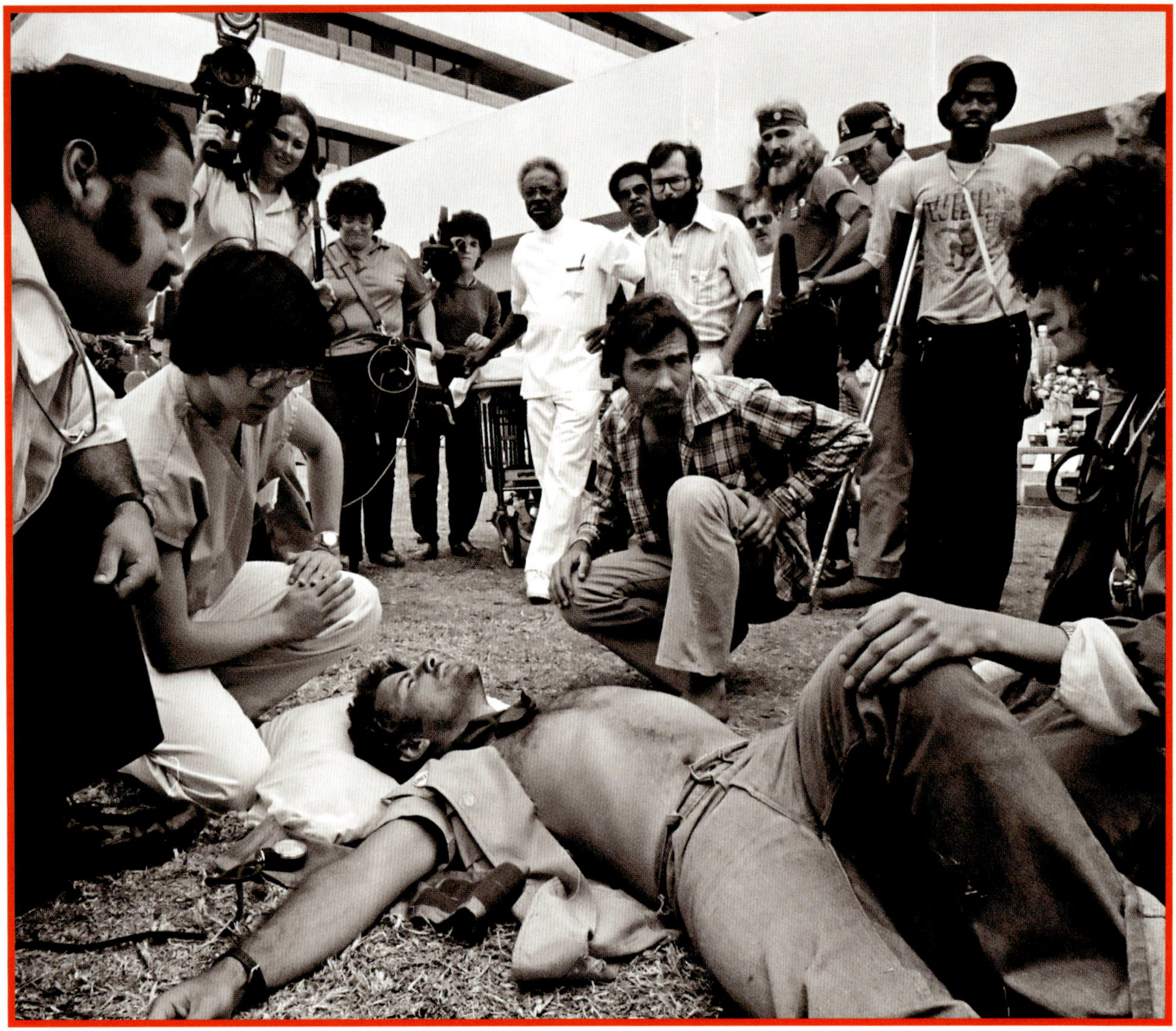

races in the States, that you also understand their plight. That more respect is owed, more action is required.

But it is more than just the veterans, it is about all the rest left behind, and Springsteen knows there is still much to be done to create a more just America.

Forty years on, the working class remains marginalized, veterans still fight for fundamental rights, and the country's reckoning with its own symbols and promises continues.

"Born in the USA" stands as a defining American protest song, a roaring anthem in a nation that sang along initially without listening. It is Springsteen's great contradiction: misunderstood at first glance, but impossible to ignore once its truth is heard. His loudest, boldest call for a better America, the anthem they never wanted, still singing the truths they struggle to face.

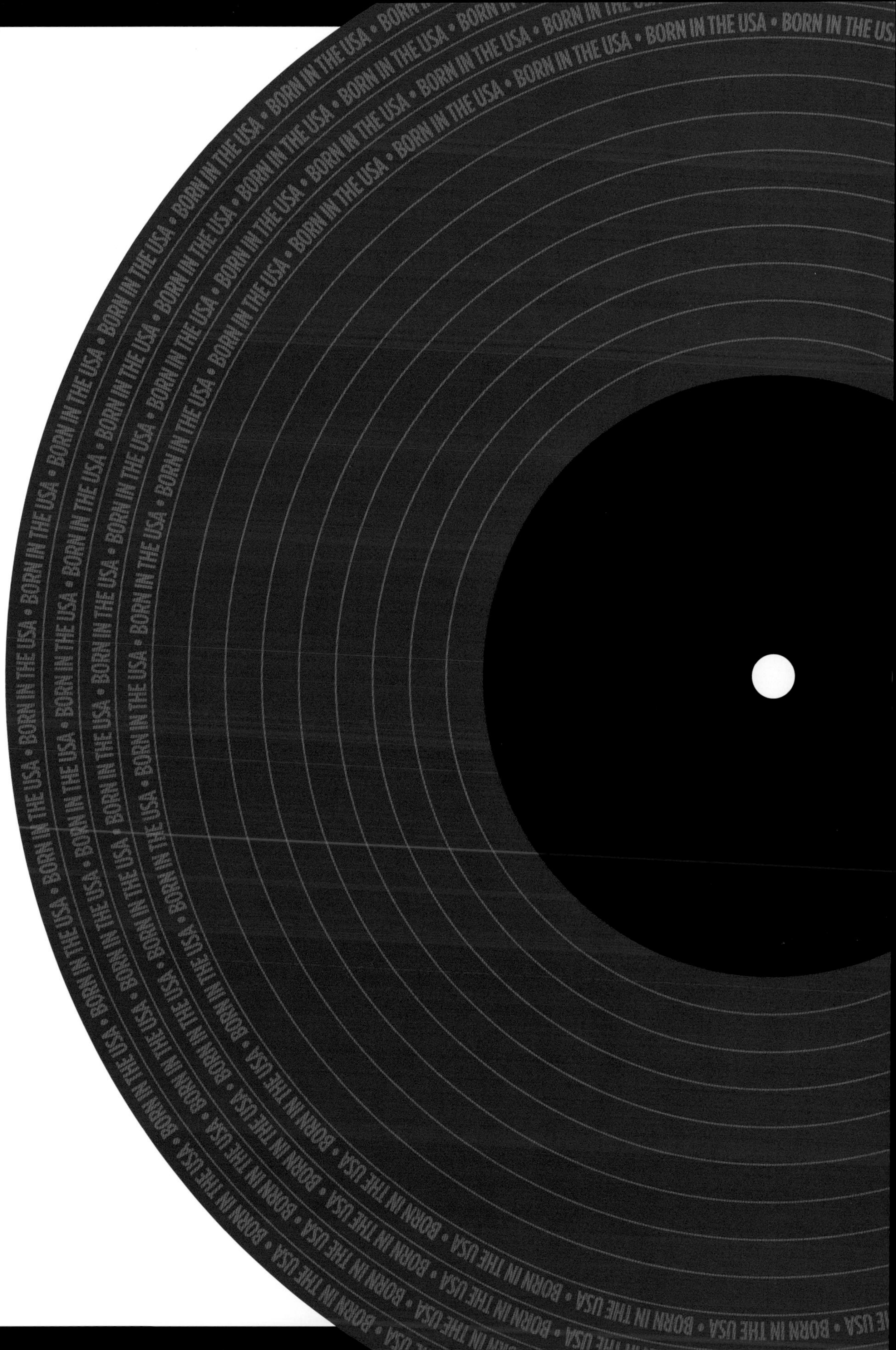
BORN IN THE USA • BORN IN THE USA • BORN IN THE USA

1984, UK

DO THEY KNOW IT'S CHRISTMAS?

BAND AID

BOB GELDOF & MIDGE URE, PHONOGRAM

RECORDED 25 NOVEMBER 1984 AT SARM STUDIOS, LONDON

On December 3, 1984, the world of popular music changed forever. "Do They Know It's Christmas?" by Band Aid wasn't just a charity single; it was the conscience of the British music world on display. A cultural flashpoint that proved music could drive not just donations, but global awareness. It rewired how artists, audiences, and the media responded to humanitarian crises, opening a door that many would walk through in the decades to follow.

At its heart was an unlikely leader. Bob Geldof, the outspoken frontman of The Boomtown Rats, a fringe band on the edges of the UK and Irish scenes, wasn't pop royalty. The Rats had scored a handful of hits, including "I Don't Like Mondays" which was a song about a school shooting in the USA. However, by the mid-1980s, they were fading from relevance. "I Don't Like Mondays" was a global hit, ironically missing out on chart success only in the US.

That song was the first time the world took notice of Geldof's conscience and songwriting skills. He had determination, outrage, and the conviction that music could be more than entertainment. He put it on the line and wrote and sang about what mattered to him.

And in 1984, what mattered was Ethiopia's famine and the reports on the BBC that shocked him into action. Encouraged by his partner, television presenter Paula Yates, who many called the driving force behind Band Aid, Geldof did something.

Together with Midge Ure of Ultravox, Geldof wrote "Do They Know It's Christmas?" and did what no one thought possible. In a single, whirlwind session at London's SARM West Studios in November 1984, he pulled together 40 of the biggest names in British and Irish pop. Bono, George Michael, Sting, Boy George, Paul Young, and Simon Le Bon were in and out of the studio to record their parts. Egos were shelved; they were there to make a difference.

The name "Band Aid" said it all. A group of musicians trying to patch a wounded world, hastily, imperfectly, but with purpose. Geldof wasn't after a one-off charity single. He was after a movement, starting in Britain but calling on the world to act.

"Do They Know It's Christmas?" exploded onto the charts. It became the fastest-selling single in UK history, moving over 3.8 million copies at home and millions more worldwide. In its first week of sales, it sold more records

than every other record on the charts combined. Its message was blunt, some said simplistic, contrasting Western holiday excess with the stark reality of famine in Africa. But for millions, especially younger audiences, it was the first time pop music had called on them to care about global injustice.

The chorus cut through not just as a song but as a challenge. In the wealthy West, Christmas meant abundance, tables heavy with food, shops crowded with gifts, whole cultures built around seasonal indulgence. Set against that was the stark reality in famine-stricken Ethiopia, where a single full meal could itself be an indulgence. The song worked because it forced listeners to face that contrast, to hear their own celebrations against the silence of empty plates elsewhere.

In its first year, the single raised £8 million, equivalent to more than £30 million today, which was channeled directly into famine relief. But the fundamental shift wasn't just in the money, it was in the mindset. Band Aid showed that pop culture could mobilize mass attention faster than politics, and with a heart that governments often lacked.

The momentum rolled across the Atlantic. In early 1985, "We Are the World" became America's answer, a USA for Africa project led by Michael Jackson, Lionel Richie, and Quincy Jones. Featuring Bruce Springsteen, Stevie Wonder, Tina Turner, and Bob Dylan, it sold 20 million copies. It raised over US$60 million for African aid.

And then came the day the world stood still: Live Aid, on July 13, 1985.

Australia actually started the concerts twice: the first show, the East Africa Tragedy (EAT)

Appeal Concert, took place in January in Melbourne, before a series of concerts played out around the globe in July. The shows started with Oz for Africa in Sydney, featuring INXS as the headline act, 12 hours before the event in London's Wembley Stadium and Philadelphia's JFK Stadium. They were broadcast globally to 1.9 billion people across 150 countries. It was the largest live television event in history at the time, a 16-hour marathon of music and conscience. I recall the parties we had in Australia at the time. After watching Australia, we woke the next day to watch the greatest concert spectacle in music history, with Wembley as its heartbeat.

Status Quo kicked it off. U2 broke through. Queen delivered a performance still hailed as one of the greatest live sets ever. Bowie, The Who, and Paul McCartney all took the stage

before a worldwide audience. The BBC's live broadcast drew over 24 million British viewers, turning the event into a national moment of pride and global solidarity.

Philadelphia mirrored Wembley's energy with its own icons: Bob Dylan, Led Zeppelin – yes, okay, they were a bunch of Brits – and a slate of American legends. But Live Aid wasn't confined to London and Philadelphia; it was global.

In total, Live Aid raised over US$250 million, much of which was donated directly to famine-stricken communities.

The criticisms emerged later, raising questions about Western paternalism, the complexities of African politics, and whether the aid effectively reached those in need. However, the impact of Band Aid and Live Aid was probably more significant than that of any other song in this book, given its global reach.

It wasn't just about raising money. It was about raising a generation's awareness, giving famine a face, a sound, and a global voice. Band Aid made charitable action part of popular culture. It showed that musicians could drive social change, not just reflect it. And that social change is, and was, undeniable.

Every major charity single or global benefit concert since, from Sun City to Stand Up To Cancer, owes something to Band Aid. The song itself became a Christmas fixture in the UK, returning for its 20th and 30th anniversaries, and raising millions more for causes such as the Darfur crisis in Sudan and the Ebola crisis.

The song itself wasn't much. Lyrically and musically, it was pulled together almost overnight, and the surge and promotions started before the studio had heard its first notes.

Band Aid didn't just patch a wound. It rewrote the rules of music's role in the world, proving that a hastily written, shallow song could start a movement that changed the world. And when the world stopped to listen, it was Wembley that became its stage, the place where pop music's conscience found its voice.

That was the power of "Do They Know It's Christmas?".

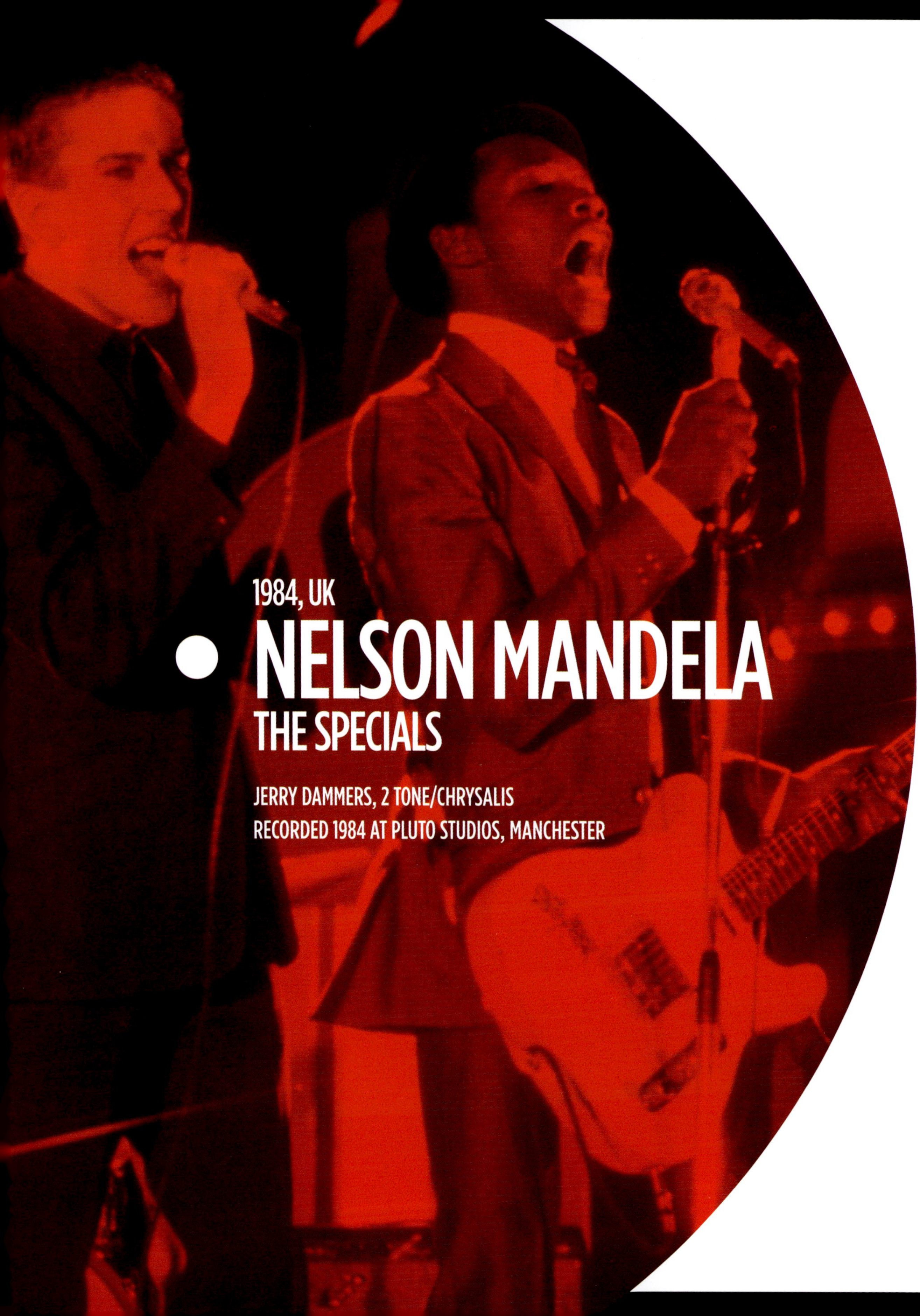

1984, UK

NELSON MANDELA

THE SPECIALS

JERRY DAMMERS, 2 TONE/CHRYSALIS

RECORDED 1984 AT PLUTO STUDIOS, MANCHESTER

When "Free Nelson Mandela" burst onto the airwaves in December 1984, it didn't sound like a protest song. It was bright, joyful, built on infectious ska rhythms with a chorus that lodged in your head. But beneath its irresistible melody lay a sharp, urgent demand, a song that carried Nelson Mandela's name from a South African prison cell onto the global stage and helped spark a worldwide justice movement.

When Jerry Dammers first wrote the song in 1983, it was simply titled "Nelson Mandela." After attending an anti-apartheid concert, Dammers was shocked at how little people in Britain and Europe seemed to know about the man who had been jailed for leading South Africa's African National Congress. Mandela had already spent over 20 years behind bars, yet his cause was almost invisible in the West. Dammers wanted that to change.

However, The Specials had fractured, and Dammers carried on under the name The Special AKA, gathering a shifting collective of musicians, with vocals from Stan Campbell and backing vocals from the likes of Elvis Costello. They recorded the song with a sense of urgency that mirrored its purpose. By its December 1984 release, the title had changed to "Free Nelson Mandela," a bold statement rather than a mere introduction.

It had also morphed from being just a song that was going to live on an album to a single that charted and impacted every part of the world in which it was heard. Released on 2 Tone Records, it became a UK Top 10 hit, spread rapidly across Europe and Australia, and seeped into the underground music scenes of the United States.

Today, protest music slips across borders with ease – even in China, where the Great Firewall still tries to keep the outside world at bay – but in the mid-1980s, getting into apartheid-era South Africa required much more stealth. "Free Nelson Mandela" was smuggled in on cassette tapes and grew through defiant sing-alongs in communities as widespread as Soweto and the Eastern Cape, its infectious chorus becoming a rallying cry for freedom.

It opened with a lonely and hollow saxophone carrying the weight of incarcerated isolation, before bursting into life,

drums snapping into a danceable groove, basslines bouncing, horns exploding in vibrant harmonies. It went from lament to hope instantly.

For a generation of young people across the world, "Free Nelson Mandela" was their first encounter with Mandela's name, and it proved that a protest song didn't need to be angry or dour to land its blow. It could lift you up and make you move while making you think.

Mandela himself was more than a political prisoner. Born in 1918 into a royal Thembu family in South Africa's Eastern Cape, he trained as a lawyer. He rose to prominence as a leader in the African National Congress (ANC). He began his activism as a believer in non-violent protest. Throughout the 1950s, he organized peaceful demonstrations, strikes, and acts of civil disobedience against South Africa's apartheid regime.

However, after the Sharpeville Massacre in 1960, when police opened fire on unarmed protesters, killing 69 people, Mandela decided that peaceful protest alone was not enough. In 1961, he co-founded Umkhonto we Sizwe (Spear of the Nation), the armed wing of the ANC.

Umkhonto we Sizwe focused on acts of sabotage, targeting infrastructure like power stations, government buildings, and military installations, aiming to damage the apartheid system without loss of life and without hurting the already marginalized communities of South Africa.

Mandela never abandoned the principle of negotiation, nor did he lead violent attacks on civilians. His shift marked a strategic turn, from peaceful protest to armed resistance, in response to a government that met non-violence with brutal repression.

He was arrested in 1962 and sentenced to life imprisonment. Mandela spent 27 years in jail, first on Robben Island, later in Pollsmoor and Victor Verster prisons. During that time, the South African government tried to erase him from public memory.

But this song cracked open the silence. It turned Mandela into a household name, a symbol of resistance known from London to Melbourne, Johannesburg to New York.

Its release coincided with a rising global anti-apartheid movement. It became a soundtrack to a wave of activism, including cultural boycotts of South African artists and sports teams, economic sanctions imposed by countries such as Australia, the United States, Canada, and the UK. The United Nations pushed for embargoes, and while governments hesitated, the people and the music spoke louder.

Other songs joined the chorus. Peter Gabriel's "Biko" (1980) mourned the death of South African activist Steve Biko and became a protest anthem in its own right. Artists United Against Apartheid released *Sun City* (1985) by Steven Van Zandt, a hard-hitting collaboration between Bruce Springsteen, Bono, Gil Scott-Heron, Bob Dylan, who all feature in this book, and others. The Specials' ska peers and punk bands lent their voices, too, making anti-apartheid activism part of pop culture's front line.

The impact of "Free Nelson Mandela" reached its symbolic peak in 1988 with the Nelson Mandela 70th Birthday Tribute at Wembley Stadium, a massive, all-star concert watched by over 600 million people worldwide. It wasn't a celebration. There was a global demand for his release. The anthem Dammers had written rang out across Wembley, turning the stadium into a pulpit for justice.

Two years later, on 11 February 1990, Nelson Mandela walked free. After 27 years, he stepped into the sunlight, the world watching. The soundtrack to his freedom? The song that bore his name. At victory rallies, Mandela danced to "Free Nelson Mandela."

In later years, Mandela thanked Dammers and the artists who had amplified his voice when the South African regime tried to bury it.

"Free Nelson Mandela" didn't end apartheid by itself. But it became part of a global groundswell of protests, boycotts, sanctions, and songs that forced the world to confront the injustice.

Apartheid officially ended in 1994 when Mandela became South Africa's first democratically elected president. But long before that election, "Free Nelson Mandela" had marched ahead of the ballots, turning protest into pop culture, a dance tune into a movement. It was a joyful, defiant anthem that helped turn a prisoner into a symbol, and a symbol into a movement.

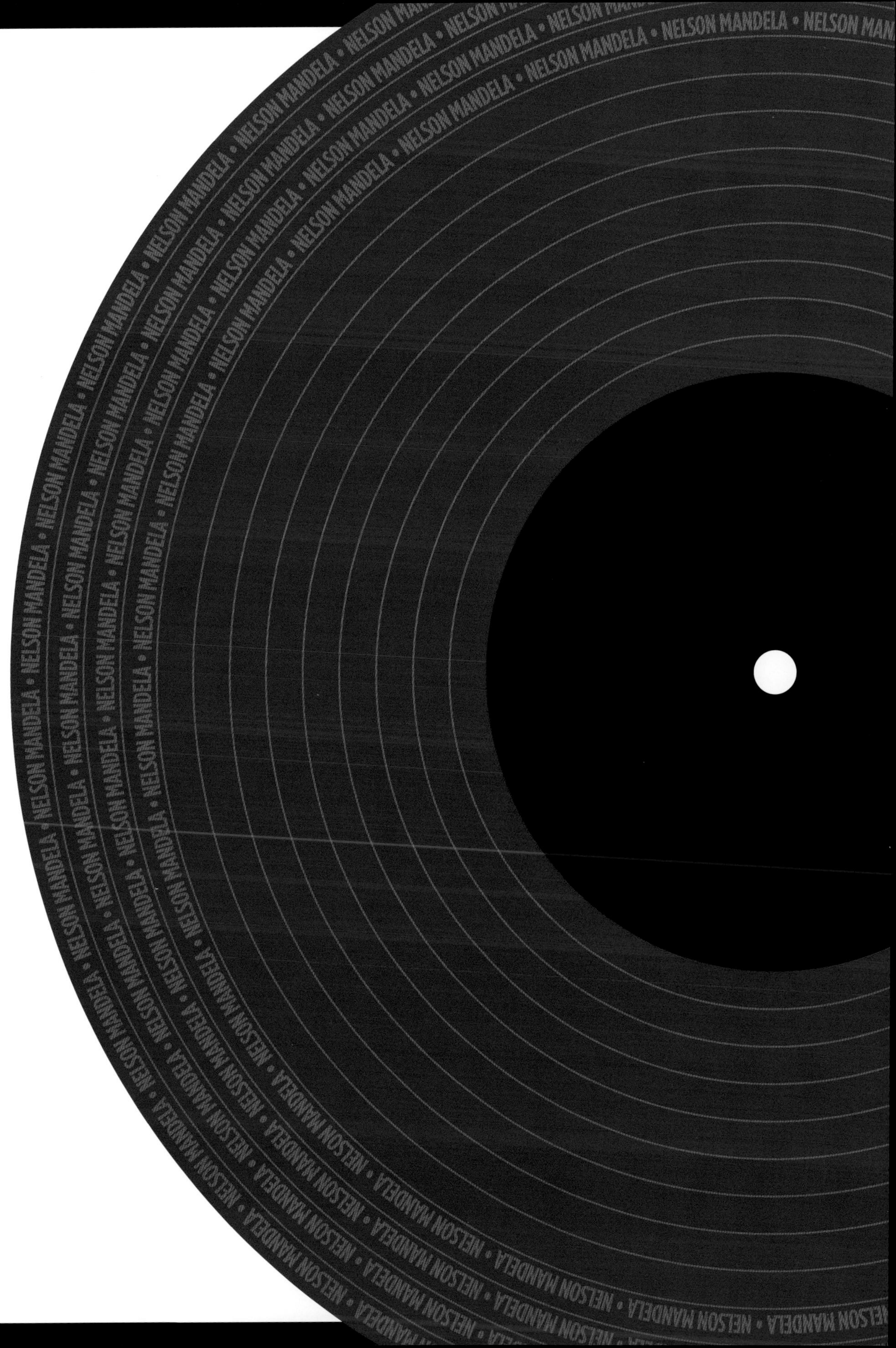
NELSON MANDELA • NELSON MANDELA • NELSON MANDELA

1984, USA

PANAMA

VAN HALEN

EDDIE VAN HALEN, WARNER BROS.

RECORDED MARCH–JUNE 1983 AT 5150 STUDIOS, HOLLYWOOD

This song is the most unusual entry in this book. "Panama" was weaponized beyond its original intent and was pure Van Halen: loud, swaggering, and unapologetically brash. With Eddie Van Halen's searing guitar riffs, Alex Van Halen's thunderous drums, and David Lee Roth's cocky vocals, it was a high-octane anthem of American rock excess.

Written not about a country, but a drag racing car Roth admired, "Panama" was built for the open road, a celebration of speed, adrenaline, and lusty abandon. It even featured Eddie's Lamborghini Miura revving in the background.

Five years after its release, in one of the strangest twists in modern music history, "Panama" was unleashed on a dictator.

Manuel Noriega was a Panamanian military dictator who ruled from 1983 until the US invasion in 1989. Once a longtime CIA asset, he became notorious for drug trafficking, corruption, and brutal repression, which eventually turned Washington against him, and President George H.W. Bush launched Operation Just Cause to remove him from power.

However, Noriega fled to the Vatican's Apostolic Nunciature in Panama City, a diplomatic sanctuary protected by international law, and the Vatican refused to turn him away, providing a haven. The United States military surrounded the compound but couldn't breach it without risking a diplomatic crisis. So instead, they turned to an unexpected weapon: rock music.

The operation became unofficially known as Rock the Dictator. Day and night, US troops blasted a relentless playlist of heavy metal and hard rock through massive speakers aimed at the compound. The soundtrack read like a rebel's greatest hits: "I Fought the Law" by The Clash, "No More Mr. Nice Guy" by Alice Cooper, "Welcome to the Jungle" by Guns N' Roses, and, at full blast, "Panama" by Van Halen.

Why "Panama"? The irony was irresistible. A song named for the country now battering the walls of its dictator's refuge. Beyond the title, its relentless energy and sonic bravado became a symbol of American resolve, a wall of sound designed to humiliate, disorient, and psychologically wear Noriega down.

The music blared for days. Windows rattled. Walls shook. The Vatican called the playing of "Panama" "a violation of dignity" when it lodged a formal protest against the action of the US military. The US eventually turned down the volume, but by then, the damage was done.

On January 3, 1990, Noriega surrendered. Whether it was the music, the political pressure, or the crushing reality of isolation that finally broke him remains debated. But "Panama," a song about speed and freedom, became part of the soundtrack to the fall of a dictatorship.

It entered military folklore, cited in Pentagon briefings as an example of psychological operations in action. In rock history, it remains one of the most surreal intersections of pop culture and geopolitical strategy: a song born of LA's Sunset Strip that ultimately became a weapon of war.

But "Panama" was no isolated case. The United States military and intelligence services have long recognized the power of music as a psychological tool, sometimes as a form of soft power, and sometimes as a weapon.

During the Iraq War and at Guantanamo Bay, the US military routinely blasted high-decibel music during interrogations, using it to disorient detainees and break their will. The playlists ranged from hard rock to pop, including "Enter Sandman" by Metallica, "Bodies" by Drowning Pool, "Babylon" by David Gray, and even "Born in the USA" by Bruce Springsteen, cruelly stripping it of its protest meaning. But it wasn't just rock; children's songs, such as the *Barney & Friends* theme, were used to induce psychological strain, with tracks from *Sesame Street* reportedly in rotation.

They'd do my head in too, and these tactics, later denounced by human rights groups, ignited a global debate about the use of music as psychological torture, a sharp contrast to its traditional role as a unifying cultural force.

The practice wasn't new. In Vietnam, Operation Wandering Soul saw US forces blasting eerie, ghostly sounds, often combined with Vietnamese funeral music, across battle zones to exploit local superstitions and break enemy morale.

Throughout the Cold War, the CIA funded Radio Free Europe, Radio Liberty, and Voice of America, beaming Western pop and rock, from The Beatles to Bob Dylan, into Eastern Bloc countries, using music as soft power to undermine communist regimes.

And perhaps the most curious twist of all, the enduring theory, neither confirmed nor thoroughly debunked, that the CIA had a hand

in the Scorpions' "Wind of Change." Released in 1990, it became the unofficial anthem of the fall of the Berlin Wall and the end of the Cold War. With lyrics that seemed too perfectly timed to history, it sparked speculation that it was less a rock ballad and more a covert message of Western triumph.

So while the role of "Panama" in ousting Noriega remains the most bizarre headline, it fits into a larger pattern where music became a weapon, a tool of influence, and a psychological lever pulled by governments and military strategists alike.

Van Halen's "Panama" had nothing to do with politics; it was a raucous, anthemic rock song ideally suited to global stadiums. Yet in a strange twist of fate, it became a battle hymn in a real-world siege. And for the CIA, the Pentagon, and those in the shadows of statecraft, it was a reminder of something every songwriter knows: music moves people, whether they want it to or not.

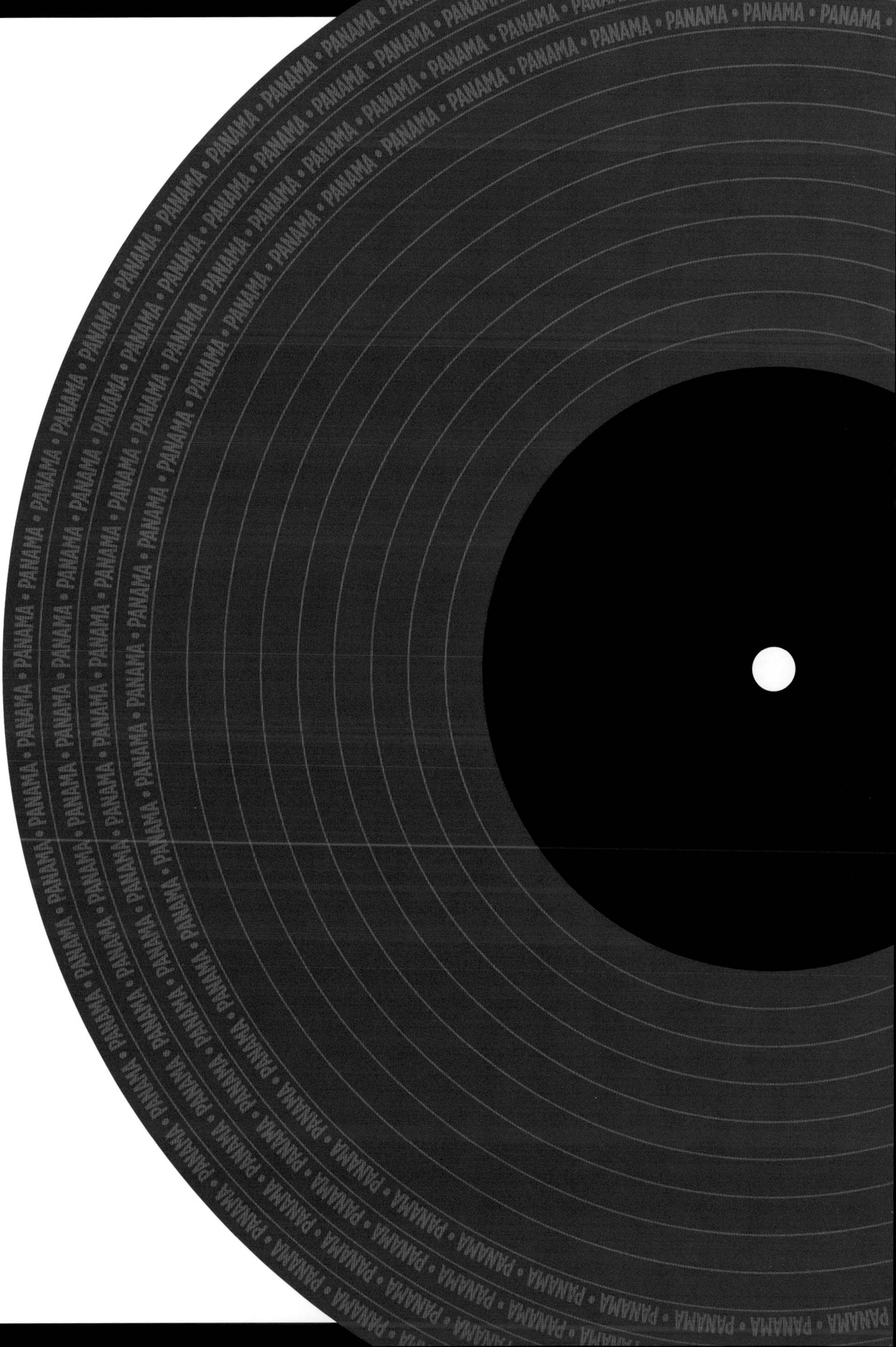
PANAMA • PANAMA • PANAMA

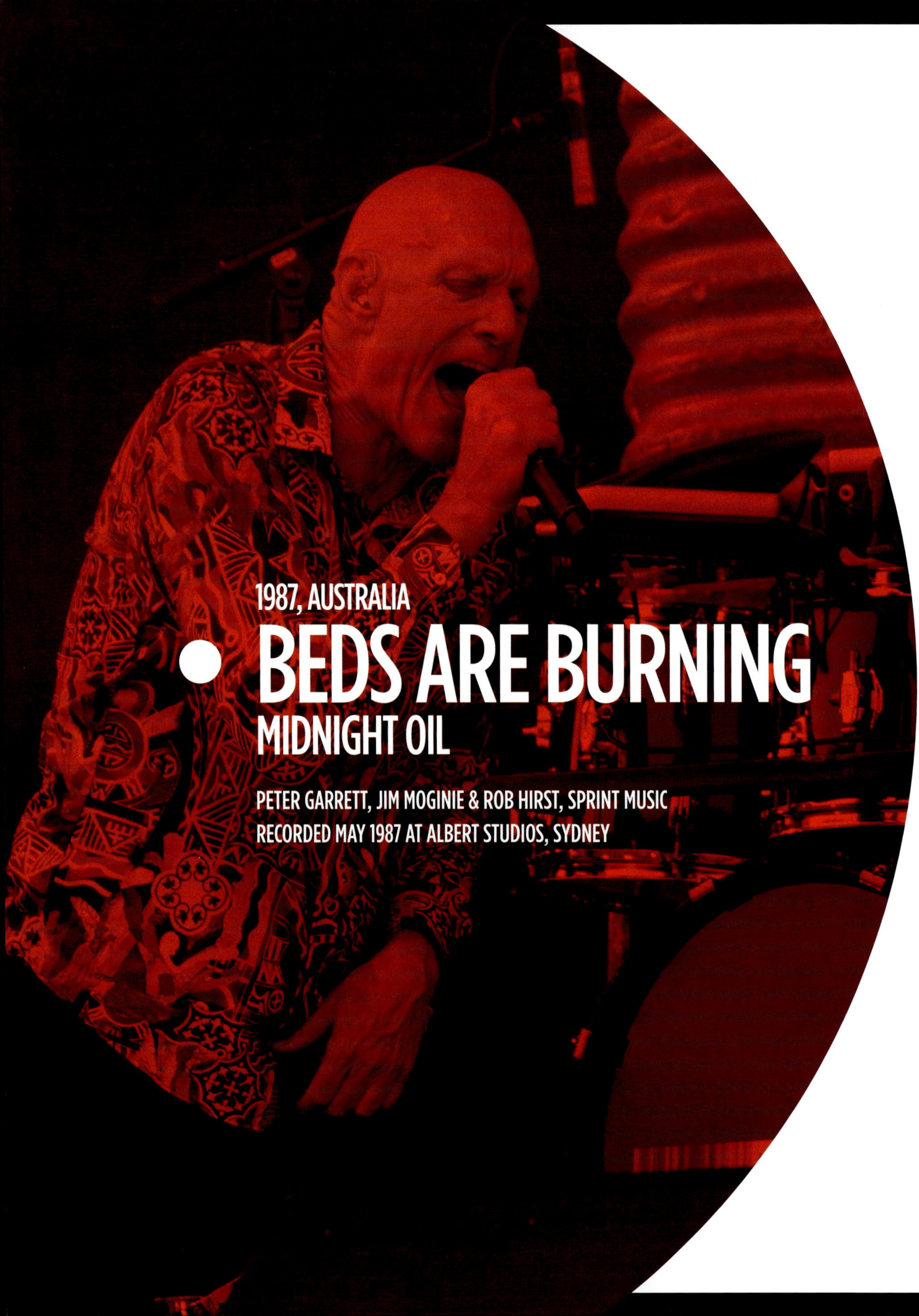

1987, AUSTRALIA

BEDS ARE BURNING

MIDNIGHT OIL

PETER GARRETT, JIM MOGINIE & ROB HIRST, SPRINT MUSIC
RECORDED MAY 1987 AT ALBERT STUDIOS, SYDNEY

When "Beds Are Burning" hit the world's radios in December 1987, it wasn't just another rock single. It was a demand set to a rhythm, a song that forced a conversation Australia had long tried to avoid. It exposed Australia's pious underbelly and forced a nation to confront a couple of centuries of wrongs.

But Midnight Oil didn't write soft protest songs; they wrote statements. And "Beds Are Burning" was their boldest effort to date. This danceable, unforgettable anthem took the fight for Indigenous Australian land rights from the remote deserts to the global stage.

This wasn't a vague plea for harmony. It was a direct challenge. Written to highlight the plight of the Pintupi people of Australia's Western Desert, who had only returned to their homelands in the 1980s after years of forced displacement, the song delivered the truth polite society didn't want to hear: the land was never ours to take, and justice meant giving it back. Its refrain was unforgettable, a demand to recognize fairness, to shoulder responsibility, and to finally pay the debt owed, and to pay rent.

When it was released, Aboriginal land rights were only just gaining recognition. Any discussion was politically charged and, more often than not, ignored, so "Beds Are Burning" crashed into mainstream consciousness. Its pounding beat, shout-along chorus, and Peter Garrett's towering presence made it impossible to ignore. It went No. 1 in New Zealand, South Africa, and Canada, and was in the top 20 globally, even cracking the US Hot Dance Club Play (*Billboard*) Top 20, a rare global success for a song with such a pointed message.

Ironically, it peaked at No. 6 in Australia, a solid hit, but a sign the country itself still had some way to go. The world embraced its chorus; Australia's reaction hinted at a deeper cultural hesitation. But as one of the biggest acts in Australia, it was hard to ignore this song and its power, and it thrust Indigenous rights into the foreground for white Australians . . . whether they liked it or not.

In many respects, "the Oils" had been working up to a statement this significant since their inception a decade earlier.

Their 1978 self-titled debut album contained "Surfing with a Spoon," which hinted at Midnight Oil's refusal to gloss over uncomfortable truths. Wrapped in bluesy rock, it was a dark reflection on heroin addiction, not a protest song, but a sign the Oils were drawn to society's darker corners.

By 1980, with the release of "No Time for Games," they turned their fire outward. It snarled at a world happy to be just another face in the crowd, a rejection of apathy and passive consumerism. Midnight Oil would not stand silent.

That stance hardened after the release of the haunting "Armistice Day" with "US Forces" and "Power and the Passion" following in 1982. "US Forces" took aim at American military influence in Australia, while "Power and the Passion" skewered political apathy and media manipulation. Both proved the Oils could deliver sharp political critique wrapped in anthemic rock. They were not afraid of speaking their minds.

By 1987, they'd honed that skill to perfection. They moved from exposing personal demons to railing against social apathy to confronting national injustice. With "Beds Are Burning," they called out Australia's great shame, the theft of Indigenous land.

Where would Indigenous rights be if one of Australia's biggest bands hadn't shoved the issue into the heart of national conversation? Midnight Oil dragged it from the margins to the middle, giving it a voice in every pub, radio station, and teenage bedroom.

Their message didn't stop there. "The Dead Heart," recorded the same year, told the story of dispossession from the Indigenous perspective. In live performances, it often began with the deep drone of the didgeridoo, an ancient instrument from northern Australia, crafted from hollowed eucalyptus and played using circular breathing. Its resonant tones grounded the Oils' message in the oldest continuing culture on earth.

Hearing "The Dead Heart" introduced by the didgeridoo brought a gravity that no electric guitar could match. One can only imagine the power if "Beds Are Burning" was performed the same way; its rallying cry carried by the heartbeat of a culture fighting to be heard.

Australia's relationship with its First Nations peoples had been defined by denial and dispossession. Aboriginal and Torres Strait Islander Australians weren't counted in the census until the 1967 referendum, a symbolic change that barely scratched the surface.

The Stolen Generations, children forcibly removed from their families under government policy, left scars that still run deep. The land rights movement of the 1970s, marked by the 1972 Aboriginal Tent Embassy and the 1981 National Land Rights Conference, fought for recognition and the restitution of traditional lands.

At that conference, Eddie Mabo sparked a legal battle that culminated in the *Mabo v. Queensland (No 2)* decision in 1992, recognizing Indigenous Australians' native title for the first time. Yet even this victory came at a price. Mabo died before the decision was handed down, and his grave was later desecrated. His family reburied him on Murray Island with traditional rites that had not been seen for 80 years.

"Beds Are Burning" didn't just top the charts. It sparked debates, fueled protests, and gave voice to a cause that had been too long ignored. Midnight Oil forced it into the cultural mainstream. When they performed at the 2000 Sydney Olympics Closing Ceremony in suits emblazoned with "SORRY," they stood as ambassadors for a movement still burning with urgency.

Midnight Oil made a point of being unmistakably Australian, refusing to sound like just another international band that could have come from anywhere. "Beds Are Burning" embodied that stance, a song rooted in the country's own land and history, and all the heavier for it.

Lead singer Peter Garrett eventually entered Federal Parliament and became a cabinet minister. Still, his voice and societal impact were strongest in the band he started with mates in the 1970s.

Its influence, however, has been recognized globally and at home, with "Beds Are Burning" regularly cited among the country's most essential songs.

Few songs have ever carried such weight, particularly in Australia, where it turned an uncomfortable truth into a global anthem. A four-minute song that forced a nation to listen.

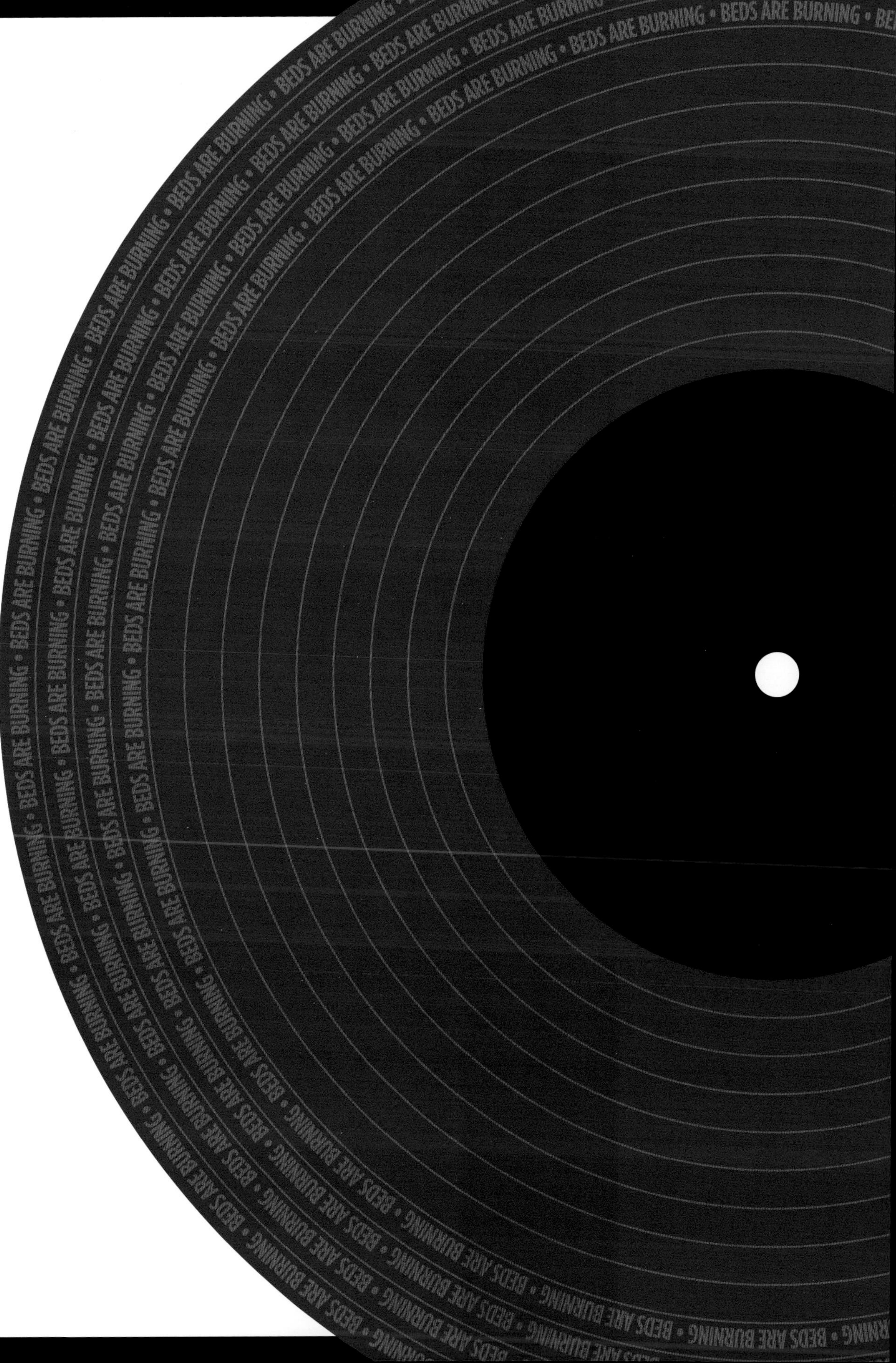
BEDS ARE BURNING

1987, USSR

PEREMEN!

KINO

VIKTOR TSOI, MOROZ RECORDS

RECORDED 1987 AT MOROZ STUDIO, LENINGRAD

In 1986, when "Peremen!" ("Changes!" in English) hit the Soviet underground, it didn't sound like a revolution, but that is precisely what it became. Viktor Tsoi and his band Kino didn't write slogans. They wrote songs. And with "Peremen!," they gave voice to a restless generation trapped between a decaying Soviet regime and a future they could barely imagine.

For most of the post-war era, life behind the Iron Curtain had been defined by repression, scarcity, and fear. The Soviet Union under Stalin had ruled by terror; under Khrushchev, by crackdowns and fleeting thaws; under Brezhnev, by stagnation and suffocating grey conformity. From Moscow to Minsk, from Leningrad to East Berlin, the Eastern Bloc staggered through decades of shortages, propaganda, crumbling housing, and a surveillance state that silenced dissent.

By the early 1980s, the cracks were showing everywhere. The economy was a rusting machine, running on empty promises and black-market deals. Supermarkets sat half-stocked. Apartments crumbled. Young people queued for bread by day and bootlegged, among other things, Western records by night. Official culture pumped out the same tired slogans about the radiant future, but nobody believed them in a life defined by the absence of freedom, truth, and hope.

Then came Mikhail Gorbachev, whose rise in 1985 brought words like *glasnost* (openness) and *perestroika* (restructuring) into the official lexicon, and he pushed for change. But his reforms felt like too little, too late for the many who felt the system was rotten to its core. The promises of communism and the idea of a superabundance of goods and services lay in ruins.

And that's when "Peremen!" arrived, the sound of a generation that had grown up in the shadows suddenly finding its voice as the fists of oppression were lifted.

"Peremen!," or "My zhdyom peremen" (We are waiting for changes), was first performed by Tsoi in the summer of 1986 and quickly became more than a song. It was the embodiment of the spirit of perestroika, a chorus that echoed the unspoken demand of a generation: enough waiting. Enough of the slogans, let's have real change.

That's how far it reached. Gorbachev himself said it. Sitting with his new pro-reform crew, telling Gromyko the old ways were done. We've got to do things differently, he said. Even pointed to Tsoi. He's out there singing about change, and the crowds are yelling it back. People want change. They're not whispering anymore, they're saying it out loud.

Yet Tsoi himself seemed reluctant to wear the badge of protest singer. In a 1988 television interview with Sergey Sholokhov, he dismissed the idea that "Peremen!" was a political statement, calling his performance of the song in the Soviet crime film *Assa* "something tacked on." His bandmate, drummer Georgy Guryanov, echoed this, insisting the song was about inner change, a creative awakening, a desire for personal freedom.

But once "Peremen!" entered the bloodstream of Soviet culture, it escaped its maker. The film *Assa* transformed the song into a national statement, framing it against scenes of Soviet corruption and repression. What began as a call for personal freedom became, in the mouths of a restless public, a cry for systemic change.

Tsoi wasn't a politician or a revolutionary in the traditional sense. He was a rock musician, and by the mid-1980s, a cult hero of the Soviet underground. Yet, with this one song, he captured the uneasy mood of a society choking on stagnation. Where official slogans talked of socialism's bright future, Tsoi spoke a simple, dangerous truth: people wanted change.

The chorus wasn't a manifesto. It wasn't politics. It was a chant. Drums and bass driving it forward, voices spitting the same word again and again: change. Not about communism, not about capitalism, not about any of that. Just a shout from the street. People were sick of being promised everything and handed nothing.

"Our hearts demand change! Our eyes demand change!"

Remarkably, "Peremen!" was not banned. In the era of Stalin or Brezhnev, such a song would have been unthinkable. However, Gorbachev's reforms created just enough space for it to exist, although never on official radio or state television. Instead, it spread in youth clubs, student dormitories, underground gigs, and endless dubbed cassette tapes. It wasn't endorsed by the Party, and that gave it power.

The authorities saw Tsoi's careful dance. He didn't name names. He didn't attack the Kremlin directly. But they also understood the risk. This wasn't dissident art; it was something more subversive, a song everyone could sing, that said everything by saying almost nothing. It was the sound of a generation holding its breath.

By the late 1980s, with the Soviet Union on the brink of collapse, "Peremen!" had become a youth anthem for a dying system. It echoed in street protests, at art shows, on bootlegged tapes played on battered stereos. It wasn't written for a political movement, but it gave one its soundtrack.

Tsoi died in a car crash in 1990, mere months before the Soviet Union began to unravel, and he was frozen in time. Graffiti in Moscow and St. Petersburg still reads "*Цой жив*" (Tsoi Lives). His James Dean-like image, complete with a leather jacket, cigarette, and dark gaze, became a symbol of Russian youth defiance.

And "Peremen!" never stopped being dangerous.

It resurfaced during the 1991 coup attempt in Moscow, sung by crowds outside the White House. In the 2000s, it became the anthem of youth protests against Vladimir Putin's tightening grip on power. In 2020, Belarusian demonstrators adopted it during mass uprisings against Alexander Lukashenko's brutal regime, proof that a song born in the Soviet underground could still rattle dictatorships decades later. In 2021, Russian protesters sang it in defiance of riot police, and once again, authorities tried to suppress its public performance.

Even now, amid renewed war and repression, "Peremen!" remains on the Kremlin's watchlist.

It was never just a song. Couldn't be. It was bigger, heavier. A symbol, raw, defiant, alive. Tsoi wasn't giving them pretty words; he was cutting through the fog. Straight through the state noise. No polish. No tricks. Just one thing hammered again and again: change. That's what people heard. That's what they grabbed onto. They wanted it bad. They were sick of waiting.

Viktor Tsoi didn't live to see the new world he sang for. But his voice still echoes in stadiums, in protests, in the whispered hopes of those who refuse to be silent. Because in any system that denies freedom, "Changes!" will always be a revolutionary demand.

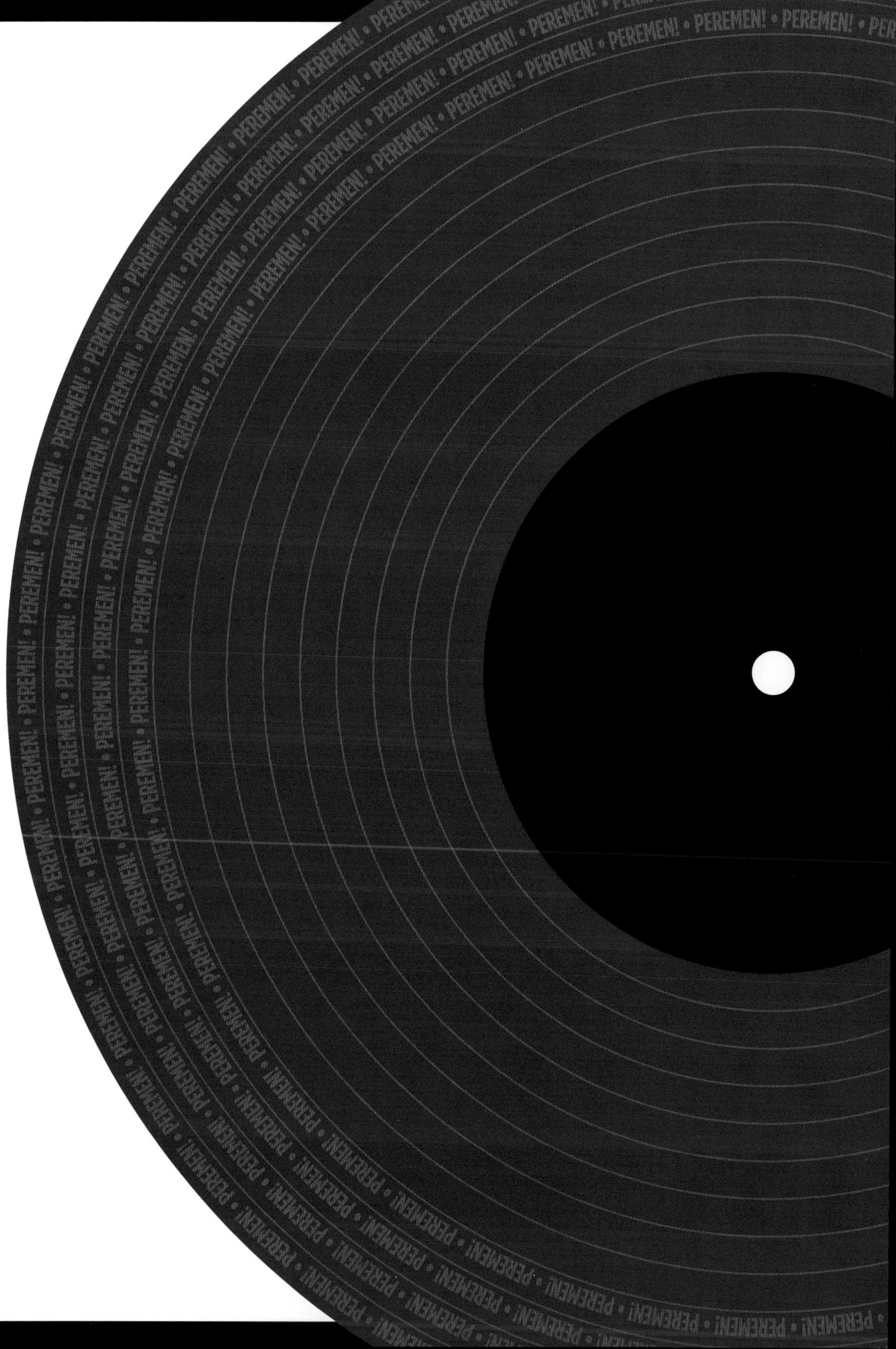
PEREMEN!

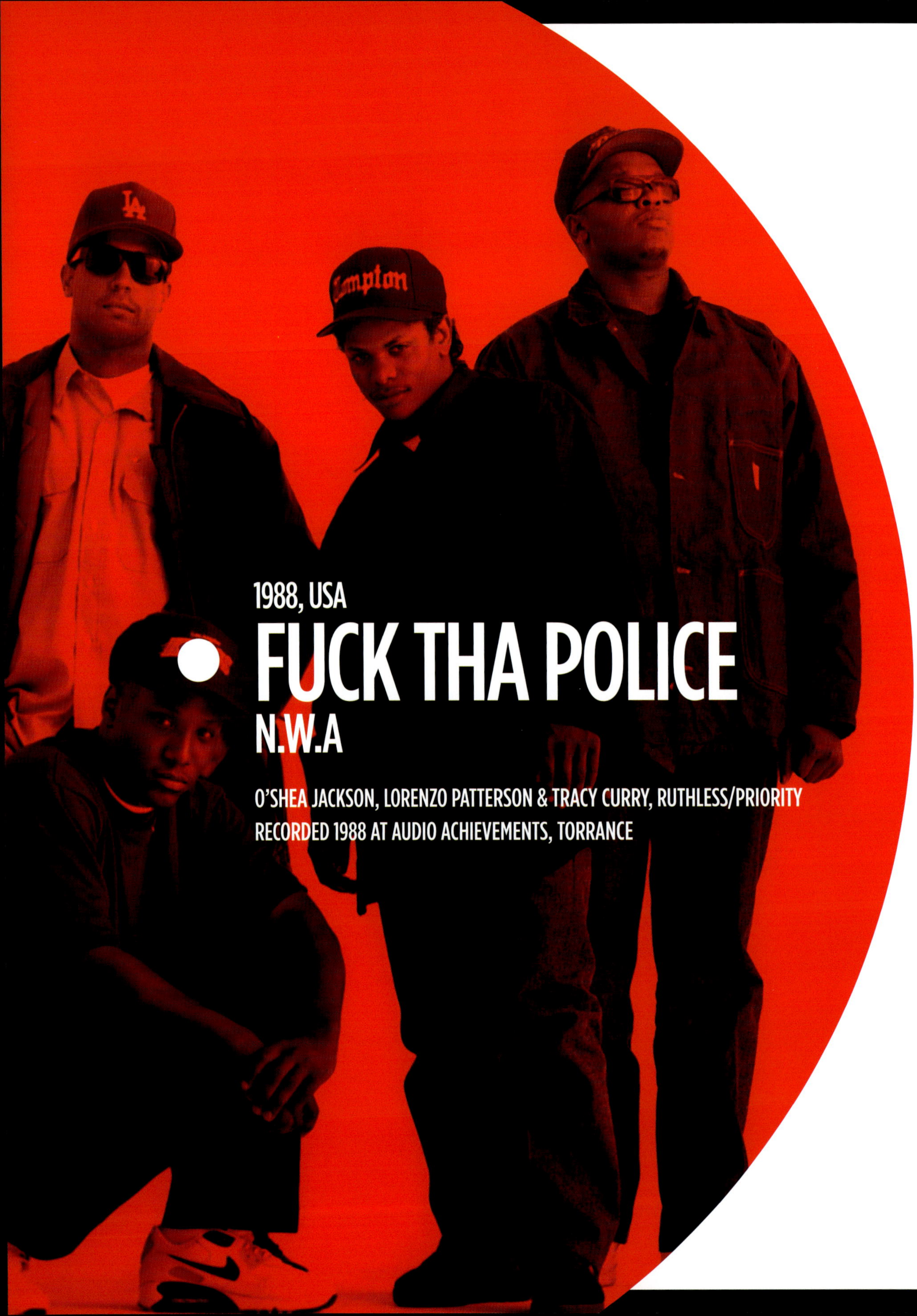

1988, USA

FUCK THA POLICE

N.W.A

O'SHEA JACKSON, LORENZO PATTERSON & TRACY CURRY, RUTHLESS/PRIORITY

RECORDED 1988 AT AUDIO ACHIEVEMENTS, TORRANCE

"Fuck Tha Police" exploded onto the American consciousness in 1988 as a declaration of war against a system of oppression many white Americans refused to acknowledge. Released on N.W.A's debut album *Straight Outta Compton*, the track didn't invent protest rap, but it defined it.

Raw, unapologetic, and confrontational, it laid bare the everyday reality of racial profiling, police brutality, and systemic injustice faced by young Black men in America's inner cities, particularly in the group's hometown of Compton, California.

Compton, a city within Los Angeles County, served as a working-class suburb of Los Angeles, located approximately 15 miles south of downtown. By the 1980s, it was a community battered by industrial decline, poverty, and violent gang culture, overshadowed by a brutal relationship with the LAPD. It became a national symbol of urban decay and police oppression, ground zero for everything N.W.A rapped about.

N.W.A – Eazy-E, Dr. Dre, Ice Cube, MC Ren, and DJ Yella – weren't polished political activists. They were angry young men speaking hard truths from lived experience as Niggaz Wit Attitudes, the long form of the group's name. "Fuck Tha Police" wasn't a rhetorical slogan. It was a direct response to relentless harassment, beatings, and racial discrimination by the LAPD under Chief Daryl Gates, infamous for his gang-suppression tactics.

The track was framed as a mock trial, with Ice Cube, MC Ren, and Eazy-E delivering their case like prosecutors for the streets. In a justice system where young Black men rarely found fairness, N.W.A flipped the script: they weren't the ones on trial, they were putting the system itself in the dock. The courtroom became a stage for ridicule, exposing the hypocrisy of institutions that demanded respect while showing none in return.

And it hit exactly where it hurt, at authority. If you want change, you have to upset people, especially those in power. "Fuck Tha Police" forced its way into the conversation, daring the establishment to try and shut it down.

The response was swift. The FBI sent a warning letter to N.W.A's label, Ruthless Records, condemning the song as a threat to law enforcement. Police unions across America

boycotted the group, and concert venues were pressured to cancel shows. Radio stations banned the track outright. But like every underground anthem before it, "Fuck Tha Police" found its way through mixtapes, car stereos, and hip-hop's fast-growing national audience.

The backlash only added to N.W.A's legend. *Straight Outta Compton* hit in the summer of 1988 like an explosion, a record that felt dangerous and impossible to ignore, sparking outrage and fascination in equal measure. The album wasn't just a hit; it was a cultural earthquake. In 2017, the Library of Congress selected *Straight Outta Compton* for preservation in the National Recording Registry, recognizing its cultural, historical, and aesthetic significance.

Although the group disbanded in 1991, their influence never faded. N.W.A bridged racial and cultural divides, bringing the raw reality of Black America to white suburban audiences and dragging hip-hop from the streets of Compton into the American mainstream. Critics who initially dismissed them would later compare their cultural shockwave to that of the Sex Pistols. Their influence extended beyond hip-hop, shaping both coasts of American rap and influencing alternative and nu-metal acts like System of a Down, Slipknot, and Korn.

The issues they rapped about were no exaggeration. In 1991, just three years after "Fuck Tha Police", the beating of Rodney King by LAPD officers, captured on video, shocked the world and ignited the 1992 Los Angeles riots. By then, "Fuck Tha Police" was a prophecy for which N.W.A didn't apologize. They didn't soften their message. They said what millions felt but few dared say. In doing so, they didn't just change hip-hop; they helped reshape America's conversation about race, authority, and the uncomfortable truth that if you want real change, you have to be willing to rattle the cage. Sometimes, you have to force people, especially those in power, to listen.

And it wasn't just in America. The song rattled cages worldwide.

In 1989, Australia's national youth broadcaster, Triple J, played "Fuck Tha Police" regularly, the only station in the world bold enough to do so. That ended when ABC management banned it following a campaign led by Liberal Senator Chris Sumner from South Australia. Triple J staff responded by going on strike, looping N.W.A's "Express Yourself" 82 times between 9 am and 4.30 pm, each spin prefaced with a statement explaining the protest. It became one of the most famous acts of media defiance in Australian broadcasting history, proving that the song's power transcended borders.

The story repeated in New Zealand. On April 10, 2011, musician Tiki Taane was arrested during a club gig in Tauranga for performing "Fuck Tha Police" while police officers were present. Charged with "disorderly behavior likely to cause violence to start or continue," Taane said later that he'd performed the song hundreds of times, but the presence of police suddenly turned lyrics into a criminal act.

"Fuck Tha Police" didn't just launch N.W.A into hip-hop legend, it cracked the American consciousness wide open. It forced a nation to confront the uncomfortable reality that the police weren't always the heroes, and that for millions of Black Americans, the justice system was a daily battlefield.

In doing so, it turned hip-hop from a party soundtrack into a political force. Where earlier rap spoke of the streets, "Fuck Tha Police" spoke to power. It gave rise to a wave of empowered, socially conscious rappers, from Public Enemy and Tupac to Kendrick Lamar. Their music wasn't just to entertain, but to indict, as well. The legacy extends beyond record sales and headlines. It normalized protest in mainstream music and shifted the way Black voices spoke to authority. It carved space for open discussion of police brutality long before body cameras and social media brought those injustices to the world.

In the years since, the song has remained a flashpoint, resurfacing with every wave of civil unrest, from the LA riots to Ferguson to the Black Lives Matter protests. When people chant against injustice today, they echo the same defiance N.W.A laid down in 1988.

"Fuck Tha Police" wasn't just a soundtrack to a fight; it was a catalyst for the changes the system didn't want.

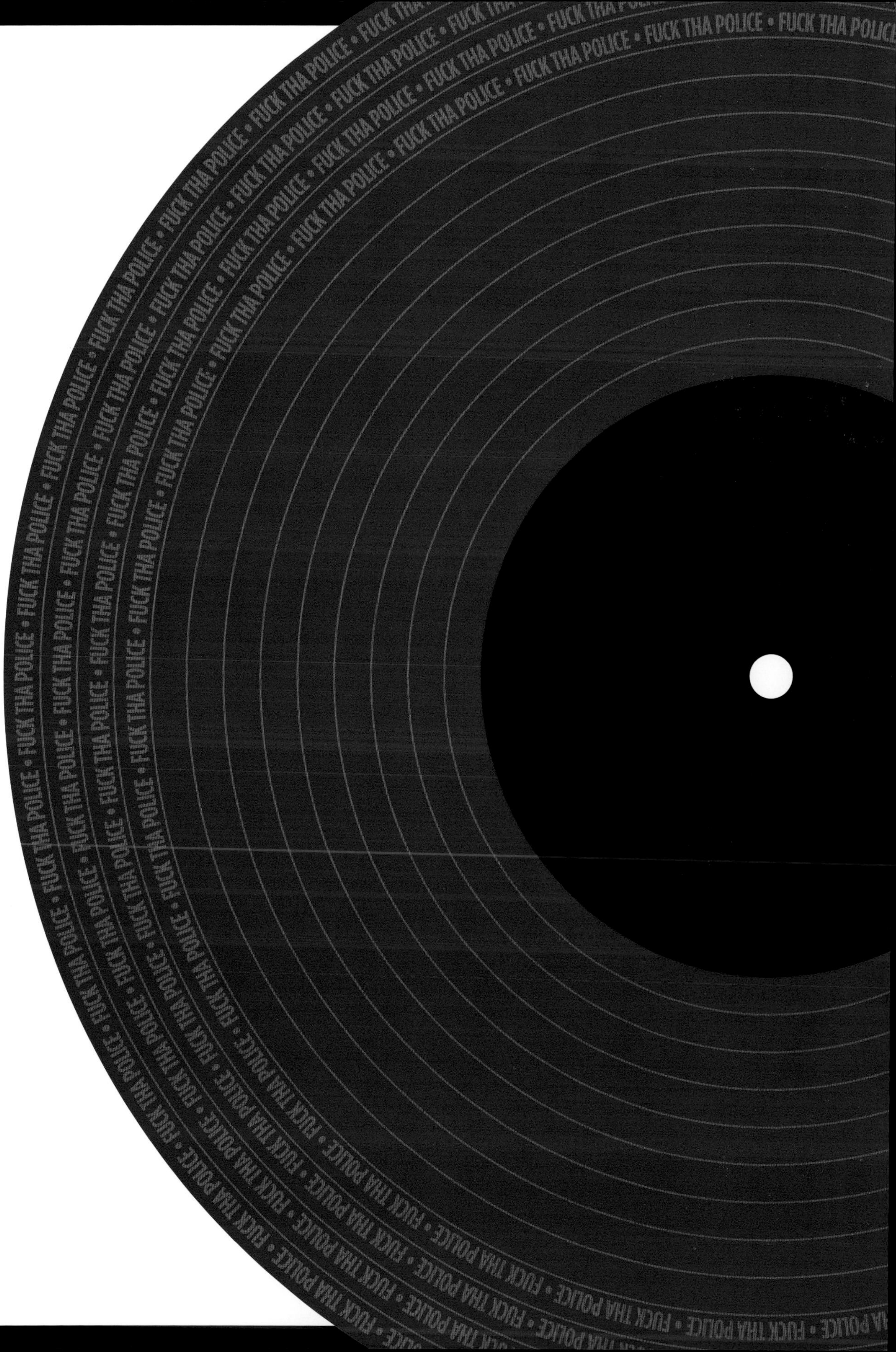
FUCK THA POLICE • FUCK THA POLICE • FUCK THA POLICE

1989, USA

FIGHT THE POWER

PUBLIC ENEMY

CARLTON RIDENHOUR, ERIC SADLER, HANK BOXLEY & KEITH BOXLEY, MOTOWN RECORDS
RECORDED APRIL 1989 AT GREENE ST. RECORDING, NEW YORK CITY

In 1989, "Fight the Power" roared into public consciousness denouncing systemic racism, cultural hypocrisy, and the sanitized myths America told itself. Commissioned by Spike Lee for his movie *Do the Right Thing*, Public Enemy crafted a track that distilled decades of anger, resistance, and pride into four-and-a-half relentless minutes.

Where N.W.A's "Fuck Tha Police" hit like a street-level haymaker, "Fight the Power" struck as a manifesto, a direct challenge to whitewashed history, political corruption, and the cultural machinery designed to pacify dissent.

Public Enemy's rise wasn't by accident. From their 1987 debut album, *Yo! Bum Rush the Show*, Chuck D, Flavor Flav, Professor Griff, and the Bomb Squad rewired hip-hop's purpose. They weren't here for party tracks. They were here to speak uncomfortable truths. Their second album, *It Takes a Nation of Millions to Hold Us Back* (1988), exploded like a cultural hand grenade, dense, sample-heavy, and underpinned by Chuck D's voice, a booming instrument of street sermons. Tracks like "Rebel Without a Pause," "Bring the Noise," and "Don't Believe the Hype" weren't just records. They were rallying cries.

But "Fight the Power" was their defining moment. It opened with the voice of civil rights activist Thomas 'TNT' Todd, framing the track as both a rallying cry and a challenge, immediately grounding it in the language of struggle and resistance. Then Chuck D stormed in, tearing into America's cultural icons with unflinching fury. He took aim at the deified image of Elvis Presley, dismissing him outright and calling out the racism embedded in the mythology. It wasn't subtle; it was a sledgehammer, smashing through polite reverence to force listeners to confront the raw anger and reality behind the music.

The line detonated like a bomb. It riffed on a long-standing, and likely apocryphal, claim that Elvis once said, "The only thing Negroes can do for me is buy my records and shine my shoes," a quote long dismissed by *Jet* magazine and others close to Elvis. But Chuck's target wasn't Elvis Presley, the man. Elvis was the myth, the so-called King of rock 'n' roll, sitting on a throne built from Black musical innovation, the very rhythms, styles, and blends of gospel, blues, and country that Black artists had pioneered. Yet while he was celebrated, those same artists were often locked out of the palace. Chuck D's frustration was less about Presley himself than about the way America sanctified its chosen cultural icons while dismissing the originators.

The shot at Elvis wasn't random. Chuck later recalled being struck by a line in Clarence "Blowfly" Reid's 1980 single "Blowfly's Rapp," where a Ku Klux Klansman mocks both Black pride and its champions, even targeting Muhammad Ali. The raw hostility of that verse stuck with him, shaping how he thought about music as a vehicle for confrontation. It pushed him to consider which white cultural icons could provoke the same gut reaction in America. The names that came to him were obvious: Elvis, long celebrated as a musical hero, and John Wayne, the embodiment of a certain kind of American masculinity. Calling them out was a way of jolting listeners, stripping reverence from figures many regarded as untouchable.

Even Public Enemy's producer Hank Shocklee admitted he was stunned when he first heard the lines. But Chuck wasn't here to pull punches. He was here to challenge the myths that held a nation together and tear them down in broad daylight.

"Fight the Power." No subtlety. None. It ripped into the myths, the airbrushed history, the double standards America was built on. Lies called out, straight up. And that chorus – you couldn't dodge it. In your head. On the block. Out of the car windows. Everywhere. A chant, over and over. Push back. Stand up. Fight. Fight the power. Repeat it, fight the power.

The lyrics in "Fight the Power" hit hard, but the Bomb Squad's audacious production pushed it into another dimension. At a time when sampling was the Wild West, the Bomb Squad didn't just loop beats. They built a hailstorm of sound, fragments of James Brown, shards of civil rights speeches, sudden blasts of horns, turntable scratches, and layer upon layer of loops, piled so thick it felt overwhelming yet precise. They pushed their equipment to the brink, layering so many samples they sometimes forgot what they'd used. Where De La Soul's *3 Feet High and Rising* and the Beastie Boys' *Paul's Boutique* used playful collages, the Bomb Squad weaponized theirs, a sonic assault that carried the weight of a Black history lesson.

And that Black history was personal. Chuck D would later credit James Brown's "Say It Loud – I'm Black and I'm Proud" (1968) as a turning point in his life, the record, he said, that convinced him to proudly say "I'm Black" instead of using the word "Negro." Public Enemy took that spirit of self-assertion, of refusing to be categorized or silenced, and poured it into every bar of "Fight the Power."

But the song didn't appear from nowhere. It stood on the shoulders of protest anthems that came before: Bob Dylan's "Blowin' in the Wind," Marvin Gaye's "What's Going On," and the Isley Brothers' "Fight the Power (Part 1 & 2)" from 1975, a sly funk groove masked as a warning. Chuck D acknowledged the Isley Brothers' song as a direct inspiration, taking their understated defiance and amplifying it for a generation facing media manipulation, police brutality, and cultural erasure.

Dylan asked questions. Gaye mourned. Public Enemy didn't bother with either. No plea, no soft edge. Just a demand, straight out. And in that moment, they linked up with the long line of artists who used music to confront a world that didn't want to hear it.

Its placement in *Do the Right Thing* burned it into cultural memory. Spike Lee didn't relegate it to background music; he made it the film's pulse, the soundtrack of unrest. As the film captured the raw tension of race and police power in Brooklyn, "Fight the Power" became its war cry.

By the summer of 1989, Public Enemy had become the political vanguard of hip-hop. This voice connected the civil rights movement to a new era of protest. The fight wasn't over. Not then. Not now. "Fight the Power" echoed at the Rodney King protests in 1991, rang out during the Ferguson protests, and blared at Black Lives Matter marches in the 2010s. In 2020, Public Enemy rewrote it with new verses, proving its core message hadn't aged a day but sadly still had work to do.

Public Enemy dared a generation to rise up and demand change.

"Fight the Power" wasn't an ending. It was another verse in an unfinished battle. The soundtrack may change. The struggle doesn't. And as long as there are powers that be, "Fight the Power" will stand as its anthem.

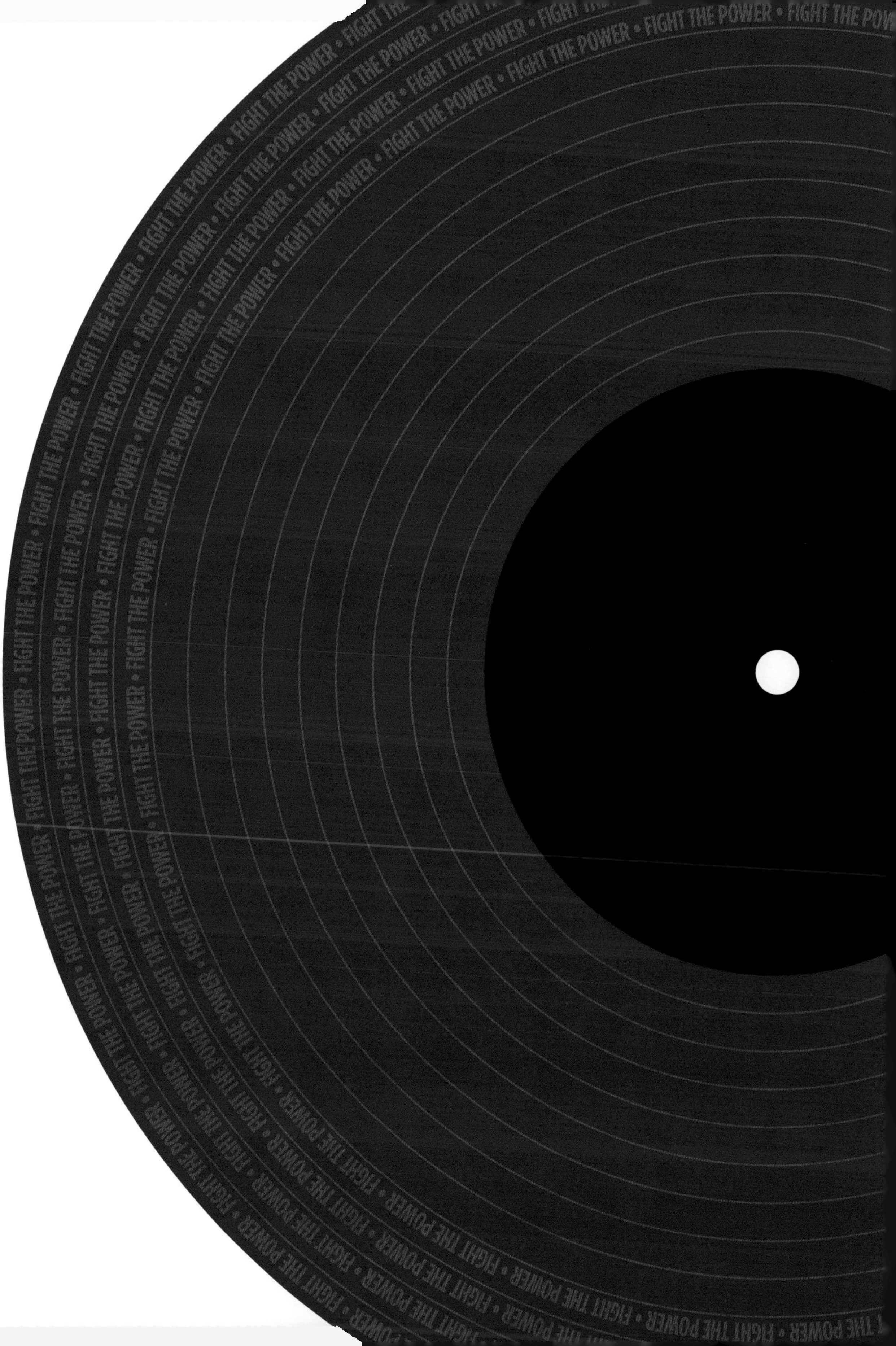
FIGHT THE POWER • FIGHT THE POWER • FIGHT THE POWER

1991, GERMANY

WIND OF CHANGE

SCORPIONS

KLAUS MEINE, MERCURY/VERTIGO

RECORDED SPRING 1990 AT WISSELOORD (HILVERSUM, THE NETHERLANDS) & GOODNIGHT LA (LOS ANGELES)

When "Wind of Change" blew across Europe in 1990, it didn't just soundtrack the end of the Cold War; it seemed to capture the fragile hope of a continent on the brink of unity. Ostensibly written by Klaus Meine, lead singer of the West German hard rock band Scorpions, the song emerged after the band visited Moscow in 1989 for the Moscow Music Peace Festival.

The image of Soviet youth standing alongside Western rock fans, flags waving inside Lenin Stadium, sparked a ballad that mixed personal longing with political hope. Its lyrics carried the spirit of Moscow itself: the river flowing past Gorky Park, a place of leisure and youth culture, and the sound of balalaikas, Russia's traditional stringed instrument, evoking both national pride and a yearning for freedom. By rooting its imagery so profoundly in the Soviet capital, the song became more than a rock ballad; it was a bridge between two worlds, carrying the symbolism of place and culture into its call for change.

"Wind of Change" was released in early 1991 in the lead-up to the dissolution of the Soviet Union. From the minute the whistling intro hit the airwaves, it was a global phenomenon. It topped charts across Europe, reached No. 4 on the US *Billboard* Hot 100, and sold over 14 million copies. In Eastern Europe and the fading Soviet sphere, "Wind of Change" became an emotional touchstone for a generation living through the collapse of old certainties, proving it was about more than just record sales.

As communist regimes crumbled across the Eastern Bloc, "Wind of Change" played from radios, echoed in public squares, and underscored spontaneous rallies. It became an unofficial anthem of revolution in Berlin, Warsaw, Budapest, and deeper behind the Iron Curtain. Not a fiery protest song, but a softly spoken hymn to hope with a gentle melody and a message of freedom that resonated in nations shaking off decades of dictatorship.

In East Germany, it became entwined with the story of reunification. In Poland and Hungary, it accompanied the first free elections in generations.

Following a failed Soviet coup attempt by a hardline communist faction in Moscow in August 1991, the Scorpions returned to

Moscow. There they performed "Wind of Change" in front of a claimed 1.5 million fans at the Monsters of Rock show at Tushino Airfield. With AC/DC, Metallica, The Black Crowes, Pantera, and Scorpions, this was no ordinary concert.

It was a symbolic celebration of the coup's collapse and the downfall of communism, a cultural turning point in a capital still reeling from the aftermath of political turmoil. For many in Russia, a German rock band singing about freedom on a Moscow stage became an improbable but powerful image of change.

In Germany itself, the song resonated just as profoundly. As the country reunited after the fall of the Berlin Wall less than two years prior, "Wind of Change" became a part of the national healing process, embraced by East and West Germans alike. It spoke of optimism, of an idea of Europe as a continent of peace and unity, which finally seemed within reach. Across Western Europe and the United States, it became a symbol of Cold War victory, not of military triumph, but of soft power, culture, and shared humanity transcending borders.

Yet the song's reach extended beyond symbolism. It softened attitudes towards the West in societies where, until recently, Western music had been banned or treated with suspicion. "Wind of Change" became one of the first Western songs to be openly embraced in former communist countries. It also helped raise funds for children affected by the collapse of the Soviet Union, and it became part of efforts to support those struggling in the chaotic aftermath of the regime's fall.

Decades later, "Wind of Change" continued to resurface at pivotal moments. It was played at the 20th anniversary of the fall of the Berlin Wall and featured prominently in the 30th anniversary commemorations in 2019. Its opening whistle remains instantly recognizable, a musical shorthand for the era when the Cold War ended, and for a fleeting moment, unity felt possible.

In 2020, the US journalist Patrick Radden Keefe launched the podcast *Wind of Change,* investigating a rumor circulating within the US intelligence community: that the song may have been written, or at least inspired, by the CIA as a covert tool of soft power. The rumor seemed outlandish at first, but placed in historical context, it wasn't entirely beyond belief.

The CIA had a long history of using culture as a weapon of soft power, funding literary magazines, art exhibitions, and jazz tours behind the Iron Curtain. During the 1950s and '60s, these covert efforts were central to winning hearts and minds in the global ideological battle.

By the late 1980s, those tactics had evolved into more direct cultural interventions, including support for initiatives like Rock the Dictator in Panama.

If the CIA had any involvement in "Wind of Change," it would have been a natural next step in this lineage, the escalation from slipping records across borders to commissioning or seeding a global anthem for a new political era. Whether true or not, the idea underscored how powerfully the song aligned with America's power objectives at the time: fostering unity, dissolving fear, and offering a hopeful vision of a post-Cold War world led by Western influence.

Even if "Wind of Change" was born purely of Meine's idealism, its effect mirrored

everything cultural diplomacy aimed to achieve, proof that sometimes a song could succeed where politics had failed.

Meine and the Scorpions categorically denied the claim. Yet the very fact that the theory persisted speaks volumes about how tightly the song had become woven into the story of the Cold War's end. It wasn't just a hit record; it was a cultural phenomenon so intertwined with the political narrative that people could believe it had been engineered by spies.

Meine would later reflect on the song as capturing a historic turning point, a piece of music that seemed to play in step with the political changes sweeping through Europe. Whether born of idealism, opportunism, or conspiracy, "Wind of Change" became far more than a power ballad. It became a vessel for a generation's hope, a cross-border hymn of unity, and a cultural artefact of a brief, shining moment when peaceful revolution seemed possible.

In an era when the Cold War ended without a shot being fired on European soil, "Wind of Change" stood as proof that, however briefly, a song could genuinely change the world. And even today, it remains a reminder of the strange places where politics, power, and pop culture collide.

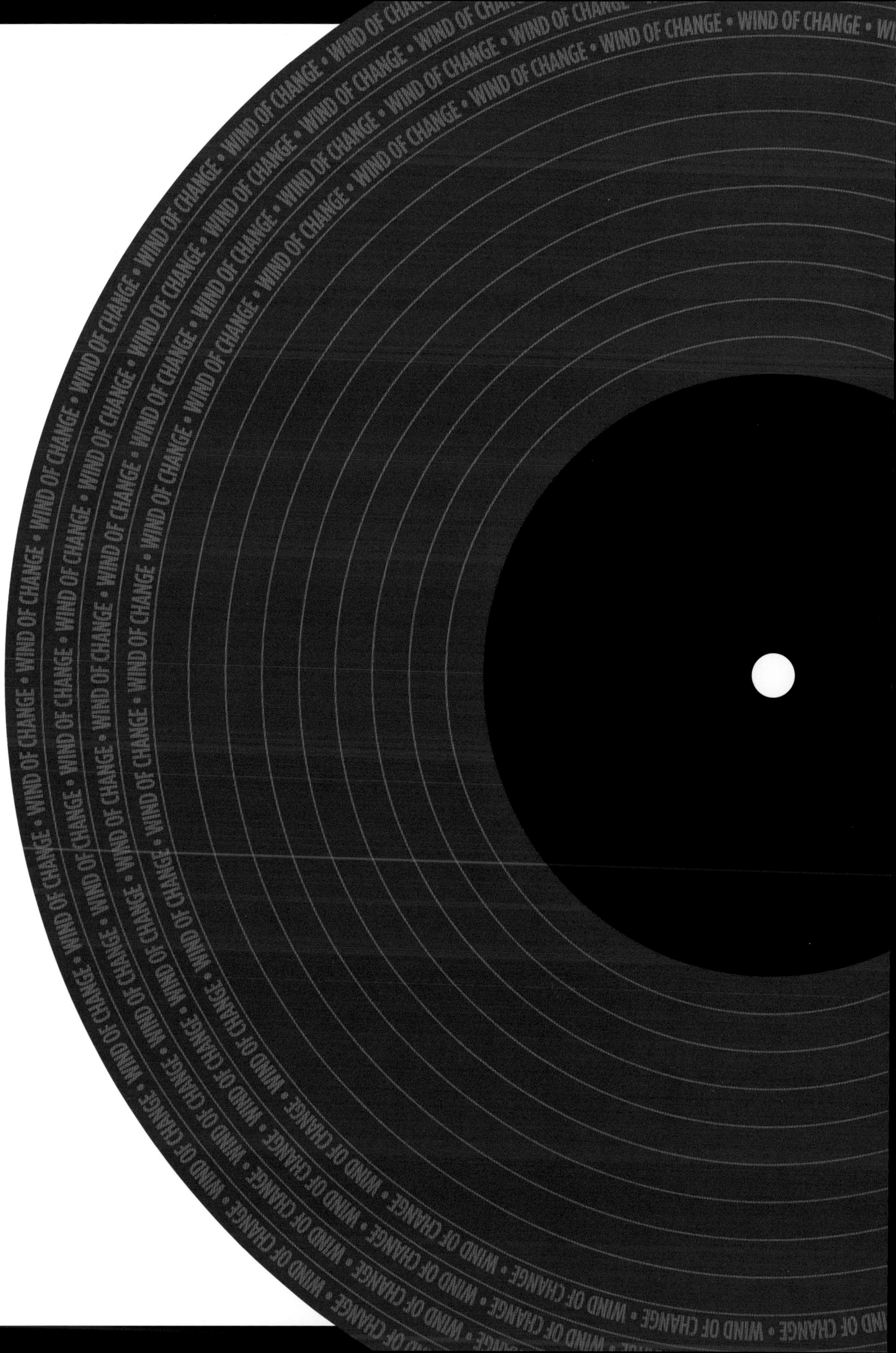
WIND OF CHANGE • WIND OF CHANGE • WIND OF CHANGE

1991, USA

SMELLS LIKE TEEN SPIRIT

NIRVANA

KURT COBAIN, KRIST NOVOSELIC & DAVE GROHL, DGC

RECORDED MAY 1991 AT SOUND CITY STUDIOS, VAN NUYS, LOS ANGELES

"Smells Like Teen Spirit" didn't just launch Nirvana; it detonated an entire cultural shift. It was released in September 1991 as the lead single from the *Nevermind* album, and smashed into a popular culture bloated on hair metal, polished pop, and the fading swagger of Reagan-era excess. With its sludgy guitar riff, ragged vocals, and half-mumbled, half-screamed lyrics, it didn't sound like anything else on commercial radio, and that was precisely its power.

Within months, "Smells Like Teen Spirit" had gone from an indie curiosity to a global anthem. By early 1992, it was topping the charts, saturating MTV, and breaking down the wall between underground alternative music and the mainstream. If "God Save the Queen" had been punk's clarion call, "Teen Spirit" became the slacker generation's anthem, a guttural howl of apathy, frustration, and alienation, lobbed at corporate America and glossy pop culture.

Nirvana had a clear sense of its identity, even if for lead singer Kurt Cobain it came with a sense of self-loathing. The connection to punk wasn't accidental.

One persistent myth claimed they occasionally played warm-up shows under the name The John Ritchie Experience, a nod to the Sex Pistols' Sid Vicious. Whether fact or folklore, it captured their refusal to play by anyone else's rules.

Where the Sex Pistols snarled at the establishment, Nirvana's rebellion was more internal, fueled by irony, self-loathing, and a deep suspicion of both authority and success. If punk screamed "no future," grunge shrugged, "whatever." But that shrug toppled glam metal, stadium rock, and corporate-friendly rebellion.

Nirvana didn't just break into the mainstream; they shattered it. They made alternative culture *the* culture. Record labels scrambled to sign every Seattle band with a distortion pedal. Grunge fashion, flannel shirts, ripped jeans, and combat boots morphed from thrift shop anonymity into a global trend.

And "Smells Like Teen Spirit" did something few thought possible; it took grunge to the world. A sound born in Seattle's underground appealed to teenagers everywhere. Nirvana made raw, abrasive rock music that even pop audiences embraced. The underground didn't just cross over, it took over.

At the heart of this shift was Geffen Records, which signed Nirvana in 1990 after they left Sub Pop. Geffen, known for mainstream rock heavyweights like Guns N' Roses, gave Nirvana a bigger stage, a sharp producer in Butch Vig, major label muscle, and professional marketing.

Yet Geffen's ambitions for *Nevermind* were modest. They reportedly hoped to sell around 250,000 copies. What followed blindsided everyone. As "Teen Spirit" exploded onto the radio and MTV, *Nevermind* knocked Michael Jackson off the *Billboard* No. 1 spot, turning the band and grunge into a global phenomenon.

Geffen gave them the platform, but couldn't control the cultural force "Teen Spirit" unleashed. The success felt less like a marketing triumph and more like an accidental revolution.

For a generation, "Smells Like Teen Spirit" said what they couldn't. Restless kids, burnt on pop, too late for punk, sick of authority. The chorus wasn't just a hook; it was a sneer at the industry, at passive kids buying the lie.

The words? Half sarcasm, half nonsense, half accident. Jumbled lines that made no sense but stuck anyway. Self-mocking, accusing, all at once. Cobain never meant to explain it. Didn't need to. The mess was the point. The sound carried the anxiety, not the answers.

The shockwaves "Teen Spirit" sent through the industry reshaped the 1990s. Without Nirvana's breakthrough, there's no Pearl Jam at the top of the charts, no Soundgarden on mainstream radio, no flood of alternative bands entering the mainstream. It wasn't just a change in sound, it was a change in attitude.

Where punk tried to tear everything down, grunge mourned that nothing better had come along, and hollow disillusionment was wrapped in distorted guitars. Cobain's cracked voice landed perfectly in the heart of a drifting generation, not understanding the point of it all.

"Smells Like Teen Spirit" wasn't just the next step after punk; it was punk's darker, more haunted echo. If the Sex Pistols were the explosion, Nirvana was the fallout. The fire might have burned out, but the smoke refused to clear.

And when Kurt Cobain took his own life in 1994, the song only grew in power. What began as a generational anthem hardened into a cultural marker, the sound of a generation's brightest star burning out in full view of the world.

The rawness that once sneered at mainstream culture came to feel like a warning, a soundtrack to alienation and mental health struggles. Cobain didn't seek fame; he just wanted to write songs and sing. When he found fame, it was corrosive.

Over time, the song became more than a hit; it became a cultural artefact. It regularly tops lists of the greatest rock songs ever recorded. It's been covered, remixed, sampled, and endlessly referenced in pop culture.

Its opening riff alone evokes not just a band or a genre, but a mood that many have tried to emulate, and few have even come close to recapturing. Instantly identifiable, it is usually accompanied by exclamations of joy. That lonely guitar, strummed away with indifference, eventually gets buried by a wall of sound led by

Dave Grohl on drums and the less likely Krist Novoselic on bass, before settling back again as part of the journey.

It was a musical journey of highs and lows, of emptiness and contentment: the sound of a generation that never quite escaped its own discontent.

It swept away the cartoonish bravado of hair metal, dismantled the slick polish of late-1980s pop, and rewrote the idea that authenticity couldn't coexist with mainstream success. Its impact lingered long after grunge faded.

It made rawness profitable and gave a generation a soundtrack that didn't offer easy answers, only a reflection of their disillusionment.

If the Sex Pistols lit the fuse, "Smells Like Teen Spirit" was the flare that lit up the sky, a signal from a generation too angry to care, too smart to conform, and too restless to stay silent. And in Cobain's absence, the song only echoed louder, the anthem of a movement, and the ghost of a cultural moment that would never come again.

And you know what? It is OK to be yourself. It is OK to feel disenfranchised. It is OK to wonder "what's next?" One billion streams on Spotify, two billion views on YouTube and more than 30 million album sales tell you that.

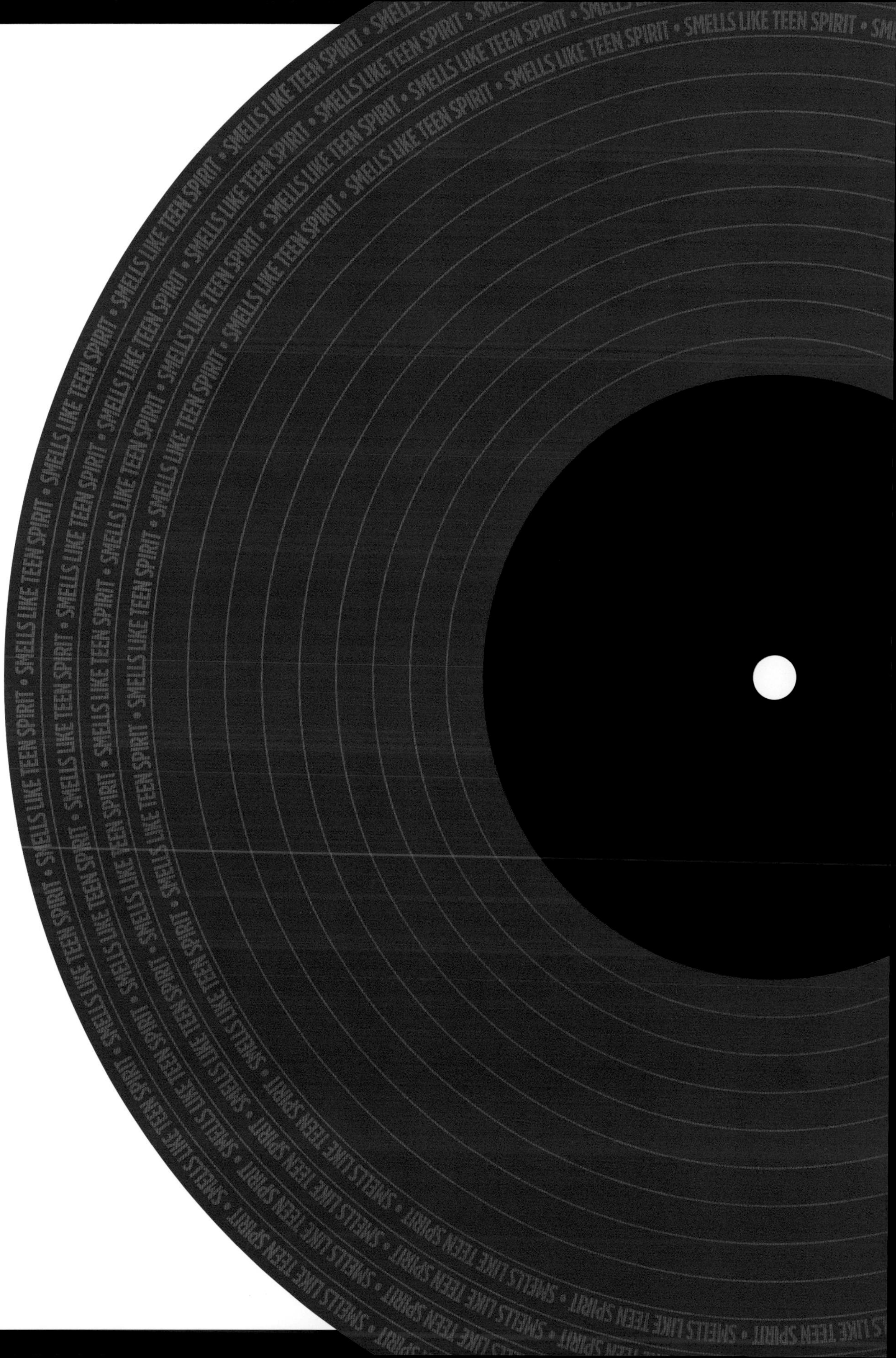
SMELLS LIKE TEEN SPIRIT • SMELLS LIKE TEEN SPIRIT •

1997, RWANDA

FREEDOM

BEN KAYIRANGA

BEN KAYIRANGA, LOCAL INDEPENDENT
RECORDED 1997 IN KIGALI

In 1997, in the fragile aftermath of the Rwandan genocide, Ben Kayiranga's "Freedom" emerged, not as a chart hit, but as a whispered anthem of hope and resistance with reggae undertones. Written and performed by Kayiranga, a Rwandan singer-songwriter living in exile in Belgium, the song became a rare voice of unity against the tide of ethnic division and authoritarian control that had torn Rwanda apart.

Where most of Rwanda's pop culture had either skirted politics or echoed government propaganda, "Freedom" dared to call for reconciliation, justice, and humanity. Sung in a mix of Kinyarwanda, French, and English, he sang for the Rwandan people and their diaspora, scattered across Africa, Europe, and elsewhere. But the message was the same in any tongue and every translation: unity, peace, and the urgent need to rebuild a broken nation.

Its sound mattered as much as its words. "Freedom" drew unmistakably from reggae, with its off-beat guitar skank, rolling basslines, and soft, syncopated percussion, as found in roots reggae protest songs. Kayiranga infused the track with East African folk rhythms and Rwandan melodic phrasing, softening reggae's sharper edges into a contemplative plea. His voice didn't rage; it mourned. If Bob Marley sang of uprising, Kayiranga sang of a world desperate to avoid the need for one. Both craved a world filled with love, it was just about how you get there.

Though war had ended in 1994, Rwanda remained a nation in mourning, its society fractured and scarred. The genocide of the Tutsi had claimed over 800,000 lives in just a hundred days, roughly 10% of the Rwandan population. In this shattered landscape, "Freedom" didn't call for vengeance; it whispered of healing. Unlike the loud, defiant anthems of other protest movements, "Freedom" traveled hand to hand on cassette tapes, shared quietly in exile communities, played at remembrance gatherings, and whispered across community radio. It was a lament, a prayer, and a fragile hope set to music.

The song was written and performed by Kayiranga, who, along with his mother and family, left Rwanda at the age of 17, relocating to France in 1984. Exiled in Europe, Kayiranga became part of the Rwandan diaspora in

Belgium and France, a community deeply opposed to the rising ethnic nationalism and government repression he had left behind.

Kayiranga's exile was both political and geographical. Although not a militant, his calls for peace and justice placed him firmly in opposition to a regime that regarded even gentle dissent as a threat to its authority. In 1994, he lost much of his family in the genocide, and he longed for a return to a better homeland, one not haunted by division.

"Freedom" became his defining work. At its heart was a call for reconciliation and renewal: a belief that peace was only possible if people stood together, that forgiveness was the path to moving forward, and that lasting stability required justice and human rights to be entrenched.

The song's true power lay in its timing. Writing for *BBC News Magazine* in 2013, Rwandan-Swedish writer and photographer Rafiki Ubaldo described Ben Kayiranga's 1997 song "Freedom" as a bold work, not because of its dancehall or reggae colors but because of the message it carried. He argued it offered a rare sense of hope to a nation still in mourning and said it lifted the spirits of an entire country, to the point where, if Rwanda represented the world, the song genuinely shifted it. Like many songs that have had to play in the underground to avoid suppression, "Freedom" isn't defined by sales or chart positions; it made its mark by infiltrating a culture that had been repressed and suppressed, striking a chord in Rwanda and among the diasporas.

Over time, its legacy has grown, crossing borders as well, which is more a measure of its impact than anything else. It has become a guiding hand for Rwandan artists who have followed.

Ben Kayiranga's legacy extends well beyond music. He has been a tireless humanitarian and advocate for social justice.

As an active supporter of the Ibuka Foundation, a coalition of genocide survivor associations, Kayiranga participated in the UNESCO commemoration of the 10th anniversary of the Tutsi genocide in 2004. In 2005, he returned to Rwanda to help lay the foundation stone for Maïsha Africa, an organization founded by Sonia Rolland to support children traumatized by genocide.

His activism also embraced environmental causes. Deeply concerned about climate change, Kayiranga has championed renewable energy initiatives, including solar and

geothermal projects. In 2017, he co-created the anthem "Île Hans" with students from the Lycée Blaise-Pascal in Orsay, supporting the Hans Insula Universalis movement, an international project symbolizing the global fight against climate change.

In 2024, he launched Memory and Biodiversity in Dialogue, a collaborative project between French and Rwandan students that produced "Slam Bibe Ihame," blending humanist reflection with environmental activism.

Kayiranga's contributions have been recognized on both cultural and civic stages. In 2013, the BBC honored "Freedom" among the 20 songs bringing a message of peace to the world. The Île-de-France Region awarded him its Silver Medal in 2014 for his musical career and, in 2019, its Medal of Honor for his educational work with students. In 2018, at the proposal of the French Minister of Education, Prime Minister Édouard Philippe appointed him a Knight of the Order of Academic Palms, a rare recognition for his service to culture and education. In 2023, he was awarded the Vermeil Medal of Honor by the Île-de-France Region for his dedication to local communities.

If "Smells Like Teen Spirit" captured the disillusionment of a Western generation, "Freedom" became a soft-spoken prayer against political collapse in Africa. It had a profound impact on Kayiranga's homeland, where it gave people hope and a dream to aspire to.

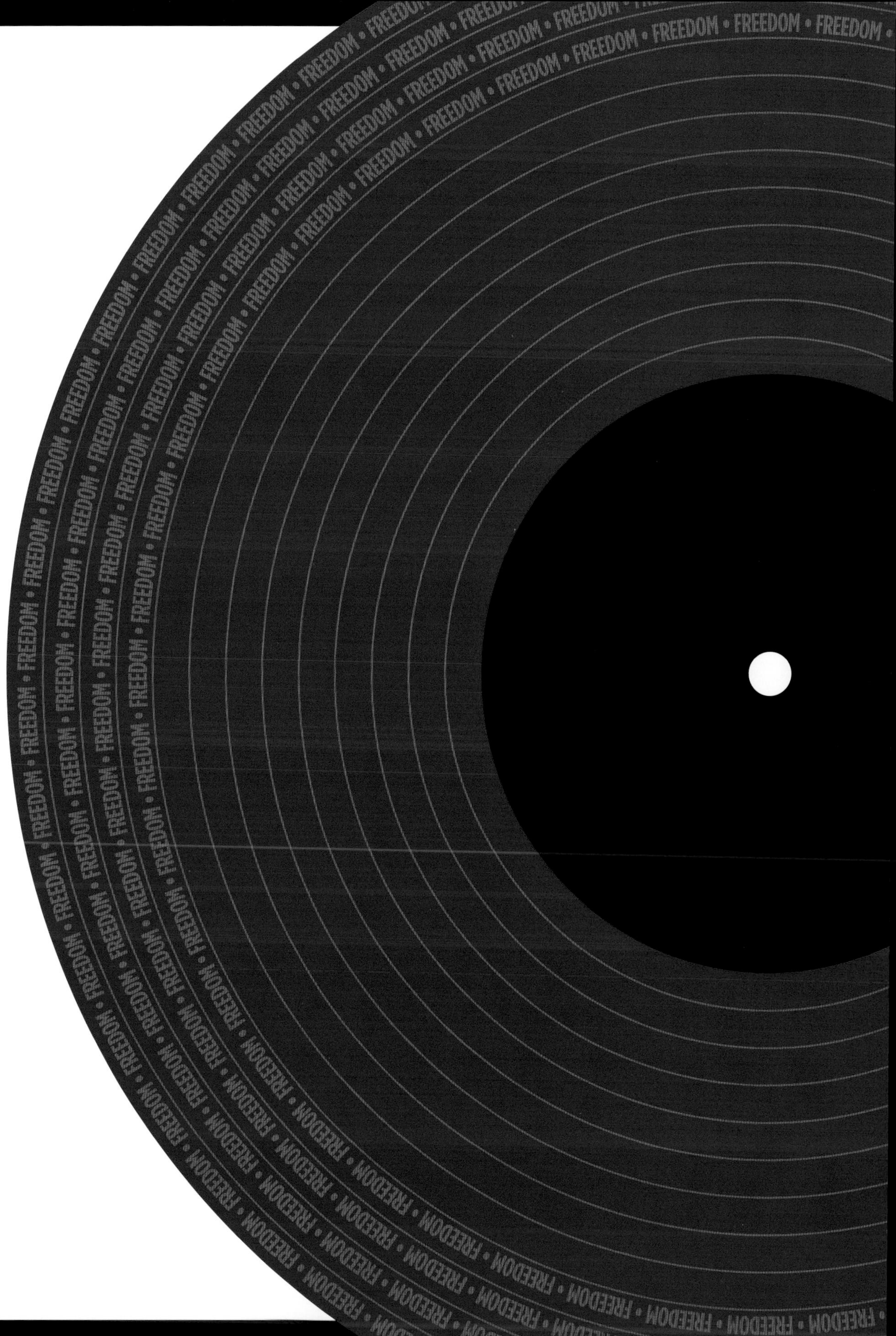
FREEDOM • FREEDOM • FREEDOM

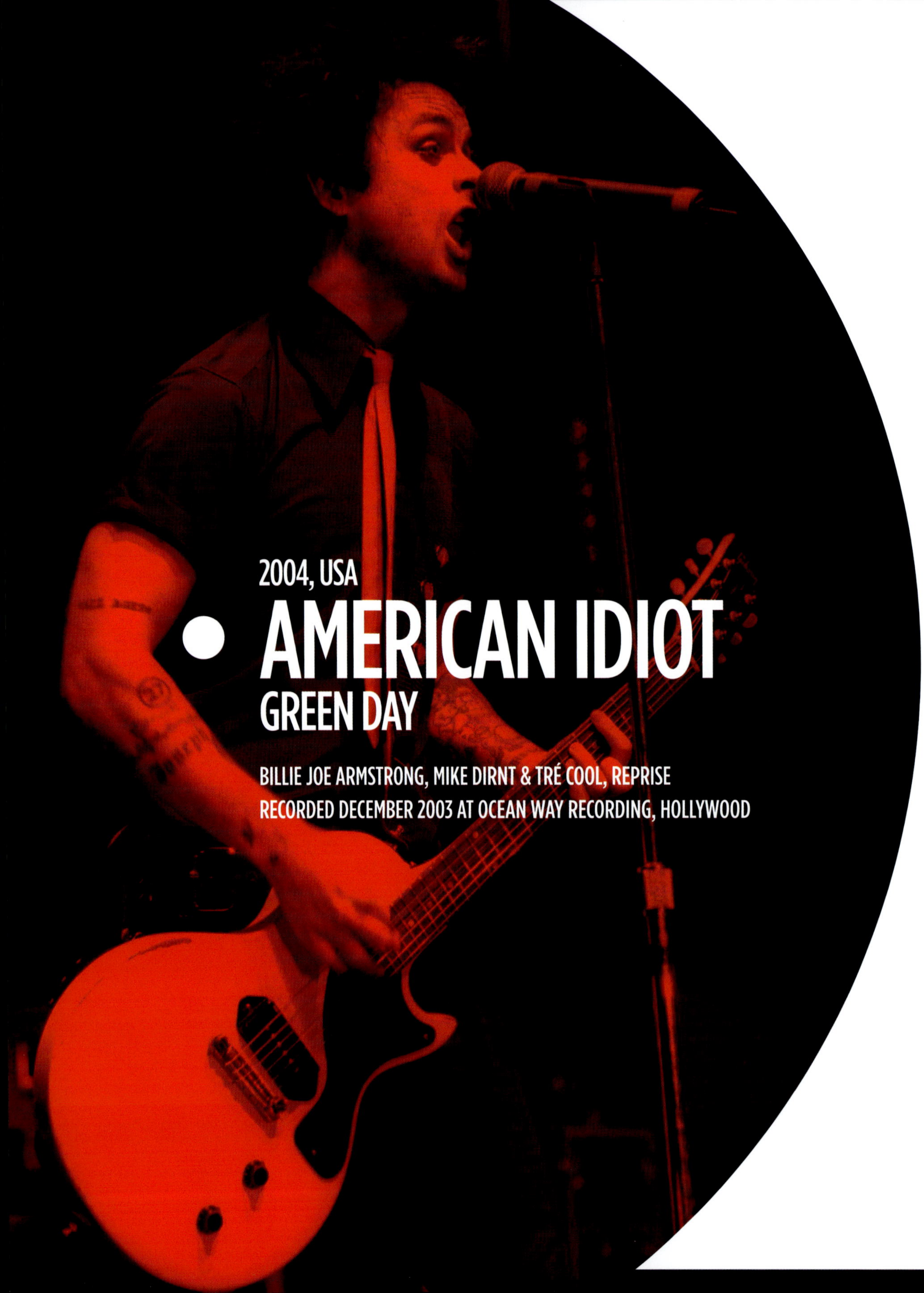

2004, USA

AMERICAN IDIOT

GREEN DAY

BILLIE JOE ARMSTRONG, MIKE DIRNT & TRÉ COOL, REPRISE

RECORDED DECEMBER 2003 AT OCEAN WAY RECORDING, HOLLYWOOD

"American Idiot" wasn't just a song and the title track to a brilliant album; it was a declaration. When Green Day dropped it in 2004, it wasn't aimed at a single political party or a passing controversy. It was a rejection of the post-9/11 climate of fear, conformity, and media-fed hysteria that had seeped deep into American life.

It was transformative for the band. Green Day shifted from high-energy, three-minute or less bursts of neo-punk into the crafted story of a concept album built around the issues raised in the title track. It wasn't a pivot, it was an evolution. *American Idiot* became a punk opera chronicling a generation adrift, manipulated by politics, sedated by the media, and betrayed by a system that is happy to trade in fear and outrage.

This wasn't a protest wrapped in metaphor. "American Idiot" hit hard and direct, a blast of punk rock that named its target and dared people to listen. It called out a society whipped into submission by infotainment, war drums, and political hysteria. But Green Day didn't stop at a single anthem. Billie Joe Armstrong, Mike Dirnt and Tré Cool crafted a narrative following a path led by Jesus of Suburbia, a lost soul swallowed by spin, hollow rebellion, and broken promises, that gave the record its punch.

That shift changed their songwriting. Until then, Green Day had rarely broken the four-minute mark, the only exception being "Misery" from *Warning* (2000). On *American Idiot*, longform tracks like "Jesus of Suburbia" extended the clock as a nine-minute suite. Even the shorter tracks felt expansive, threaded by common themes and linked without silence.

Yet the title song stood out for its precision. At just 2:54, it delivered a scathing, multi-layered political attack, making it the shortest stand-alone track on the album. It took direct aim at media fearmongering and rising jingoism. Armstrong wrote it after hearing Lynyrd Skynyrd's "That's How I Like It," recoiling at its pride in redneck identity. He slammed the Iraq War's television coverage, calling out the reality-show spectacle of embedded journalists. Dirnt later said many would feel insulted, but the song was less an angry finger-point than a call for individuality, a stand against herd mentality.

Even its provocative language, juxtaposing "faggot" and "America," was deliberate. Armstrong wanted a voice for the disenfranchised, a song to strip away pretense and wake people up. When it came to the subject of flag desecration, Green Day didn't bother with subtlety. Their message was blunt, a rejection of patriotic pieties and a deliberate provocation aimed at shaking their audience.

American Idiot didn't just shake the culture, it stormed the charts. Green Day's first-ever No. 1 album on the *Billboard* 200, it sold over 267,000 copies in its first week in the USA and to date has sold more than 16 million worldwide. The single peaked at No. 61 on the *Billboard* Hot 100 but soared to No. 3 in the UK and debuted at No. 1 in Canada. In Australia, it cracked the Top 10 and placed No. 22 in Triple J's Hottest 100 of 2004. Green Day performed it at the 2005 Grammys.

The album won the Grammy for Best Rock Album and earned nominations for Album of the Year and Record of the Year. For a band once known for bratty anthems and pop-punk hooks, *American Idiot* was a reinvention that stunned the industry. Its impact was likened to that of the Sex Pistols in 1977, the return of punk as a political lightning rod.

Its influence reached beyond music. Critics hailed it as a voice for a disenfranchised suburban class, and a defining soundtrack to a growing backlash against George W. Bush's presidency. "Wake Me Up When September Ends," written about Armstrong's father, became a post-Hurricane Katrina anthem, its sorrow fused with scenes of devastation.

Kerrang! credited it with dragging rock back into the mainstream. *Rolling Stone* sealed its legacy in 2020, ranking it No. 248 on their 500 Greatest Albums of All Time list.

Two decades later, the "redneck agenda" Armstrong sneered at has only darkened. In the Trump-MAGA era, the politics of outrage became mainstream. The "information age of hysteria" Green Day warned of matured into a barrage of disinformation, culture war bait, and grievance politics dressed up as patriotism. The hand grenade of *American Idiot* feels less like a symbol now and more like a daily reality, outrage hurled like a weapon across media and politics.

The song itself kept evolving as a protest anthem. In 2016, Armstrong turned its fury directly on Donald Trump during live performances. Two years later, a fan-driven campaign pushed "American Idiot" back into the UK charts to coincide with Trump's state visit, climbing to No. 25 on the Singles Chart and No. 2 on the Downloads Chart. The line continued to resurface, reworked on *New Year's Rockin' Eve* in 2024 and then adapted again in 2025 in South Africa, this time aimed at Elon Musk.

"American Idiot." Still sharp. It could be sharper now. A sneer at blind flag waving, at

bigotry dressed up as patriotism, at outrage turned into a product. Swap the word, swap the slogan; it still lands. Green Day wasn't just raging at one man in the White House. They were swinging at the whole machine. Fear sold as identity. Hate packaged and sold back to you.

And here's the twist. Some fans who once screamed "American Idiot" back at the band turned on Green Day when they spoke out against Trumpism, greed, and injustice, and missed the point. "Stick to music," they barked, but Green Day didn't shift. The world did, and the majority of the fans understood.

The heart-shaped grenade is still there, clenched tight, daring the world to look. Green Day saw it coming. They threw their warning into the world with a three-chord anthem. And as the years proved them right, they never sat down quietly.

Because "American Idiot" wasn't just a song. It was the prophecy many ignored, and the hand grenade is still ticking.

2005, TUNISIA

RAIS LEBLED

HAMADA BEN AMOR (EL GÉNÉRAL)

HAMADA BEN AMOR, LOCAL LABEL
RECORDED 2005 IN TUNIS

In December 2010, as Tunisia simmered with silent anger, a young rapper from Sfax gave that fury a voice. Hamada Ben Amor, "El Général," was 21 when his song "Rais Lebled" shot across the internet, carried by a hollow, menacing beat and the raw, unfiltered rage of a generation pushed to the edge.

"President of the country, here I am today, speaking to you."

That president was Tunisia's dictator, Zine El Abidine Ben Ali, a security chief turned president who built a police state on fear, corruption, and silence. His regime controlled everything: the courts, the media, the economy. The Ben Ali family and his wife's Trabelsi clan plundered the country while Tunisia's youth faced chronic unemployment, constant harassment from corrupt officials, and a future drained of hope. Speaking out meant jail, torture, or disappearance. Most people learned to keep their heads down.

"Rais Lebled" was more an act of open defiance than it was a protest song; it took aim and lobbed a hand grenade straight at the heart of the regime with a plea for dignity and liberty. With the stripped-back sound of a stark drum loop, a pulsing synth, and El Général's cracked, urgent voice, it didn't carry the bravado of Western hip-hop. Instead, it throbbed with menace. Its hollowness felt like the soundtrack to a nation's emptiness; every word had meaning, and it rang a warning bell.

And the words hit hard. The song did not speak in metaphors or coded messages, it looked power in the eye and called it out. A message aimed straight at the president, it demanded accountability while describing the desperate reality of daily life. It evoked images of a nation abandoned by its leaders: families scrounging in rubbish heaps just to stay alive, children going hungry while officials sat in comfort, and communities forced into lives stripped of dignity.

The voice in the song wasn't standing outside the pain, it came straight out of it. It sounded like ordinary people worn down, shoved to the edge, made to live in ways no one should. Stripped of dignity, treated more like animals than humans. What gave it power was that it

Ben Ali. El Général did. He wasn't just making music. He was throwing a match on dry grass.

And the fire came soon enough.

A week before Mohamed Bouazizi's fatal protest, El Général turned on a handheld camera, pulled a baseball cap low over his eyes, and filmed himself rapping "Rais Lebled" after opening with a scene of the president intimidating a young child in a school, and then a desolate street scene. There was no studio, no production. Just a young man staring into a camera, words laced with fury.

He didn't dress it up. No metaphor, no soft landing. Just a straight shot at the president: your people are dying.

YouTube and Facebook were the vehicles for this song, and it went viral on both platforms, moving from one phone to the next. The Qatari government-owned news outlet Al Jazeera picked it up, adding more fuel to the fire. He was shouting his anger in a country that for more than two decades had only whispered angst in private. The image of El Général, head bowed, eyes hidden, became as powerful as his words.

On December 17, in the town of Sidi Bouzid, 26-year-old Mohamed Bouazizi,

didn't try to make any of this polite or easy to take. It was a howl, part rage, part despair, and it demanded to be heard, even by those who wanted to look away.

And those words hit hard.

"Mr President, your people are dying."

"People are eating garbage."

"Speaking to you from suffering, we're living like dogs."

Rapped in a street blend of Tunisian Arabic and French, "Rais Lebled" cut through the fear like a blade. Until then, Tunisia's small underground rap scene had grumbled about poverty and injustice, but no one dared name a street vendor, had his cart seized by municipal officers for the second time. When he tried to complain, he was dismissed and allegedly slapped in public. Humiliated, broke, and broken by a system that gave him nothing, Bouazizi doused himself in petrol outside the governor's office and struck a match. His death wasn't planned as a political act. It was a final cry of despair.

But it lit the fuse.

Protests exploded in Sidi Bouzid. Within days, they spread across Tunisia. And wherever the crowds went, "Rais Lebled" followed, blasted from phones, speakers, chanted in streets, daubed on walls.

If Bouazizi's death lit the fire, El Général poured on the fuel. The revolution had begun.

On December 24, Tunisia's secret police came for him. El Général was dragged from his home in Sfax and taken into custody. His family said he disappeared without warning. For three days, he was held by the regime's security forces, interrogated, warned, but not tortured. His detention sparked outrage. Far from silencing him, it fanned the flames. His arrest made global headlines, with coverage from Al Jazeera, CNN, the BBC, and the video of "Rais Lebled" spreading even further.

El Général was not crushed by his incarceration. When he was released on December 27, he returned to Tunisia as a symbol of hope. "Rais Lebled" was now a battle cry. In Tunis, the capital of Tunisia, protesters marched with lyrics from the song scrawled on banners. It blared from car radios, crackled over loudspeakers, and echoed from Tahrir Square to Tripoli.

Tunisia's uprising quickly found both a face and a soundtrack. The song helped tear down the wall of fear, showing people that it was possible to stand up and speak the truth. It didn't spark the revolution, but it became its anthem.

On January 14, 2011, Zine El Abidine Ben Ali fled Tunisia, a dictator toppled by a people who, with the help of a young rapper, had found their voice.

El Général was a reluctant hero and voice to a revolution. He didn't want to be a national figure or a symbol, he simply wanted to make music and be allowed to express himself and live with dignity. He continued making music, releasing tracks like "Tounes Bladna" (Tunisia is Our Country), which urged unity and warned against betrayal, but "Rais Lebled" was his magnum opus. Its impact was tied to its moment in time as a perfect storm of truth and courage.

El Général wasn't a lifelong agitator or a hardened activist. He was a young man who, in one fearless moment, said what everyone else was too afraid to say and helped change the world around him.

And that was enough.

2011, USA

BORN THIS WAY

LADY GAGA

STEFANI GERMANOTTA, JEPPE LAURSEN, FERNANDO GARIBAY & PAUL BLAIR, INTERSCOPE

RECORDED 2010 AT ABBEY ROAD (LONDON) & GERMANO (NEW YORK CITY)

In February 2011, the reigning queen of pop transformed a dance track into a global declaration of pride. Lady Gaga's "Born This Way" wasn't just another chart-topping single, it was a manifesto, a bold, joyous anthem that told LGBTQ+ people, people of color, and anyone who had ever felt different that they were perfect exactly as they are.

From the moment it was released on February 11, the message was impossible to miss. Gaga didn't soften it with metaphor or disguise it in euphemism. Instead, she delivered what no mainstream pop star had dared before, an open embrace of every identity, declaring survival and pride as universal rights.

Two nights later, on February 13, she belted those words live at the 53rd Annual Grammy Awards, three and a half minutes into her high-energy performance, a moment watched by millions around the world. Emerging from a translucent egg in a symbolic rebirth, Gaga took the biggest stage in music and turned it into a pulpit for radical inclusion.

"Born This Way" wasn't just pride. It was a fight. A dig at the tools used to keep people small. A beat you could dance to, sure, but underneath it was faith twisted back against the preachers. Gaga turned their language on its head. If God makes no mistakes, then He didn't screw up making queer kids. Simple as that. No begging for tolerance. No asking permission. A claim. A truth. Take it or leave it.

And she didn't pull up. Verse two hit like a slap. People clapped, people fumed. She went straight at the church, straight at the old lines about sin and shame. Flipped it. Said love was clean, holy even. A shot was fired right back at the pulpit.

With that, Gaga wasn't mocking religion. She was reclaiming it. Raised Catholic, she invoked the traditional Christian title for God, "capital H-I-M," and tied it directly to acceptance and love. It was her way of challenging centuries of faith used as a weapon against queer people.

The backlash came quickly. Religious conservatives accused her of blasphemy. Right-wing commentators railed against her for promoting sin. In the mainstream press, some critics dismissed her Grammy performance as gimmicky or derivative, highlighting its clear echoes of Madonna's "Express Yourself." Others said the spectacle of her arrival in an egg overshadowed the song's deeper meaning.

Even within LGBTQ+ circles, questions arose, not about the heart of the message, but about whether the "born this way" framing reduced complex human experiences to biological determinism. Others wondered whether Gaga's megastardom risked drowning out the voices of grassroots queer artists.

None of that dulled the song's impact, nor should it.

"Born This Way" was a personal anthem so many in the LGBTQ+ community could relate to. It spoke a truth on radio, in clubs, at rallies, and on the world's biggest stages that many were frightened to express. It was a declaration of belonging.

And it did more than rally the converted. Fueled by her chart dominance and cultural ubiquity, "Born This Way" landed far beyond activist circles. It was on mainstream radio playlists; it echoed in shopping centers, clubs, and sports arenas . . . places where LGBTQ+ issues had rarely been addressed, let alone celebrated. Gaga wasn't just affirming queer identity to those who already agreed, she was planting a flag in the heart of popular culture and daring the world to look.

The personal testimonies flowed. Fans, many of them young LGBTQ+ people, flooded social media with stories of how the song helped them come out, accept themselves, or feel less alone. How it saved their lives. Her concerts became sanctuaries, places where identity wasn't just accepted but celebrated.

Social psychology talks of the contact hypothesis, which says that exposure to positive representations of marginalized groups can help reduce prejudice. And in 2011, it didn't get much more positive than "Born This Way."

In terms of exposure, the song exploded commercially. "Born This Way" debuted at No. 1 on the *Billboard* Hot 100. In the United States it sold 448,000 digital copies in its first three days and went on to break records on iTunes with more than a million downloads worldwide in its first five days. It topped charts in more than 25 countries, including the United Kingdom, Canada, Australia, and Japan.

The album of the same name, released in May 2011, debuted at No. 1 in the US with 1.1 million copies sold in its first week, the largest opening for a female artist since 2000. It topped charts in over 20 countries and went on to sell more than six million copies worldwide.

Awards followed. "Born This Way" won the MTV Europe Music Award for Best Song in 2011 and Best Female Video at the MTV Video Music Awards. It earned nominations for Song of the Year and Best Pop Solo Performance at the Grammys. The album won Best Album at the MTV Europe Music Awards and was Grammy-nominated for Album of the Year.

But the real legacy lived beyond the charts. Gaga launched the Born This

Way Foundation, dedicated to youth empowerment, mental health, and fighting bullying. She kept performing the song, at Pride events, humanitarian concerts, and even a presidential inauguration. In 2021, she re-released it with LGBTQ+ artists for its 10th anniversary, reaffirming its place as a living, breathing anthem.

It arrived at a cultural crossroads. In 2011, the "Don't Ask, Don't Tell" policy had just been repealed, which meant those serving in the US military no longer had to hide their sexual orientation. Marriage equality was getting closer to reality. The LGBTQ+ rights movement was on the rise. Gaga didn't just reflect the changes that were underfoot, she gave it a voice.

Her Grammy performance wasn't universally embraced, but it became a defining moment for everything she was singing about. That night a global star took the biggest stage in music, stared down controversy, and didn't flinch.

When Gaga hit the chorus it didn't feel like just another pop hook. It came across like a demand, like armor thrown up for anyone who needed protecting. A dare to the rest of the world. For millions who heard it, it landed more like a blessing. Not just something to dance to, but something to hold onto, a song to get through life with.

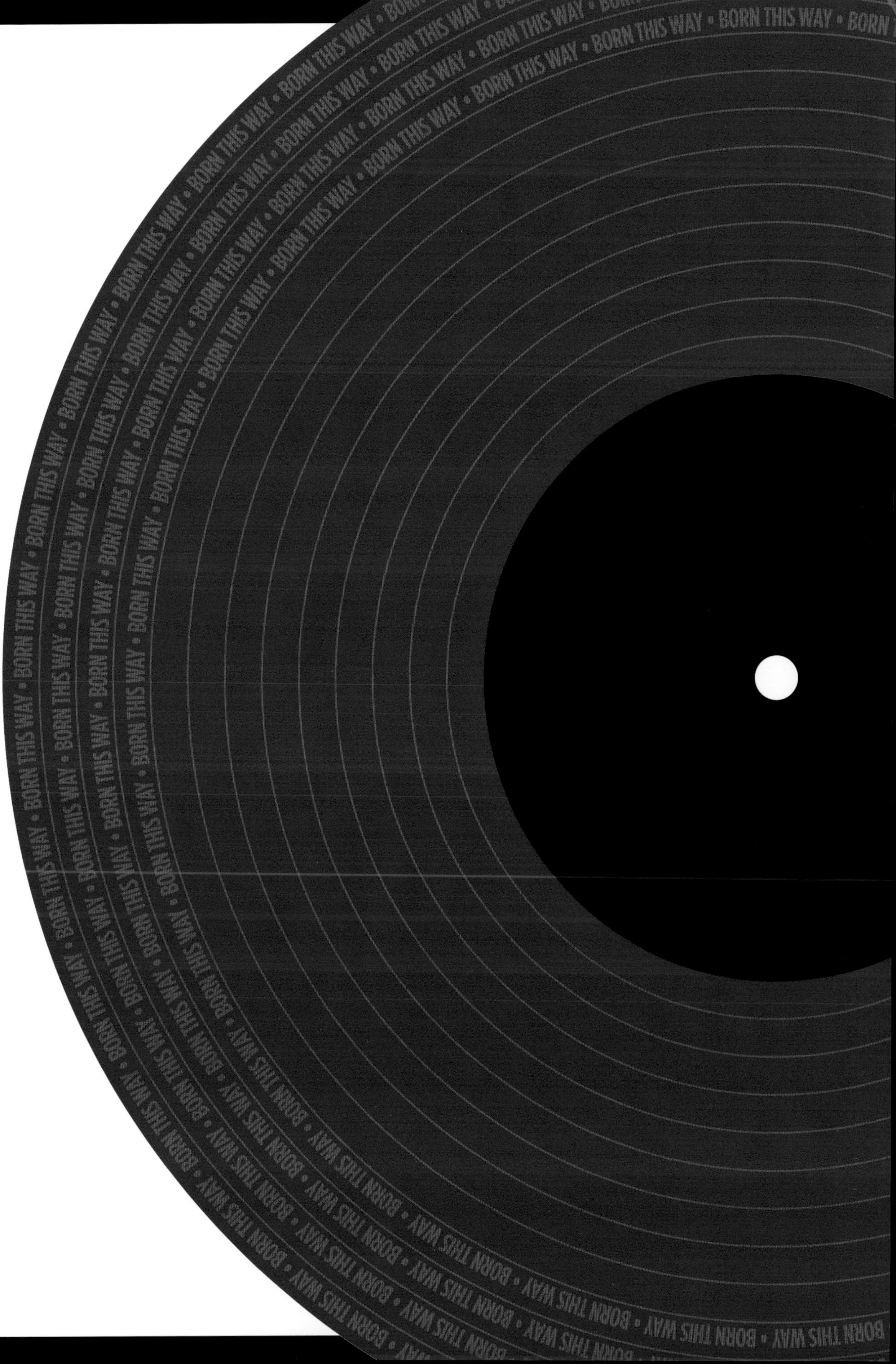
BORN THIS WAY • BORN THIS WAY • BORN THIS WAY

2015, USA

ALRIGHT

KENDRICK LAMAR

KENDRICK LAMAR, TOP DAWG/AFTERMATH

RECORDED 2014 AT CHALICE RECORDING STUDIOS, HOLLYWOOD

By 2015, America was facing a rising tide of protest and demands for racial justice, and one refrain rose above the noise. It was simple, defiant, and unforgettable, a promise of survival and hope that became the movement's rallying cry.

Kendrick Lamar's "Alright" wasn't crafted as a traditional protest song. It didn't name movements, chant slogans, or issue political demands. He wrote it in 2014 during the sessions for *To Pimp a Butterfly*, drawing on his own experience, the weight of systemic racism, the scars left by police violence, and his personal battles with depression, survivor's guilt, and the haunting fear of dying young in a hostile world.

By the time Lamar spoke with MTV News in mid-2015, the song was already being played at protests all over the country. He said it was about hope, about hanging on. Not just a chant to shout and forget, but a push to face what was in front of you, to keep going, to survive by sheer strength.

"Alright" carried a message of hope, but it didn't sugarcoat a thing. From the opening breath, it was clear this wasn't going to be dressed up for radio. The word "Nigga" got thrown in like a punch to the chest, not to shock for the sake of it, but to make a point. It was a challenge to White America, a demand to face the reality that Black America lives with every day.

The track didn't dance around the subject. It went straight at the system, straight at the cops. The song didn't pull aside or soften the blow. Nothing dressed up, nothing cleaned. Just anger. Raw. The kind of talk you hear shouted on a corner, scribbled on cardboard, spat through a megaphone. The same truth people had been saying for years: the ones meant to protect are the same ones pulling the trigger.

That's where the strength hit. Just hammering the word, over and over, until it turned inside out. Not an insult anymore. A spit of defiance. Saying: this is us, this is what we've carried, and you don't get to turn your head away.

That reality ran through every verse of "Alright," a vivid portrait of a man navigating a world stacked against him. However, it was the chorus that transformed the song into something more than the sum of its lyrics. It's OK, we are going to be alright.

The key lyric was simple and direct. Repeated like a mantra, and remarkably positive.

When "Alright" dropped in March 2015, America was in the throes of unrest. The Black Lives Matter movement had erupted in response to the killings of Michael Brown in Ferguson, Eric Garner in New York, and Freddie Gray in Baltimore. Protesters flooded streets, facing down riot police, tear gas, and the brutal machinery of a justice system that had failed them over and over again.

In those marches, "Alright" took on a life that Lamar may never have anticipated. The chorus leapt from speakers and headphones onto the frontlines of protest. Demonstrators chanted it in unison, scrawled it on cardboard signs, shouted it through megaphones, and sang it in the faces of armored police.

It wasn't just a song anymore. It was a living, breathing anthem of defiance and survival.

Black America responded with fierce affirmation. "Alright" became more than a soundtrack for activists. It was a new battle cry, a modern freedom song in the long tradition of civil rights anthems, which began with the likes of Billie Holiday, Bob Dylan, and Sam Cooke.

It was embraced and claimed in churches, barbershops, community centers, and block parties. For many, Lamar's voice wasn't celebrity commentary from a safe distance; it was the voice of someone who knew the streets and the struggle.

Not everyone was on board, though. Some cultural critics debated whether its hopeful chorus risked softening the searing reality of police brutality and systemic racism. Others questioned whether its crossover success and mainstream industry embrace might blunt its political edge.

Really? But these critiques confirmed how deeply "Alright" had become embedded in Black culture. It could not be ignored.

Not even by White America, which lived in blissful ignorance of the plight of the racial divide when it came to police brutality. They never had to confront it as an issue beyond the gangs, and the response was as divided as the country itself. Progressives hailed it as a cultural watershed that forced conversations about systemic injustice, racial identity, and Black resilience.

Critics, writers, and academics praised it as a reflection of a generation's anger and hope. This was "Strange Fruit," 75 years on.

But conservative commentators lashed out. When Lamar performed "Alright" at the 2015 BET Awards, standing atop a vandalized police car, the American flag waving defiantly behind him, right-wing media bristled. Fox News led the chorus of condemnation, with Geraldo Rivera famously calling the performance "disgusting" and claiming that hip-hop culture, Lamar included, was doing more harm to young Black Americans than racism itself.

Lamar dismissed the outrage with unwavering defiance. He stood by its purpose. He explained about confronting harsh truths and giving his community a voice and a source of hope in a hostile world.

It refused to stay suppressed in the underground. It sold more than one million copies, earning platinum status in the United States.

"Alright" secured four nominations for the 2016 Grammys and won Best Rap Performance and Best Rap Song. It was critically acclaimed, too. *Rolling Stone* named it the Best Song of 2015, with similar honors from *Pitchfork*, *Billboard*, *The Guardian*, and NPR.

But "Alright" wasn't made to sit on award lists or hover on charts. It lived where Lamar had always placed it, in the streets, in whispered mantras, in shouted chants, in the living, breathing heartbeat of Black America's resistance.

Lamar didn't intend to write a protest anthem, but he did. He offered a song that refused to beg for justice by giving voice to hard truths and deep wounds, while also proving hope. It declared with the quiet force of those who have endured for generations that Black America would survive.

"Alright" wasn't universally embraced, but it became a cultural reckoning. This song exposed a nation's divides and dared it to listen.

"Alright" wasn't a promise, and nor was it a cliché. But it was a challenge to a nation still searching for its answer.

2019, ALGERIA/FRANCE

LA LIBERTÉ

SOOLKING

SOOLKING & SKALPOVICH, POLYDOR

RECORDED 2018–19 AT STUDIO DAVOUT, PARIS

In the spring of 2019, as Algeria's streets filled with chants, banners, and the urgent, peaceful roar of a people reclaiming their future, one song rose above the crowd, not from a politician, nor a veteran revolutionary, but from a young Algerian rapper with roots in the diaspora and his heart still in the casbah.

When Abdelaziz Bouteflika, a president who had ruled Algeria for two decades, announced in February 2019 that he would run for a fifth term despite being incapacitated by a stroke, it triggered something Algeria had not seen in a generation: a mass, youth-led uprising that would be known as the Hirak, from the Arab word *al-Ḥirāk*, meaning "The Movement."

It started as a protest against a single politician, but that wasn't enough, so it became a full-scale demand for systemic change, a rejection of entrenched military dominance, corruption, censorship, and the suffocating weight of a post-colonial elite that had ruled since independence.

Soolking's "La Liberté" landed in this atmosphere as a cry for freedom that resonated across generations and social divides. It was part *raï* (Algeria's traditional popular music style), part pop, part hip-hop, a fusion that reflected the complexity of Algerian identity and allowed it to land perfectly.

Soolking, born Abderraouf Derradji in Algiers, was a singer and rapper with a following in 2019 among young Algerians and the North African diaspora for his distinctive blend of styles. But "La Liberté" struck a different chord.

Its most powerful line was its simplest: "Freedom, freedom, freedom . . ."

Three words endlessly repeated and pleading across language barriers, borders, and generations. It was sung in the streets by protesters, shouted from balconies, and blasted from car radios. It became the chant of the Hirak, a sonic emblem of peaceful defiance. It was a collective heartbeat, as direct as it was universal.

In a country and time when free speech was muzzled, state-controlled media suppressed dissent, and protest songs were often censored, "La Liberté" found its audience by bypassing traditional channels. Uploaded to YouTube and spreading virally across social media, it garnered

millions of views within days. It wasn't just played, it was shared, reposted, and sung aloud by crowds gathered in Algeria's public squares. The internet became its radio, the people its amplifiers. It has now been viewed more than 425 million times.

Soolking wrote in the language of the people by singing in Darija, the Algerian Arabic dialect, and blending traditional North African rhythms with modern production. "La Liberté" wasn't just about a call for reform. It was about reclaiming identity, asserting dignity, and reconnecting with a national spirit that had long been stifled by authoritarian rule.

Algeria's story is one of layered oppressions: colonization by France, a brutal war of independence, and decades of authoritarian governance by a post-independence elite that traded revolutionary credentials for political power. The Hirak wasn't just anti-Bouteflika. It was anti-fear, anti-corruption, anti-apathy, and "La Liberté" captured that mood perfectly with a hopeful defiance.

The Hirak was characterized by its unwavering commitment to non-violence, and its crowds marched in their millions, refusing to be provoked by their oppressors. "La Liberté" reflected that ethos by not carrying threats or anger. It had a calm demand for dignity and a belief that freedom was not just a possibility, but a certainty waiting to be claimed.

And "La Liberté" didn't stop at Algeria's borders. With Soolking's position as a transnational artist, born Algerian and living in

France, the song transcended the diaspora. It resonated with Arab communities in Paris, Brussels, and Montreal, giving the Algerian cause a voice in global conversations about freedom, identity, and post-colonial struggle. When the international media began reporting on the protests, it latched onto the song that had become an unofficial anthem of the movement. Soolking took the cry for Algerian freedom to the world stage.

The impact extended beyond the lyrics. "La Liberté" was a rallying cry and a way for Algerians, especially the younger generation raised under layers of silence and control, to say: "We matter."

It was more than a song. It was also a statement that music and culture could carry the resistance where politics had stalled. That standing side by side in streets, in cafés, and across social media could mean something. It was their song, and it gave them hope.

"La Liberté" had already written itself into Algeria's modern history when Bouteflika finally stepped down in April 2019, pushed out by relentless public pressure. For Soolking and the Hirak, victory wasn't celebrated as such because this was just the beginning. But the messages remained alive inside the new and growing democracy, with a growing refusal to forget.

In "La Liberté," there was a melody that lifted instead of provoked. It celebrated unity, dignity, and the quiet, powerful belief that freedom begins when people stand together and raise their voices. There was no venom, no call to arms, no incitement.

"La Liberté" didn't bring down the regime, but it lit a fuse. It gave the Hirak a voice, a chant that carried its hopes. It was sung in the streets as a clear and simple statement: "The future is ours to claim."

Freedom. Freedom. Freedom.

Once again, music had found its place. Not just to move, but to move people forward.

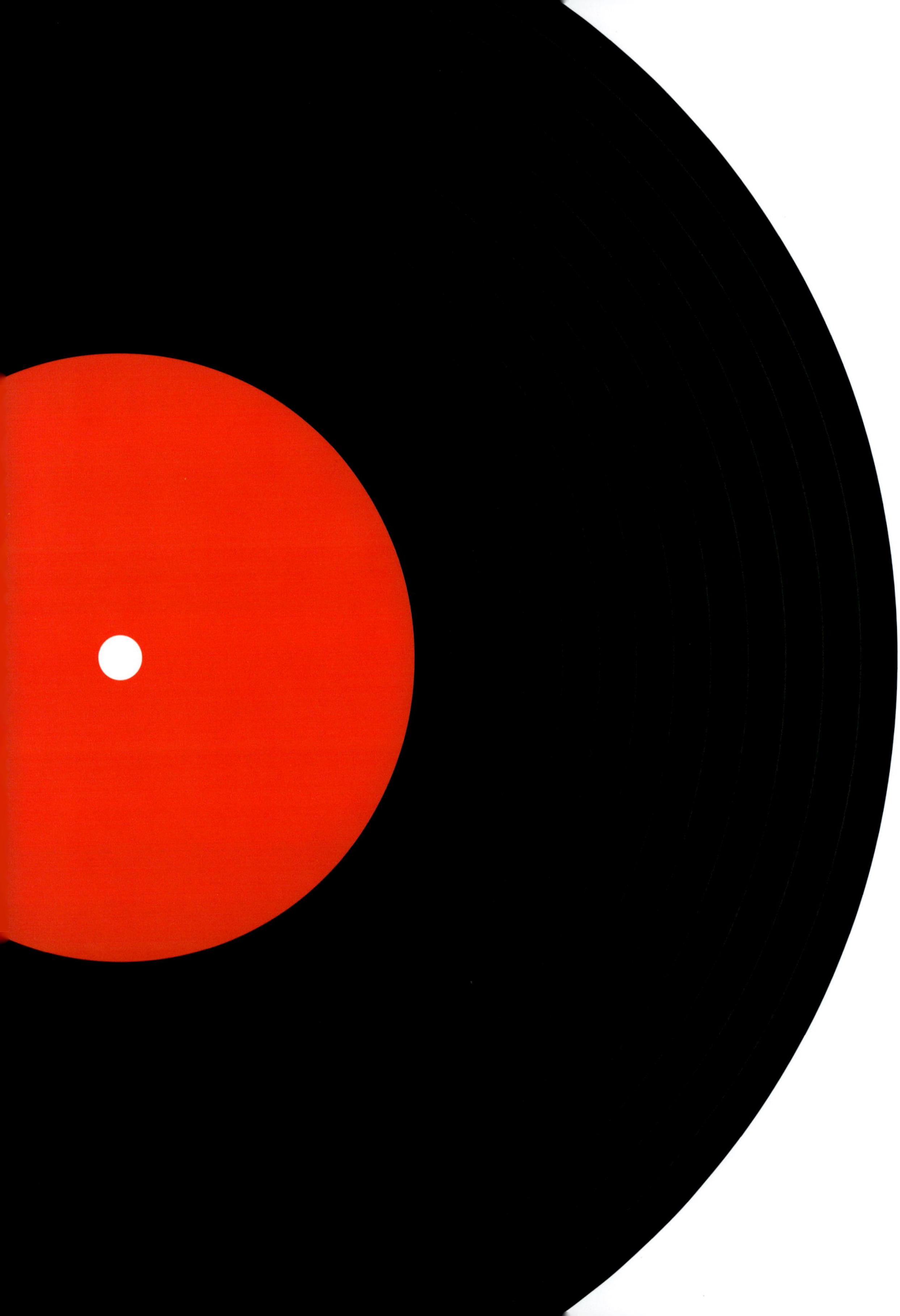

ACKNOWLEDGMENTS

I said at the start that this book isn't simply a playlist of the music I like, but it is very much about songs I appreciate. Songs I respect. Thankfully, many great writers, journalists, and historians have come before me and told the stories of these songs in books, magazines, newspapers, and on stages.

Much has been written about music's role in change, especially protest music. But not every song in this collection is a protest song. Some are quiet ballads of hope, others accidental agents of change, a few written with revolution in mind. This is a book about moments when music mattered, sometimes loudly, sometimes softly, but always when it counted.

Researching this meant diving deep into books, journals, interviews, and liner notes, chasing not just the songs, but the times and places they changed. This book could never have happened without those who did the digging before me: the authors, the journalists, the critics, and, most of all, the songwriters who penned the words and music that gave these moments their voice. The people who changed history.

Closer to home, there are people in my life who have endured this strange, obsessive process, which starts as a melody in my head, often leads to weekends lost down research rabbit holes or weeks chasing stories across the world. My children, now grown-up, Byron and Gabi, still lose me to this madness, and I don't say it enough: I write for you both. Yes, Gabi, there is no Taylor Swift, Billie Eilish, or Harry Styles, and Byron, AC/DC, and Black Veil Brides weren't even close, but I hope you like this anyway. I'm delighted that you love music . . . especially now that Gabi can fund her own obsessions.

I added Sam Cooke to keep Elaine happy. No, that's a lie; he was always going in. But I'm pleased it made her happy.

Zakk, Rexx, Skye, and Greg, you are part of this too, because you indulged me in the '90s and were a big part of my musical journey with people like Josie, Peter, Kevin, Graham, Jimi, Liza and way too many others to mention. I had some of the best times of my life with you guys, and I learned about the struggles of an artist's life and the stories you want to tell.

To my mother, Margaret, who passed away while I was writing this book, and my father, Geoff, whom I lost many years ago, thank you for raising me with music as a constant presence in my life. I can still picture myself as a kid, sitting in the back room of our house in Dromana every Sunday night, watching *Countdown* and seeing your reaction to the Sex Pistols, which to be honest kind of inspired the rebel in me. That moment stayed with me. It shaped how I understood the raw emotion that music could unleash, and how powerful that could be. It didn't matter whether you loved or loathed it; you felt something, as did I.

You encouraged me to do it my way, and I have, even if I am more Sid than Frank.

Every list-based book I've written has involved spirited debates in pubs, often arguing over the merits of the names and moments that help cut the lists. But this one? This one opened up bigger conversations. Unlike motorsport or Australian football, music crosses every boundary, and that meant even more arguments, in even more places. Often in the bars and bandrooms that give my hometown of Melbourne its own unique and vibrant musical heartbeat.

If we had a discussion and you tried to guess the list or expressed disappointment that "Dancing Queen" by Abba didn't make it in, or that I couldn't accept that disco changed the world, thank you. Who knows, surely there is a *More Songs That Changed the World* book waiting?

To the crew at Gelding Street Press, you take the raw demos I hand you and somehow mix them into a finished record. Raquel and Katie, you are my brilliant producers rolling into my world like Flood or Butch Vig with ideas that make me look better. Vicky, you get these stories into readers' hands and somehow make me look more professional than I sometimes appear, which is perhaps me channeling Kurt Cobain. Paul and Lisa, my publishers, thank you for believing in me.

So yes, my name's on the cover. But, like every great album and every sold-out show, it takes a crew to bring it all together. And this book is our latest record.

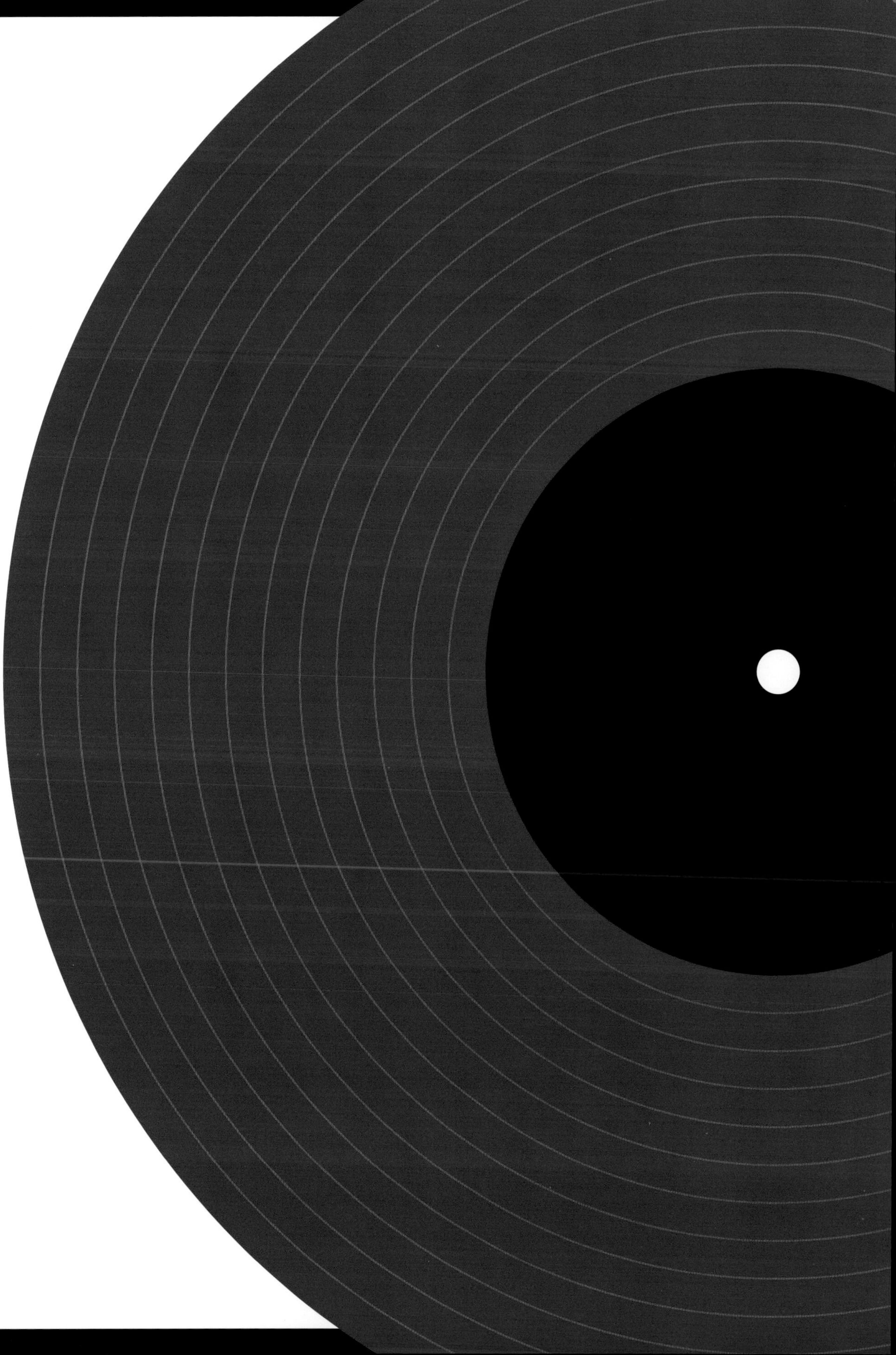

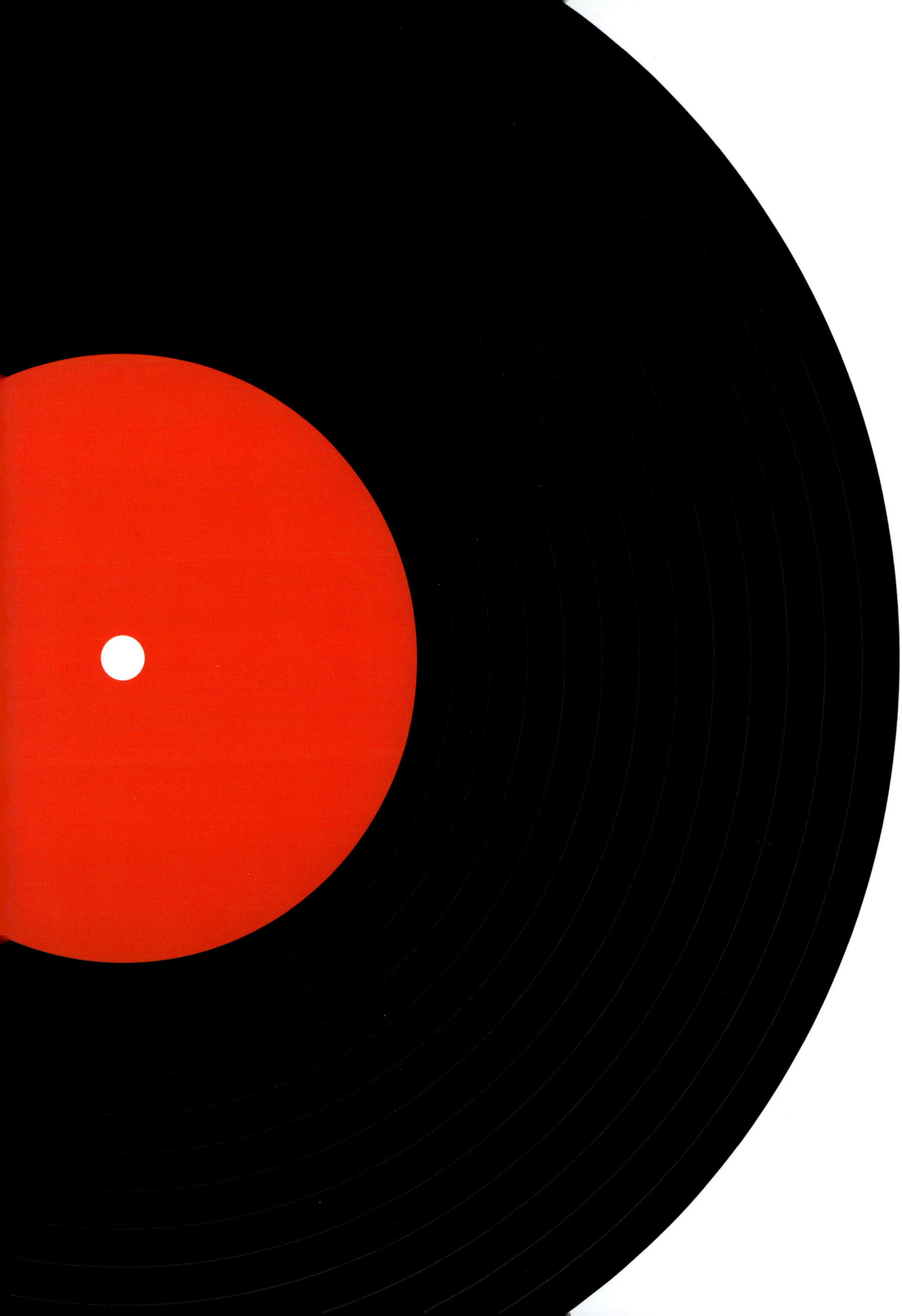

BIBLIOGRAPHY

BOOKS

Aussie Rock Anthems – Top 40 – Glen Humphries, Gelding Street Press, 2024

Australia's 1967 Referendum: Race, Power and the Australian Constitution – Bain Attwood & Andrew Markus, Aboriginal Studies Press, 2007

Born to Run – Bruce Springsteen, Simon & Schuster, 2016

Disco Files 1973–78: New York's Underground, Week by Week – Vince Aletti, DJhistory.com, 2009

Edward Koiki Mabo: His Life and Struggle for Land Rights – Noel Loos & Eddie Koiki Mabo, University of Queensland Press, 1996

Everything Was Forever, Until It Was No More: The Last Soviet Generation – Alexei Yurchak, Princeton University Press, 2005 (pb 2006)

Fight the Power: Rap, Race, and Reality – Chuck D with Yusuf Jah, Canongate/Delacorte, 1997

Glory Days: Bruce Springsteen in the 1980s – Dave Marsh, Pantheon Books, 1987

Is That It? – Bob Geldof, Sidgwick & Jackson, 1986

Notes from Underground: Rock Music Counterculture in Russia – Thomas Cushman, State University of New York Press, 1995

Parental Discretion Is Advised: The Rise of N.W.A and the Dawn of Gangsta Rap – Gerrick D. Kennedy, Abrams Press, 2017

Perestroika: New Thinking for Our Country and the World – Mikhail Gorbachev, Harper & Row, 1987

Red Wave: An American in the Soviet Music Underground – Joanna Stingray with Madison Stingray, Post Hill Press, 2020

Songs – Bruce Springsteen, Avon/HarperEntertainment, 1998

The Aboriginal Tent Embassy: Sovereignty, Black Power, Land Rights and the State – Gary Foley, Andrew Schaap & Edwina Howell (eds.), Routledge, 2014

The Encyclopedia of Popular Music (5th ed.) – Colin Larkin (ed.), Omnibus Press, 2011

To Be Young, Gifted and Black: Lorraine Hansberry in Her Own Words – Lorraine Hansberry (ed. Robert Nemiroff), Prentice-Hall, 1969

U2 by U2 – Bono, The Edge, Adam Clayton & Larry Mullen Jr. (with Neil McCormick), HarperCollins, 2006

The Village People: Camp, Culture, and Code – Jack Fritscher, Palm Drive Publishing, 1994

We Are the World: The Photos, Music, and Inside Story of One of the Most Historic Events in American Popular Music – David Breskin (with Cheryl McCall & Robert Hilburn), Perigee/Putnam, 1985

MAGAZINE / SPECIAL ISSUES

"The Day the World Rocked" (Issue #454) – *Rolling Stone Magazine*, 1985

ARTICLES AND ONLINE SOURCES

"Alright: How Kendrick Lamar's Song Became the Anthem of the Black Lives Matter Movement" – Daniel Kreps, *Rolling Stone*, December 17, 2015

"Tsoi Lives!" – Anna Aslanyan, *London Review of Books*, June 13, 2018. https://www.lrb.co.uk/blog/2018/june/tsoi-lives

"Aretha Franklin Took 'Respect' to the Top, 50 Years Ago This Week" – Detroit Free Press, July 31, 2017

"Aretha Franklin: The Queen of Soul Looks Back on a Mighty Career" – Aretha Franklin (interview by Linda Wertheimer), NPR – All Things Considered, December 277, 1999

"Belarus Protests and the Song of Change" – BBC News, 2020

"Born This Way: The Story Behind Lady Gaga's Equality Anthem" – Stephen Daw, *Billboard*, February 11, 2021

"Celebrating 10 Years of Lady Gaga's Hit Born This Way in Time for Pride" – *Irish Examiner*. https://www.irishexaminer.com/lifestyle/artsandculture/arid-40316312.html

"Coldplay – Viva La Vida," Vinyl Record Album LP, New – Joe's Albums. https://www.joesalbums.com/products/coldplay-viva-la-vida-sealed-vinyl-record-album-lp

"Fight the Power: The Most Provocative Song Ever?" – Christian Blauvelt, BBC Culture, June 28, 2019

"Gorbachev's Recollection of Peremen! in Leadership Context" – *The Independent* (London), 1995

"Green Day: Taking on the World" – Ian Winwood, *Kerrang!*, Bauer Media Group, February 2005

"Green Day: The Q Interview" – *Q Magazine*, Bauer Media Group, October 2004

"Green Day's Angry Anthem" – Jon Pareles, *The New York Times*, September 2005

"How Viktor Tsoi's Most Famous Song Became the Post-Soviet World's Protest Anthem (Against the Rock Legend's Own Wishes)" – Meduza, June 21, 2017

"Interview with Rob Hirst" – *Songwriting Magazine* (UK), 2016

"Kendrick Lamar Opens Up About the Message Behind 'Alright'" – Rob Markman, MTV News, July 1, 2015

"Kendrick Lamar's 'Alright' Is a Protest Song Fit for Ferguson" – Alexis Petridis, *The Guardian*, July 1, 2015

"Kendrick Lamar's 'Alright' Is a Song for Hope" – NPR Music, June 30, 2015

"Kendrick Lamar's 'Alright' Is the Soundtrack to Black Lives Matter" – Jamilah King, Mic, July 15, 2015

"La Liberté de Soolking devient l'hymne du Hirak" – Jeune Afrique, March 20, 2019

"La Liberté de Soolking, hymne de la révolution algérienne" – *Le Monde*, March 29, 2019

"Lady Gaga Reflects on 'Born This Way' 10 Years Later" – Chris Willman, *Variety*, May 21, 2021

'Lady Gaga's 'Born This Way' Turns 10: How a Pop Anthem Inspired a Generation' – Brittany Spanos, *Rolling Stone*, February 11, 2021

'Lady Gaga's Bold Message on Religion and LGBTQ Identity' – Trudy Ring, *The Advocate*, February 12, 2011

"Nirvana – Smells Like Teen Spirit" – TV90s. https://tv90s.com/nirvana-smells-like-teen-spirit/

"One Night in Miami: The True Story Behind Sam Cooke's Stirring 'A Change Is Gonna Come'" – Patrick Ryan, *USA Today*, January 17, 2021

"Paste Magazine's 50 Dancefloor Classics" – *Paste Magazine*, 2017

"Russia's Protest Soundtrack" – *The Moscow Times*, 2021

"Soolking et La Liberté, la bande-son du Hirak algérien" – France 24, March 25, 2019

"The 10 Best All-American Rejects Songs of All-Time" – ChaosPin. https://chaospin.com/best-all-american-rejects-songs/

"The 100 Best Protest Songs of All Time" – *Rolling Stone* staff, *Rolling Stone Australia* – Music Lists, January 28, 2025.

"The American Idiot Story" – John Colapinto, *Rolling Stone*, March 2005

"The Elvis Controversy" – Louie Robinson, *Jet Magazine*, August 1, 1957

"The Grammys 2011: Lady Gaga's Eggstraordinary Entrance" – Paul Harris, *The Guardian*, February 14, 2011

"The Hirak Movement in Algeria: A Peaceful Uprising" – Middle East Eye, April 16, 2019

"The Protest Song That Became Algeria's National Chant" – The New Arab, March 27, 2019

"TIME 100: Songs of the Century" – *Time Magazine*, December 31, 1999

"Tunisia: Diary of a Revolution" – Olivier Piot, *Le Monde diplomatique* (English edition), February 2011. https://mondediplo.com/2011/02/04tunisia

"We Wait for Change: The Meaning of Tsoi's Peremen!" – Radio Free Europe / Radio Liberty, 2020

"Victor Willis Denies Y.M.C.A. as Gay Anthem and Threatens Legal Action" – *Variety*, December 2024 https://variety.com

"Village People Blacklisted by Soviet Youth Wing" – Associated Press, 1985

REPORTS, DATA, AND MEDIA

"500 Greatest Albums of All Time" – *Rolling Stone*, September 2020

58th Annual Grammy Awards – Winners & Nominees – The Recording Academy, 2016

Billboard Hot 100 – *Billboard*, various issues, 1958–present (archived at https://www.billboard.com/charts/hot-100)

Broadway Idiot – directed by Doug Hamilton, FilmBuff, 2013

Chart Performance Data – *Billboard,* various dates

Interview with Hamada Ben Amor – Al Jazeera, January 2011

Mabo v Queensland (No 2) – High Court of Australia, June 3, 1992

"Rolling Stone's Best Songs of 2015" – *Rolling Stone*, December 2, 2015

Triple J Hottest 100 – Australian Broadcasting Corporation, January 2005

UK Singles Chart Records – Official Charts Company, July 2018

VH1's 100 Greatest Dance Songs – VH1, 2000

Village People's Y.M.C.A. Inducted Into National Recording Registry – Library of Congress, 2020

WEBSITES

AllMusic Artist Biography: Village People – Ron Wynn, AllMusic, 2019 – https://www.allmusic.com/artist/village-people-mn0000806745/biography

Born This Way Foundation – Our Story – https://bornthisway.foundation

NPR.org – https://www.npr.org/

The Beatles Bible – https://www.beatlesbible.com/

Robert Christgau: *The Village Voice* Reviews – 1978–1981 – https://www.robertchristgau.com

Violeta Parra » Cronología de Violeta Parra – www.violetaparra.cl (archived 12 November 2011)

ADDITIONAL MUSIC REFERENCES

Cruisin' (Album Liner Notes) – Village People, Casablanca Records, 1978

To Pimp a Butterfly (Album Liner Notes) – Kendrick Lamar, Top Dawg Entertainment / Aftermath / Interscope, 2015

PHOTO CREDITS

ALAMY: pp. 10, 13, 14, 16, 18, 22, 28, 29, 35, 36, 38, 42, 43, 50, 54, 56, 61, 67, 71, 72, 74, 78, 81, 84, 88, 91, 94, 104, 112, 113, 116, 119, 122, 124, 125, 130, 132, 136, 138, 141, 143, 144, 146, 148, 154, 158, 159, 160, 168, 171, 174, 177, 178, 182, 184, 186, 189, 198, 206, 214, 219

GETTY IMAGES: pp. 4: © CORBIS/Corbis, 6: HUM Images/Universal Images Group, 20: Bettmann, 24: ullstein bild, 32: Hulton-Deutsch Collection/Corbis, 44: Bettman, 46: Marcelo Benitez/Latincontent, 60: Koh Hasebe/Shinko Music, 62: Michael Ochs Archives, 68: Brian Rasic, 87: Michael Ochs Archives, 92: KEMAL ASLAN/AFP, 98: Michael Ochs Archives, Lynn Goldsmith/Corbis/VCG, 134: Brooks Kraft LLC/Sygma, 162: Joanna Stingray, 166: Joanna Stingray, 183: Koh Hasebe/Shinko Music, 190: Michel Linssen/Redferns, 192: Per-Anders Pettersson, 194: Patrick Robert/Sygma/Corbis/Sygma, 204: Fethi Belaid/AFP, 210: Kevin Mazur/WireImage, 216: Joel Saget/AFP

SHUTTERSTOCK: pp.201, 209, 212, 218

WIKICOMMONS: pp.7: William P. Gottlieb/Library of Congress's Music Division, 8: Public domain, 9: Carl Van Vechten Collection, Prints & Photographs Division (Library of Congress), 19: Public domain, 26: U.S. News & World Report Magazine Photograph Collection, Prints & Photographs Division (Library of Congress), 30: New York World-Telegram and the Sun Newspaper Photograph Collection (Library of Congress), 40: Daniel Kramer (Albert Grossman Management), 48: Public domain, 52: Koch, Eric/Anefo, 55: Public domain, 58: Cal Montney, Los Angeles Times Photographic Collection at the UCLA Library, 64: Ron Kroon/Anefo, 76: Public domain, 77: Public domain/Arquivo Nacional Collection, 82: Public domain, 96: Los Angeles Times Photographic Collection at the UCLA Library, 101: Los Angeles Times Photographic Collection at the UCLA Library, 102: ETH-Bibliothek Zürich, Bildarchiv/Photograph: Lüthy, Patrick, 106: Public domain, 109: Public domain, 110: Public domain, 114: Koen Suyk/Anefo, 120: Ben PL, 126: TomKern/Pixabay, 128: Joseph Mischyshyn/Geograph project collection, 129: Paul Martin Lester, 140: European Union, 1998–2026, 147: Bernard DUPONT, 150: Public domain, 152: Public domain, 153: Public domain, 156: Thesupermat, 165: Public domain, 170:

ABOUT THE AUTHOR

Aside from the obvious family, pets, and a good wine or whisky, Andrew Clarke loves three things: Australian rules football, car racing, and music. With this book, he has now completed the trilogy for Gelding Street Press, having previously written *The Immortals of Australian Football, Australian Football's 100 Year Club,* and *The Immortals of NASCAR* for the Australian-based publisher.

But his story is much deeper and more long-winded than that, tracking back to the 1980s with his first book and then through another 30 or so on his way to this book. He has also ghostwritten autobiographies with seven athletes and personalities, helping to tell their stories.

Words have always been important, and the impact of words has always been a curiosity to him, from some of the greatest speeches of all time to those that fire off meaning and inspire change in four minutes or less. Sticks and stones may break bones, but words can cause a lifetime of harm, or they can lift you out of the mire and inspire you with hope.

Through his darkest days, music gave him hope. He understood he wasn't alone; that he wasn't the first and he won't be the last. That the world can be a better place thanks to words spoken and words sung.

With his holy trinity complete, he could stop. But he won't. And just like Springsteen, Bono, or Dylan, he'll keep writing: because words matter.

ad42.com.au
ad42media

ALSO IN THIS SERIES

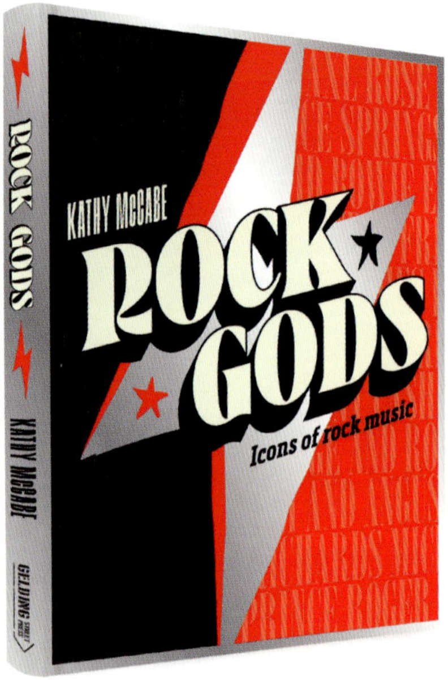

ROCK GODS
Kathy McCabe
ISBN: 9781922662347

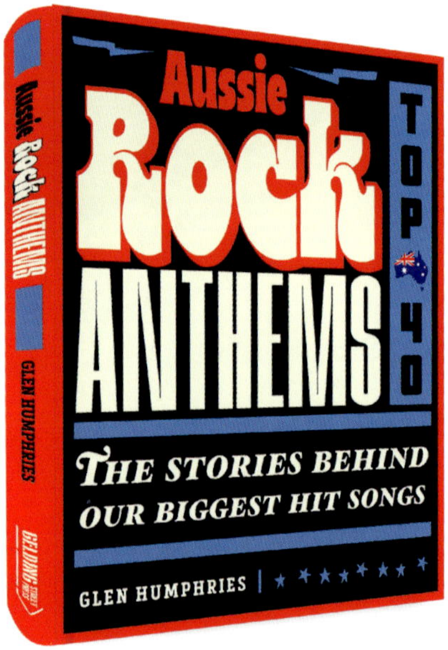

AUSSIE ROCK ANTHEMS
Glen Humphries
ISBN: 9781922662057

Available in all good book stores
geldingstreetpress.com